A LEGACY OF

Catholic-Jewish Dialogue

THE JOSEPH CARDINAL BERNARDIN JERUSALEM LECTURES

Thomas A. Baima, STD

EDITOR

LTP
LITURGY
TRAINING
PUBLICATIONS

"Introduction: What we have Learned from 40 years of Catholic-Jewish Dialogue," © 2005 Thomas A. Baima; "Antisemitism: the Historical Legacy and the Continuing Challenge for Christians," © 1995 Joseph Cardinal Bernardin; "Jewish-Christian Relations after the Holocaust: Toward Post-Holocaust Theological Thought," © 1996 Emil L. Fackenheim; "Catholic-Jewish Relations: A New Agenda?" © 1997 Edward Cardinal Cassidy; "The Theological Significance of Israel," © 1998 David Hartman; "Christian Anti-Judaism: the First Century Speaks to the Twenty-First Century," © 1999 Anthony J. Saldarini; "Bethsaida: Home of the Apostles and the Rabbis," © 2000 Richard A. Freund; "An Ancient and Venerable People," © 2001 Robert Louis Wilken.

"Medieval Christians and Jews: Divergences and Convergences" © 2002 Robert Chazan; "How Jewish and Christian Mystics Read the Bible" © 2003 Bernard McGinn; "Christian-Jewish Relations in the Enlightenment Period" © 2004 Arthur Hertzberg; "Catholics, Jews and American Culture" © 2005 Francis Cardinal George, OMI; "Afterword" © 2012 Michael Kotzin.

A LEGACY OF CATHOLIC-JEWISH DIALOGUE: THE JOSEPH CARDINAL BERNARDIN JERUSALEM LECTURES © 2012 Archdiocese of Chicago: Liturgy Training Publications, 3949 South Racine Avenue, Chicago IL 60609; 1-800-933-1800, fax 1-800-933-7094, e-mail orders@ltp.org. All rights reserved. See our website at www.LTP.org.

Background photograph of the Dome of the Rock in Jerusalem is Image Copyright Renewer, 2012. Used under license from Shutterstock.com. The cover photograph of Cardinal Bernardin is by Joel Fishman.

Printed in the United States of America.

Library of Congress Control Number: 2012943754

16 15 14 13 12   1 2 3 4 5

ISBN 978-1-61671-063-7

LCJD

Contents

Preface

I am grateful that one of the prerogatives of an editor is having the opportunity to write the preface of the collection. This project began many years ago, without any of us knowing that we were setting out on a journey which would one day result in this book. In 1995, after many years of joint projects, the Archdiocese of Chicago and our four Jewish institutional partners, the American Jewish Committee, the Chicago Board of Rabbis, the Jewish Federation of Metropolitan Chicago, and the Spertus Institute of Jewish Studies planned a most ambitious dialogue project. Joseph Cardinal Bernardin would lead a delegation of Catholic and Jewish leadership to the Holy Land for the Chicago Catholic-Jewish Dialogue Visit to Israel, the West Bank and Gaza. The Catholic delegation consisted of Sister Diane Bergant, Sister Joan Monica McGuire, OP, Fr. Daniel Montalbano, Fr. John T. Pawlikowski, OSM, Fr. Michael D. Place, Robert Quakenbush and myself. The Jewish delegation included William E. Rattner, Jonathan Levine, Maynard I. Wishner, Michael C. Kotzin, Rabbi Peter S. Knobel, Rabbi Byron L. Sherwin, and Rabbi Herman E. Schaalman.

The center piece of the visit was an address by Cardinal Bernardin in the Senate Hall of the Hebrew University of Jerusalem on Anti-Semitism. This event quickly came to be called "The Jerusalem Lecture."

For the Jewish community, the trip would be an opportunity to share with the Cardinal and the Catholic members of the delegation the meaning of Israel in the life of Jews. For the Catholic members, it would be a personal pilgrimage to the places of the origin of Christianity and an opportunity for our Jewish friends to understand our faith. Together, we hoped to add our voices to so many others in support of the peace process, which in 1995 was at a high point, sadly not seen since.

The success of the Chicago Catholic-Jewish Dialogue Visit also depended on our dialogue partners in Israel, the West Bank and Gaza. Leaders, both political and religious along with scholars and community activists helped us to deepen the Catholic-Jewish dialogue through our encounter with the realities "on the ground" in the Middle East. They included Yossi Alpher, Zvi Brosh, Fr. (now Bishop) Denis Madden, Gabriel Padon, Adolfo Roitman, Danny Pins, Patriarch Michel Sabbah,

Shimon Peres, Ezer Weizman, Yehuda and Hanna Amichai, Fr. Marcel Dubois, Emil Fackenheim, Reuven Dafni, Rabbi Adin Steinsaltz, Fr. Peter Vasko, OFM, Elias Freij, Fr. Thomas Stransky, Patriarch Diodoros I, Archbishop (now Cardinal) Andrea Cordero Lanza di Montezemolo, Ehud Olmert, Chief Rabbi Yisrael Meir Lau, Rabbi David Hartman, Yitzhak Rabin, Ze'evi Kahanov, Bishop Giacinto-Boulos Marcuzzo, Yassir Arafat, Giora Lev, Yehuda Danon, and Teddy Kollek.

The visit was also an opportunity to teach our two communities in Chicago about interreligious dialogue, so each of the television network affiliates and the major daily newspapers were invited to send reporters to travel with the delegation. The visit captured the imagination of Chicago and was featured five times a day on television news and daily in the papers.

After the dialogue visit was complete, four of us met to debrief on the project. Fr. Michael Placc, Jonathan Levine, Michael Kotzin, and I discussed the idea of a ten-year lecture series as a follow up to the Jerusalem Lecture was born. I presented the idea to Cardinal Bernardin who both approved it and gave us a grant to fund the project.

The basic idea was to follow the two communities through 2,000 years of history. The dialogue visit had shown us that each encounter today carried the entire weight of the history of each community and our interactions with each other over these many centuries. Since the goal of dialogue is to understand the other person or group, to clear away misconceptions, and to foster inter-group harmony, we felt that the study of history would be another tool to foster our relationship. As we had journeyed together to Israel, the West Bank, and Gaza, so too we could journey across the centuries together. By making the journey together we would uncover the complex relationship that has existed between Jews and Christians from the first century until the present day and hopefully gain insight into its many nuances.

And so the Jerusalem Lectures were born. Professor Emil Fackenheim agreed to give the first (or second, depending on how you count) in Chicago in 1996. The rest is our history, which I describe in my essay in this volume.

This book is a record of this ten year conversation. Like all books, it would not have been possible without the help of many people. Certainly, I must begin by thanking the authors without whom there would have been nothing to collect into this anthology. Professor Emil L. Fackenheim,

Edward Cardinal Cassidy, Rabbi David Hartman, Professor Anthony J. Saldarini, Dr. Richard A Freund, Dr. Roberet Louis Wilken, Professor Bernard McGinn, Dr. Robert Chazan, Rabbi Dr. Arthur Hertzberg and Francis Cardinal George, OMI each devoted themselves to this project and produced the most sustained engagement of public intellectual dialogue on Catholic-Jewish relations in the United States. Dr. Michael Kotzin concludes the collection with his "Afterword."

But a book is produced by more than authors. A number of other individuals must be recognized as well. In this list are the secretaries and assistants and colleagues of the principals who supported the project at every turn. My special thanks goes to Janet Virva, Becky Galler, Paula Harris, the Late Barbara Feldt, and Jason Renken for the "details."

Personally, I must thank my archbishop, Francis Cardinal George, for his support of the exercise of my priestly ministry through the intellectual apostolate. I also thank my colleagues at the University of Saint Mary of the Lake / Mundelein Seminary for their support of my research and publishing program. In a special way, I want to thank the Rector/ President, Msgr. Dennis J. Lyle for understanding the desire of his vice rector for academic affairs to remain an active scholar. I also want to thank Fr. Douglas Martis and Kevin Thorton and the staff of the Liturgical Institute of the University of Saint Mary of the Lake and John Thomas at Liturgy Training Publications for agreeing to publish this work. They supported the publication project from the first time I called them. Additionally, I must mention Eileen D. White who assisted me with the professional editing and preparation of the manuscript and with many editorial suggestions. It was Kevin Thornton who then saw the manuscript through to completion.

Finally, I should note that a number of the people who were so much part of this long endeavor have died before it was completed: Joseph Cardinal Bernardin, Emil Fackenheim, Barbara Feldt, Arthur Hertzberg, Daniel Montalbano, and Anthony Saldarini. I dedicate this work to their memory.

Thomas A. Baima
Mundelein, Illinois

Introduction

What We Have Learned from 40 Years of Catholic–Jewish Dialogue[1]

Thomas A. Baima
April 9, 2005

*Following the completion of the tenth Jerusalem Lecture, the
Reverend Dr. Thomas A Baima, associate professor of systematic
theology and Vice-Rector for Academic Affairs of the University
of Saint Mary of the Lake, and the former ecumenical officer of the
Archdiocese of Chicago, delivered an academic paper at the
American Academy of Religion regional meeting at DePaul University
April 9, 2005, in which he surveyed the lessons of forty years of
institutional Catholic-Jewish dialogue in metropolitan Chicago. Father
Baima situates the theme of the lecture in the context of the academy's consideration of Religion in the Public Sphere. He then offers a
summary of the manifold ways in which the Archdiocese of Chicago
has engaged its several Jewish partners in dialogue through initiatives
promoting the common good, through scholarly engagement of
the two communities' sometimes mutually exclusive religious claims.
This summary provides an overview of this volume of collected
lectures and situates the individual lecture and even the lecture series
in the wider context of Catholic-Jewish relations in Chicago. Father
Baima argues that the Chicago relationship is a microcosm of the*

---

1. In the American Academy of Religion lecture, Father Baima explored the engagement of the
Archdiocese of Chicago and the Jewish community in the interfaith organization, the Council
of Religious Leaders of Metropolitan Chicago by analyzing two public acts. That section is omitted here. In the version of the paper presented in this volume, Father Baima has replaced the final
section with a description of a subsequent Catholic-Jewish collaboration, between Cardinal
George and the Jewish Federation of Metropolitan Chicago, *the Fassouta Project.*

global Catholic-Jewish engagement occurring since the end of the Second Vatican Council. By careful study of the particular dynamics in Chicago, we can learn much about the overall relationship between these two world religious communities.

IN our proposal to the Midwest American Academy of Religion, we explained this session in the following way:

> The public sphere is changed by the fact and awareness of inter-religious dialogue. The reality that religious groups with certain common roots but competing and mutually exclusive claims and mixed histories of coopera-tive but often hostile interaction have initiated, expanded, and continue to develop ways of conversing and pursuing initiatives for the common good has great potential for changing the shape of the global future. The fact that such dialogue exists and is expanding has been slow in impacting the public consciousness, even perhaps the awareness of many of the adherents of those religious groups. It is a means of accessing the public square, bringing a prior engagement of parties with each other and seeking a larger voice with a larger public. The quality of an already-in-process mode of action distinguishes it from the voices of individual religious bodies acting alone. In bringing their conversation public as well and seek-ing to engage the other participants in public dialogue and influence, reli-gious groups in dialogue demonstrate the possibilities for seemingly diverse elements to fruitfully engage and interact.

In my section of this seminar, I hope to do three things. First, I will narrate the rich history of how Catholics and Jews have "conversed and pursued initiatives for the common good" in Chicagoland. This history is one of great pride to the two communities and is one of the reasons Chicago is seen as an important center of interreligious dialogue on the world stage. Secondly, I want to explore the intellectual engagement of the "competing and mutually exclusive claims" through a survey of the Joseph Cardinal Bernardin Jerusalem Lectures. Finally, I will describe how the two communities engaged one such case of competing claims in the public sphere by examining the response of the Archdiocese of Chicago and the Jewish Federation of Metropolitan Chicago to the problem of Christian emigration from the Holy Land.

Part One: Conversed and Pursued Initiatives for the Common Good

For a full week in 1995 it was impossible to turn on the television in the Chicago area and not see images of the Catholic-Jewish dialogue. On March 20, 1995, Joseph Cardinal Bernardin, the Archbishop of Chicago, ordained three priests as bishops of the Catholic Church. That event was quickly overshadowed; for immediately after the service, the archbishop took off his vestments and then, garbed in the simple black dress of a cleric, drove to O'Hare International Airport where he met the top leadership of Chicago's Jewish community and together they began his historic dialogue visit to Israel, the West Bank, and Gaza. For a full week, at the top of every local newscast, five times a day, the citizens of Chicago saw images of Jews and Catholics accompanying the senior prelate of the Catholic Church in the United States journeying together on a mission that included fact-finding, promoting the peace process, exploring the plight of Palestinians, all the while undertaking a religious pilgrimage to Jerusalem, a city holy to Jews, Catholics, and Muslims, although holy to each group in radically different ways.

Ten years later, the current archbishop, Francis Cardinal George, would deliver the memorial lecture which recalled his predecessor's dialogue visit. In that address, Cardinal George would push the dialogue in some dramatic ways, calling on Jews and Catholics to engage the public sphere together around serious issues of secularism and post-modernism. And the Cardinal would propose a new role for interreligious dialogue, which would move it beyond relations between the religions themselves, and toward engagement in the public debates about the post-modern world.

How did Chicago come to be a place where events like these could happen and happen so easily? The answer to that question lies in history.

The story of Catholic-Jewish relations in Chicago begins in 1958. It was in that year that the first of the institutional expressions of that relationship can be documented. This was the year that the Archbishop of Chicago, Albert Cardinal Meyer, established the Archdiocesan Office for Urban Affairs. This new agency of the archdiocese, under the direction of Monsignor John J. Egan, was charged with the task of engaging the world outside the Catholic Church for the sake of the common good. It was through that engagement, that the Catholic Church of Chicago and the Jewish community formally met each other, as both groups looked at the critical issues facing the city and its people.

The two communities would further formalize their relationship during the civil rights movement. The Chicago Conference on Religion and Race (CCRR)was one of the first interfaith roundtables to engage the matter of civil rights. Composed of the Archdiocese of Chicago, the Chicago Board of Rabbis, the Church Federation of Greater Chicago, and the Episcopal Diocese of Chicago, CCRR was a vehicle for interfaith engagement in the early days of the relationship. Through CCRR, the interfaith community addressed the sin of racism in what has been called by some critics, the most segregated city in America.

At the same time, the Catholic Church was changing. From 1962 to 1965, the Second Vatican Council was meeting in Rome and forging a program of engagement with the modern world. Out of that program would come the historic document, *Nostra Aetate*, the Declaration on the Relationship of the Church to non-Christian Religions.[2] Largely aimed at healing the rift between Catholics and Jews in the aftermath of World War II and the Holocaust, the document became a watershed in Jewish-Catholic relations since its teaching represented the highest level of authority in the Catholic Church, an ecumenical council presided over by the Pope. That same year, 1965, Archbishop John Patrick Cody of the Archdiocese of Chicago established the Commission on Human Relations and Ecumenism to succeed the Office for Urban Affairs. At its head was Monsignor Edward M. Egan, who today is Cardinal Archbishop Emeritus of New York. Under his leadership, the archdiocese organized itself for ecumenical and interreligious engagement. The commission was responsible for setting up a network of parish ecumenical representatives and writing the first *Interdiocesan Ecumenical Program*, which set out guidelines for the practice of ecumenism and human relations for the archdiocese of Chicago and the dioceses of Gary, Rockford, and Joliet.[3]

Father William Lion would succeed Msgr. Egan as ecumenical officer and pursue a program of personal relationships with the various judicatory heads. Father Lion was the executive director of the Catholic

---

2. See *Nostra Aetate:* The Declaration on the Relationship of the Church to Non-Christian Religions, in *The Documents of Vatican II,* Walter M. Abbot, ed. (New York: American Press, 1966), 662–663.

3. *Interdiocesan Ecumenical Program,* ed. Edward M. Egan (Chicago: Archdiocese of Chicago, 1965).

Conference of Illinois and under his leadership, a Department of Ecumenical Affairs would be established at the state level, including all of the dioceses in the province. The department would author another version of the *Interdiocesan Ecumenical Program* for the six dioceses in Illinois.[4]

In 1982, after the death of Cardinal Cody, Archbishop Joseph L. Bernardin would become the Archbishop of Chicago. That same year, in anticipation of the new *Code of Canon Law,* the Department of Ecumenical Affairs would begin work on a comprehensive set of norms to guide ecumenical and interreligious affairs in the province. The new code would be promulgated in 1983, the same year that the department would publish the *Province of Chicago Ecumenical Guidelines.*[5]

Cardinal Bernardin would increase the diocese's commitment to interreligious engagement through the establishment of a fully staffed Office for Human Relations and Ecumenism. Under the direction of Msgr. John J. Egan, the new office would pursue both the human relations agenda of the former Office for Urban Affairs and the newly developed ecumenical and interreligious agenda of the Catholic Church. It was during this period that the interfaith program of the archdiocese would take shape.

One of the first Catholic-Jewish programs was begun by Sister Anna Marie Erst. Working with the American Jewish Committee, she established the Institute for Catholic-Jewish Religious Education. This institute is today headed by Sister Mary Ellen Coombe and continues to provide training for Catholic and Jewish educators who introduce Jewish and Catholic school children to the other religion.

The relationship between the archdiocese and the Chicago Board of Rabbis also developed. Institutionally, the principal venue was the Chicago Conference on Religion and Race. That organization had been a vital force in the early days of the civil rights movement, but as time went on, the issues the several religious communities wished to confront had broadened beyond civil rights alone. So, under the leadership of Rabbi Herman Schaalman, Dr. Sterling Cary, Bishop Paul Erickson, and Msgr. John Egan, CCRR evolved into the Council of Religious Leaders of Metropolitan Chicago (CRLMC). Since 1984, CRLMC has become the principal

---

4. *Ecumenical Guidelines*, ed. Robert Jackson (Chicago: Catholic Conference of Illinois, 1981).

5. *Province of Chicago Ecumenical Guidelines,* ed. Thomas A. Baima (Chicago: Catholic Conference of Illinois, 1983).

roundtable for the bishops and heads of religious communities to build personal relationships and confront together the critical issues which face Chicago. In the third part of this paper I will examine one incident which will illustrate the maturity of the interreligious engagement.

The Office for Human Relations and Ecumenism began a program for the reception of the decrees of Vatican II in the archdiocese. Conceived as a twenty year process, the office began with having the archbishop model the behavior. This was followed by a process of covenant relationships to highlight the elements of commonality which already existed between communities. The third phase was to repeat the covenant process at a more local level to involve parishes and schools. The final phase was one of ecumenical formation of ministers, through which the ecumenical attitude would be infused into all the ministries of the archdiocese.

Catholic-Jewish relations followed along this same pattern as Christian ecumenism, though with appropriate modifications. The modeling step was accomplished through a major celebration of the twentieth anniversary of *Nostra Aetate,* the Declaration on the Relationship of the Catholic Church to Non-Christian Religions. Held at Mundelein College, this major event launched the Catholic-Jewish relationship on the public scene. Cardinal Bernardin moved the relationship into the public square with this major celebration. The visibility had an animating effect on the parish/synagogue dialogues.

That event also marks the point where the archdiocese reached out to a wider institutional engagement with the Jewish community. While maintaining its long-standing collaboration with the Chicago Board of Rabbis, the archdiocese forged new institutional relationships with other Jewish institutions, such as its newly formed connection with Spertus College. One of the few Jewish liberal arts colleges in the United States, Spertus was in a unique position to partner with the archdiocese. Anticipating the goal of formation of ministers, Spertus and the archdiocese developed an unprecedented project. Cardinal George has described it this way:

> A unique project developed at Spertus College in the Joseph Cardinal Bernardin Center for the Study of Eastern European Jewry. Since Chicago is the largest Polish city after Warsaw, it was appropriate for Spertus and the Archdiocese to develop this project together. A high point for the Center

was the visit to Chicago of a group of seminary professors from Poland, who spent seven weeks here studying Judaism and interreligious dialogue.[6]

Alongside all of this, Catholic Charities and the Jewish Federation forged a number of collaborations in the area of social welfare and public policy. The American Jewish Committee continued to work with the archdiocese on formation of the clergy and developed the Priest/Rabbi Retreat, a project which continues to the present day. The Jewish Community Relations Council (JCRC)addressed defamation issues and other public policy questions. In the late 1980's the Catholic-Jewish Scholars Dialogue was established between the Federation, the Board of Rabbis, the JCRC and the archdiocese to provide a roundtable which considered issues of theology and public policy.

The history of the relationship between the archdiocese and the Jewish community was based on relationships forged through efforts to promote the common good. What is significant about the Chicago relationship is that unlike many other cities, these efforts didn't stop in Chicago. Cardinal Bernardin's dialogue visit to Israel, the West Bank and Gaza set in motion a public intellectual project which would take the engagement into an exploration of the competing and mutually exclusive claims of the two religions.

Part Two: Exploring Competing and Mutually Exclusive Claims

The pinnacle of the dialogue came in Senate Hall of the Hebrew University of Jerusalem. The President of the university conferred an honorary fellowship on the Cardinal after which he delivered the fellowship lecture, *Antisemitism: The Historic Legacy and the Continuing Challenge for Christians.*[7]

Cardinal Bernardin detailed the development of Christian thought on anti-Semitism, in particular pointing out how in recent years the Catholic Church

---

6. Francis Cardinal George, OMI, "Catholics, Jews and American Culture" the 2005 Jerusalem Lecture (Chicago: Archdiocese of Chicago, February 21, 2005).

7. Joseph Cardinal Bernardin, *Antisemitism: The Historical Legacy and the Continuing Challenge for Christians.* (Chicago: Archdiocese of Chicago, March 23, 1995). See also, *A Blessing to Each Other: Cardinal Joseph Bernardin and Jewish-Catholic Dialogue* (Chicago: Liturgy Training Publications, 1996).

xvi   *Thomas A. Baima*

has undertaken important efforts to acknowledge responsibility for that legacy. He repudiated any remaining vestiges of antisemitism in the Church's contemporary teaching and practice as sinful. The Cardinal called upon Jews and Christians to recommit themselves to counter any resurgence of antisemitism, together with other forms of racial and ethnic violence.[8]

For a cardinal of the Roman Catholic Church to say these things was not new. In essence they repeated the teaching of the Second Vatican Council. But for a cardinal to journey to Israel with a group of Jewish leaders and to deliver this lecture in Jerusalem out of the context of the long-term relationship they shared was unprecedented. The real significance of the Jerusalem Lecture, however, was not what it said about the past, but what it demanded of the future.

> In responding to these realities, Cardinal Bernardin [suggested] several ways that Jews and Christians [could both] together and separately, build a better future of relations. He [called] for renewal of Catholic teaching material on antisemitism, expansion of awareness of Vatican II's rejection of anti-Jewish theology. The Cardinal [called] for Jewish educators also to rethink the Jewish community's understanding of its relationship with the Church. In these and other ways, Jews and Christians can, together, build a new relationship for the future.[9]

Some initial steps were taken at once back in Chicago through the publication of a guide for teaching about Catholic-Jewish relations by Deborah Levine.[10] But more directly, the challenge was embraced by the four Jewish organizations and the archdiocese in the creation of the Jerusalem Lecture series. Through this effort, which has now extended over ten years, the archdiocese and the Jewish community have reflected in public on the serious theological and historical issues which separate them. I would argue that it is precisely the sustained engagement of these questions which has produced the fruits of dialogue. I would also suggest that the choice of conducting the dialogue as Cardinal Bernardin did, in the public forum rather than in closed meetings which typically

---

8. Joseph Cardinal Bernardin, *Antisemitism: The Historical Legacy and the Continuing Challenge for Christians* (Chicago: Archdiocese of Chicago, March 23, 1995).

9. Ibid.

10. See Deborah J. Levine, *Teaching Christian Children about Judaism* (Chicago: Liturgy Training Publications, 1995).

conclude with both parties producing joint statements, has contributed to the overall dynamics of dialogue in Chicagoland.

It is instructive to examine the themes covered by the Jerusalem Lectures. Like Gaul, they may be divided into three parts. The first part of the series dealt with a further expansion of the themes raised by Cardinal Bernardin in the Hebrew University lecture. The second part consisted of a diachronic study of the relationship of Christians and Jews from the first century to the twentieth. The third part consisted of a study of the modern period and identified modernity as a third partner in the conversation between Christians and Jews. The lecture series celebrated its tenth anniversary with Cardinal George proposing a provocative next step for the conversation with his lecture, *Catholics, Jews and American Culture.*[11]

Professor Emil Fackenheim was the first lecturer to engage the themes raised by Cardinal Bernardin at Hebrew University. Possibly his most provocative insight was a quote from an unnamed Christian he met at a conference in Germany. Professor Fackenheim wrote:

> Christians must begin again at the beginning, with the first two questions of the Bible: "Where are you, Man?" and "Where is your brother?" Christian anti-Judaism will never end until Christians relate positively to Jews, not despite their non-acceptance of [Jesus] Christ, but because of it.[12]

This quotation touches directly on the theme we are considering, the competing and mutually exclusive claims of two religions. Note especially how Fackenheim's quote also contains within it the path forward. Christians must find in their own religious identity a way to accommodate the religious self-identity of Jews. This is the basis for the inclusivist school of the theology of religions, and I would argue, the only approach that can actually answer Fackenheim's provocative question. The exclusivist school fails to ever engage the question of accommodation and the pluralist school denies that it is a question. But more on that later.

Edward Cardinal Cassidy was the next Jerusalem Lecturer. He asked the participants to consider what principles support an engagement of

---

11. George, op. cit.

12. Ibid., 21. (Professor Fackenheim cites these statements as follows: "The first two statements I heard at a Jewish-Christian conference, held in the Pabst Johannes Haus, Krefeld, Germany in 1983.")

the conflicting and mutually exclusive claims. He wrote: "The first such principle is the fact that we are speaking in this context of joint action in favor of the moral values which as faith communities we share. We are not two humanitarian societies, far less are we two debating clubs. We are two faith communities and as such we are being called to respond to a common challenge."[13] Another key principle he noted, was the Catholic Church's understanding of its relationship to Judaism as unique among all the other world religions. "It is important for us to keep this "unique" aspect of our relationship in mind, especially when we enter into a wider interfaith dialogue. [Jews and Christians] have an agenda based on what John Paul II has described elsewhere as being 'linked together at the very level of their identity.' With no other faith community, not even Islam, do Christians have such a relationship."[14] Christianity is organically related to Judaism. Jews are Christians' elder brothers and sisters. In this we see the beginnings of an answer to Professor Fackenheim's provocative question.

If for Christians the fundamental question is what do you think of Jesus, then for Jews in the late twentieth century, an equally important question (though not equivalent in the strictly theological sense) is to ask Christians what they think of Israel. The equivalence has to do with identity and the other's acknowledgment of one of its key components. I remember on my first trip to Israel, how I had to confront my own inaccurate notion that Jewish identity was rooted solely in biblical Judaism. One of the Jewish staff on our mission was trying to explain to me the phenomenon of a "secular" Jewish identity. She said: "[f]or many Jews today, both here in Israel and in America and Europe, their identity is grounded in the twin events of the Holocaust and the establishment of the State of Israel." The religious Jews on the trip at once began to challenge the sufficiency of her description, but none questioned that Israel was one of the terms of the identity equation. The most Orthodox among them said, "You see we disagree about everything, except, of course, Israel."

---

13. Edward Cardinal Cassidy, *Catholic-Jewish Relations: A New Agenda?* (Chicago: Archdiocese of Chicago, April 30, 1997), 6.
14. Ibid. See *Attività della Santa Sede 1982*, pp. 184–185.

It was Rabbi Dr. David Hartman who put this question of identity to the Chicago dialogue with his lecture on "the Theological Significance of Israel."[15] In speaking to a group of Christians who define their self-identity in the term "catholic," meaning universal, Dr. Hartman wrote:

> Israel is not the embodiment of the universal. Israel is an expression of the dignity of particularity. In the eighteenth century, Jews felt that in order to speak ethically, you had to embody the universality of Kantian ethics. In order to be dignified, you had to embrace universality and reject particularity, which many of them did by giving up their particular traditions. Jews assimilated in droves because they believed mistakenly that you became universal by discarding the particular. The reborn State of Israel is an intensified expression of a people's particular identity. And it is this very particularity that can teach us the meaning of universalism as an outgrowth of a commitment to particularities.[16]

Assimilation, which Dr. Hartman mentions, was a deliberate strategy of both Jews and Catholics after immigration to America. Both communities are now questioning that strategy's continued value to their future. The significance of Dr. Hartman's contribution to the dialogue is to allow both Catholics and Jews to see that there is profound theological significance behind any authentic answer to the assimilation question. Even in our divergent claims and mutually exclusive identities, there are points of commonality and unity which are deeper than the practical.

Dr. Hartman's lecture brought the first phase of the project to a close. From there, the Jerusalem Lecture series turned its attention to history. The dialogue had uncovered a serious lack of knowledge of the other communities' history. It was as if both Jews and Christians stopped paying attention to each other in (after?) CE 70! In place of good historical knowledge, both communities were operating on assumptions, most of which were either false or so in need of nuance as to be functionally useless.

The second phase of the lecture series, then, sought to expose the degree to which we misunderstand each other's history. It would be an impossible task to correct this in a few short lectures, so the goal was

---

15. David Hartman, *The Theological Significance of Israel* (Chicago, Archdiocese of Chicago, March 17, 1998).

16. Ibid., 25.

rather to create a group of conscious incompetents, "people who know that they do not know."[17]

What were the things that Christians and Jews "didn't know they didn't know"?[18] We didn't have a clear sense of Christian anti-Judaism as it existed in the earliest days of the Church. So, Professor Anthony Saldarini explored the history of the first century and offered his insights on how a better historic understanding of this first century phenomenon can inform our own confrontation of anti-Judaism in the twentieth century. Another element of history that needed attention was the continued relationships between Christian and Jews in the first centuries. The separation of the Church and the synagogue was a more complex process than most Christians understood. Gaining insight into that process furthered our understanding of Cardinal Cassidy's claim to an organic relationship between the two religions which Richard A. Freund argued was historical as well as theological.[19] Professor Robert Wilken would continue this theme with his study of Jewish peoplehood in the period of Christian antiquity.[20]

The key insight that this historical survey shows is that in addition to competing and mutually exclusive claims, the two religions have areas of significant commonality. I would argue that this commonality is not merely coincidental, but since it consists in elements which are constitutive of each religion's self-identity, the commonality also provides the bridge for understanding conflicting claims in terms of one's own faith claims. So, a better understanding of the Jewishness of Christianity creates the condition of the possibility of a Christian theology of Judaism.

Nowhere was this clearer than in the section of the lectures which dealt with the Middle Ages. Catholics remember that in the Middle Ages the three religions of Judaism, Christianity, and Islam all discovered Aristotle. For a time, their theologians were speaking the same language. Yet the Middle Ages were some of the worst for practical relations between

---

17. I borrow this expression from Charles R. Hobbs and his lecture series *Insight on Your Time and Your Life* (Morton Grove, IL: Nightengale-Conant, 1985).

18. Anthony J. Saldarini, *Christian Anti-Judaism: The First Century Speaks to the Twenty-First Century* (Chicago: Archdiocese of Chicago, April 14, 1999).

19. Richard A. Freund, *Bethsaida: Home of the Apostles and the Rabbis* (Chicago: Archdiocese of Chicago, April 10, 2000).

20. Robert Louis Wilken, *An Ancient and Venerable People* (Chicago: Archdiocese of Chicago, March 18, 2001).

the communities. These complexities were considered by Robert Chazan and Bernard McGinn.[21]

The Middle Ages gave way to the Modern period, where the two religions had quite different responses to modernity. Modernity also represents a new conflicting claim in the religious dialogue, or perhaps I should say trialogue.[22] (The spell check on my computer insists that trialogue is not a word, which is another proof of modernity's presence in the world of conflicting claims). Rabbi Dr. Arthur Hertzberg explores these matters in his lecture on the two religions in the Enlightenment period.[23] In doing so, he both brings the historical section of the lectures to a close and becomes the immediate interlocutor to Cardinal George, whose response positions the lecture series for the future. Dr. Hertzberg and the cardinal constitute the third phase of the lecture series. Closing phase two, Dr. Hertzberg wrote:

> . . . the revolutionary and scandalously difficult point that the Enlightenment itself, and some of its leaders, represented a secular counter-religion which persecuted and even excommunicated those who did not join their "church." But Judaism and Christianity did part company in the modern era when the Enlightenment led the European intellectuals toward enmity toward religion. In widely varying degrees, the bulk of the Jewish community and the bulk of the Catholic community reacted quite differently . . . in its battle with the Enlightenment, the church lost. With its encounter with the Enlightenment, the synagogue had to redefine itself in many ways but the Jews, who [in Christendom] had long been a persecuted and embattled people, won. Therefore, two hundred years later, we have to re-estimate what this historic turning means now for both of our faiths.[24]

Cardinal George opened the next phase in the lecture series with a provocative development of Dr. Hertzberg's findings. It is at this point in my narrative that the Jerusalem Lecture series speaks directly to the topic of this year's meeting of the Midwest American Academy of

---

21. Robert Chazan, *Medieval Christians and Jews: Divergences and Convergences* (Chicago: Archdiocese of Chicago, March 14, 2002); Bernard McGinn, *How Jewish and Christian Mystics Read the Bible* (Chicago, Archdiocese of Chicago, March 3, 2003).

22. George, op. cit.

23. Arthur Hertzberg, *Christian-Jewish Relations in the Enlightenment Period.* (Chicago: Archdiocese of Chicago, May 10, 2004).

24. Ibid.

Religion. To give you the fully developed idea, I want to quote Cardinal George at length:

> Rabbi Hertzberg went on to assert that the opinion of these Enlightenment Jews was that it would be "better that religion should be removed from its central and dominant role in human society," and that [religion] "accept a much more modest definition of itself as the faith of individuals. . . ."[25] Dr. Hertzberg gives us a very good definition of the problem which confronts us as we enter this 21st century. The problem, simply stated, is that, with the advent of the Enlightenment, a new dialogue partner has entered our conversation: secularism. And with the entrance of secularism on the stage of public life, the Jewish-Catholic dialogue takes on the quality of a trialogue. We have not sufficiently recognized this fact, I believe, in our bilateral conversations, because we share it without too much conflict. Given that the form of secularism we have in the United States is different in significant respects from its counterpart in Europe or even Canada, our consideration of it must recognize that secularism, like religion, inculturates in particular ways in different societies. It is for this reason that I titled my lecture *Catholics, Jews **and** American Culture,* instead of *Catholics and Jews **in** American Culture.* American Culture is an actor in our mutual relationship; it is a semantic system, which interacts with the semantic systems of our respective faiths as they dialogue with one another. Following Dr. Hertzberg, I would argue that it is a religious competitor with Judaism and Catholicism, sometimes helpful and sometimes malign.[26]

Cardinal George went on to say:

> We are two ancient faith communities entering the 21st century and called to respond to a common challenge—two pre-modern faiths in a postmodern culture.[27] That challenge includes, among other things, the universalist pretensions of nation-states and how their claims affect the particularity

---

25. Ibid.

26. George, op. cit.

27. Cardinal George writes in a footnote on this passage, "There is a sense in which Catholic faith, founded in Christ's resurrection from the dead two thousand years ago, nevertheless sees itself reaching back to creation itself. Without succumbing to supersessionism, theologians such as Yves Congar, OP, can write about *Ecclesia ab Abel,* 'the Church from Abel.'" See Yves Congar, OP, "Ecclesia ab Abel," *Abhanglungen uber theologie und Kirche,* Heinrich Elfers and Fritz Hoffmann, eds., (Dusseldorf: 1952), 79–108.

of peoples, and the presence of a secularism with all the qualities of a religion co-opting society for its own ends.[28]

His conclusion is that both Judaism and Christianity are in a privileged position to contribute to the next phase in the development of American culture. While he is critical of the current state of American culture and, in a particular way, of how the Calvinist antecedents of the dominant Protestant culture have created a kind of secularism which is hardly benign, but more resembles Puritan New England, the cardinal nevertheless sees a future in the interreligious dialogue especially by the ability of such dialogues to introduce a communitarian ethos to the public debate.

I would argue that such a move can also make secularism a partner in the trialogue. Once you introduce the communitarian principle, you move into a post-modern frame of reference which severs its link to the Enlightenment, which is individualism. While Catholic philosophy takes a position which is different from communitarianism, nevertheless, contemporary communitarians such as Professor Amatai Etzione could be dialogue partners in this endeavor.[29]

Returning to our topic of religion in the public square, let me share Cardinal George's final assertion. He wrote: "At the end of my Library of Congress address in 1999, I advanced the claim that":

In the next millennium, as the modern nation state is relativized and national sovereignty is displaced into societal arrangements still to be invented, it will be increasingly evident that the major faiths remain carriers of culture and that it is more sectarian to be French, [Russian or] American than to be Christian or Muslim, [Jewish], Hindu or Buddhist. Interreligious dialogue is more basic to the future of faith, therefore, than is Church-state dialogue, important though that remains.[30]

---

28. George, op. cit.

29. Regarding the distinctions between Catholic philosophy and communitarianism see Edward T. Barrett's fine dissertation at the University of Chicago: *Personalistic Liberalism: The Ethical and Political Thought of Karol Wojtyla / Pope John Paul II.* Amatai Etzione is University Professor at the George Washington University and former president of the American Sociological Association. Professor Etzione's works are too numerous to begin to list here, but represent, in my estimation, a significant post-modern critique from the discipline of sociology, (constructive speculative sociology, if there is such a thing), and pose a corrective to some of the very issues Cardinal George raises. These, interesting though they may be, are beyond the scope of this paper.

30. George, "Catholic Christianity and the Millennium," op. cit.

With this we come to the end of the survey of the intellectual engagement of the "competing and mutually exclusive claims" through a survey of the Joseph Cardinal Bernardin Jerusalem Lectures. Finally, I will describe how the two communities engaged one such case of competing claims in the public sphere by examining the demonstration project on Christian emigration from Israel: the Fassouta Computer Literacy Project.

Part Three: The Fassouta Project

On the surface, the Fassouta Computer Literacy Project is fairly straightforward. It was a project to create and staff a computer lab in an existing community center in a town in northern Israel. What is significant and worthy of our study is the reason behind the otherwise straightforward project. The project sought to demonstrate the problem of Christian emigration from Israel and the profound effect this was having on the life of the Church there. The project is also an illustration of the depth which the Catholic-Jewish dialogue in Chicago had achieved. Cardinal George spoke of this in the press conference announcing the Fassouta Project:

> Since becoming Archbishop of Chicago, I have enjoyed exceptional rela-
> tionships with the local Jewish leadership. This is due in large measure to
> efforts by Catholics and Jews for many years before I came back to Chicago
> for which I am grateful. The relationship is so good in fact, that I felt quite
> free to say some difficult things to Rabbi Yehiel Poupko a couple of months
> ago about my concerns over Christian emigration from Israel. You see, the
> Christian population in the Middle East is getting smaller and smaller. As
> Jews know better than anyone, unless you have a certain level of population
> it is very difficult to maintain a Jewish life. This is now sadly true for the
> Christians in the very land of our origin, the land of Jesus and the Apostles.
> In the years that I was Vicar General of the Oblates of Mary Immaculate,
> my religious order, I traveled to the Middle East and heard first-hand from
> the Arab Christian community of their struggles. They would mention
> many things, the violence, the lack of security, the way that they were a
> double minority in Israel, being neither Jewish nor Muslim. But most of
> all, they always mentioned the problem of emigration, that the youth who
> were the future of their community would leave because of the lack of job

training and opportunity. If a vital community of Christians is not maintained in Israel, then all that will be left is the shrines.[31]

The Cardinal noted that he "felt close enough to Rabbi Poupko to tell him these real concerns."[32] This friendship is the intangible product of a long-term dialogue relationship. All of the planning and research in the world could not produce the kind of personal relationship that occasioned such an exchange between a Catholic and Jew. The project was born of trust, building over many years and issuing forth with a very practical, concrete response to a real life problem. The project, Cardinal George went on to say that he hoped first

> to show how the problem of Christian emigration from Israel is a real concern both to the Arab Christians there in the Middle East and to Catholics throughout the world. Secondly, we hope to show that Jews and Christians have come to the point that we can speak freely to one another about these real, on the ground issues, and that together we can do something about them.[33]

The media was attracted to the story because Jews and Catholics were collecting money to help Christians find jobs in Israel. But the Cardinal underscored that the really noteworthy aspect of the project was not the goal but the origin of the project in dialogue.

> This project also demonstrates the effects of dialogue. There are some who question why Catholics and Jews should spend the effort at dialogue. They frequently say, it comes to nothing. What we are beginning today shows that the real fruit of interreligious dialogue is honest understanding of each others' deepest concerns and the will to engage in a dialogue of deeds to address them.[34]

Conclusion

As you can see from the rich history of how Catholics and Jews have "conversed and pursued initiatives for the common good" in Chicagoland

---

31. Francis Cardinal George, "Fassouta Project Press Conference," July 21, 2003.
32. Ibid.
33. Ibid.
34. Ibid.

and the intellectual engagement of the "competing and mutually exclusive claims" through a survey of the Joseph Cardinal Bernardin Jerusalem Lectures and finally, in my description of how the two communities engaged a case of competing claims in the public sphere, the past 40 years have been quite significant. Through a process of engagement of the other, the two communities have initiated, expanded, and continue to develop ways of conversing and pursuing initiatives for the common good. This ongoing dialogue has great potential for changing the shape of the global future. The fact that such dialogue exists and is expanding has been slow in impacting the public consciousness, even perhaps the awareness of many of the adherents of those religious groups. But, as I have demonstrated, dialogue is a means of accessing the public square, bringing a prior engagement of parties with each other into that square, and seeking a larger voice with a larger public. The quality of an already-in-process mode of action distinguishes it from the voices of individual religious bodies acting alone. In bringing their conversation public as well and seeking to engage the other participants in public dialogue and influence, the Catholic and Jewish communities have demonstrate the possibilities for seemingly diverse elements to fruitfully engage and interact.

Anti-Semitism: The Historical Legacy and Challenge for Christians

Joseph Cardinal Bernardin
Hebrew University of Jerusalem
March 23, 1995

Joseph Cardinal Bernardin, the Archbishop of Chicago from 1983 to 1996, received the honorary fellowship of the Hebrew University of Jerusalem on March 23, 1995. During a ceremony in the Senate Hall on Mount Scopus, the Cardinal delivered this address. Cardinal Bernardin detailed the development of Christian thought on the legacy of anti-Judaism, in particular pointing out how in recent years the Catholic Church has undertaken important efforts to acknowledge guilt for that legacy. He repudiates any remaining vestiges of in the Church's contemporary teaching and practice as sinful. The Cardinal calls upon Jews and Christians to recommit themselves to counter the resurgence of anti-Semitism, together with other forms of racial and ethnic violence. In responding to these realities, Cardinal Bernardin suggests several ways that Jews and Christians can, together and separately, build a better future of relations. He calls for renewal of Catholic teaching material on anti-Semitism, expansion of awareness of Vatican II's rejection of the anti-Judaic theology. The Cardinal calls for Jewish educators also to rethink the Jewish community's understanding of its relationship with the Church. In these and other ways, Jews and Christians can, together, build a new relationship for the future.

LADIES and gentlemen, I am greatly honored by your conferral upon me of the Honorary Fellowship of the Hebrew University of Jerusalem. It is a humbling experience, indeed, to receive such an honor from this distinguished scholarly community. I am also very grateful for this opportunity to address you on the subject of anti-Semitism from a Catholic point of view.

In recent years the Catholic Church has undertaken important efforts to acknowledge guilt for the legacy of anti-Semitism and to repudiate as *sinful* any remaining vestiges of that legacy in its contemporary teaching and practice. In 1989, the Pontifical Commission for Peace and Justice issued a strong declaration on racism, which had an international impact. The document, entitled *The Church and Racism: Towards a More Fraternal Society,* (24) insisted that "harboring racist thoughts and entertaining racist attitudes is a sin."[1] And it clearly included anti-Semitism on its list of continuing manifestations of racist ideologies that are to be regarded as sinful. In point of fact, *The Church and Racism* (15) calls anti-Semitism "the most tragic form that racist ideology has assumed in our century" and warns that certain forms of anti-Zionism, while not of the same order, often serve as a screen for anti-Semitism, feeding on it and leading to it.[2]

Pope John Paul II has taken up the challenge to anti-Semitism put forth by the Pontifical Commission on several occasions in recent years. During a visit to Hungary in 1991, conscious of the post-Communist era resurgence of anti-Semitism in certain parts of Central and Eastern Europe, the Pope spoke of the urgent task of repentance and reconciliation:

> In the face of a risk of a resurgence and spread of anti-Semitic feelings, attitudes, and initiatives, of which certain disquieting signs are to be seen today and of which we have experienced the most frightful results in the past, we must teach consciences to consider anti-Semitism, and all forms of racism, as sins against God and humanity.[3]

In his current book, *Crossing the Threshold of Hope,* the Holy Father repeats this theme as he calls anti-Semitism "a great sin against humanity."[4]

In my address this afternoon I will reflect on how we can work to eradicate the evil of anti-Semitism from our midst. This is not an easy

---

1. Pontifical Commission *Justitia et Pax: The Church and Racism: Towards a More Fraternal Society* (Washington D.C.: United States Catholic Conference, 1988, 34).

2. Ibid., 23

3. John Paul II, "The Significance of Anti-Semitism," *Origins,* 23:13 (September 5, 1991), 204.

4. John Paul II, *Crossing the Threshold of Hope,* ed. Vittorio Messori (New York: Alfred A. Knopf, 1994), 96.

task; it is one to which I have been dedicated for many years. My reflections will have four parts: (1) the roots of anti-Semitism in Christian history, (2) contemporary developments in Catholic theology, (3) thoughts on the relationship between anti-Semitism and Nazism, and (4) actions that can be taken to ensure that anti-Semitism is not part of the future.

Origins of Anti-Semitism

Allow me to explore briefly some of the reasons why anti-Semitism has been part of Christian life. It is important that we do this because anti-Semitism has deep roots in Christian history, which go back to the earliest days of the Church. In fact, as Father Edward Flannery has shown in his classic work on anti-Semitism, *The Anguish of the Jews,* the early Christian community inherited a cultural tradition from the Greco-Roman civilization that included a prejudicial outlook toward Jews.[5] Jews were disliked in pre-Christian Greece and Rome for their general unwillingness to conform to prevailing social mores. It is regrettable that this long history of anti-Semitism in a Christian context has been virtually eliminated from our history texts and other educational materials. Inclusion of this history, as painful as it is for us to hear today, is a necessary requirement for authentic reconciliation between Christians and Jews in our time.

In addition, there were many other factors that likely contributed to the growth of anti-Jewish feelings among Christians in the first centuries of the Church's existence. For one, the overwhelming number of early Christians came from the Greco-Roman communities with little personal acquaintance with Jews and Judaism. We now know from scholars dealing with early Christianity, such as Robert Wilken and Anthony Saldarini, that the final break between Judaism and Christianity was a far more gradual process than we once imagined, extending into the third and fourth centuries in some areas in the East.[6] Nevertheless, the *formative* influence of Jewish Christianity upon the Church as a whole

5. Edward Flannery, *The Anguish of the Jews,* rev. ed., (New York/Mahweh: Paulist Press, 1985).

6. See Wayne A. Meeks and Robert L. Wilken, *Jews and Christians in Antioch in the First Four Centuries* (Missoula, MT: Scholars Press, 1978); Robert L. Wilken, *John Chrysostom and the Jews: Rhetoric and Reality in the Late 4th Century* (Berkeley: University of California Press, 1983); and Anthony J. Saldarini, "Jews and Christians in the First Two Centuries: The Changing Paradigm," in *Shofar* 10 (1992), 34.

declined rapidly after the pivotal decision reached by Paul and the representatives of the Jerusalem Church at what is often called the Council of Jerusalem. This resulted in the loss of any countervailing positive identification with Jews and their religious heritage that could overcome the new convert's inbred cultural prejudices. This tendency toward separation from anything Jewish was further enhanced by the desire to avoid any linkage between the Church and the Jewish community after the disastrous Jewish revolt against the Roman imperial authorities (66–70 C.E.) which, besides the destruction of the Temple in Jerusalem, generated continued post-war pressure and retribution by Rome against the Jewish community.

Another factor contributing to the emergence of anti-Semitism in early Christianity may be the image of Jews that emerges from the New Testament itself. There are texts that remain open to anti-Judaic interpretation, and there is ample evidence that such interpretations emerge in the first centuries of Christian history.

Negative attitudes towards Jews in the New Testament were only the beginning of difficulties for the Jewish community. Unfortunately, there soon developed within the teachings of the early Fathers of the Church a strong tendency to regard Jews as entirely displaced from the covenantal relationship because of their unwillingness to accept Jesus as the Messiah, despite the clear teaching to the contrary on the part of St. Paul in Romans 9–11, which served as a basis for the Second Vatican Council's renewed constructive theology of the Christian-Jewish relationship.

This belief, that the Jews had been totally rejected by God and replaced in the covenantal relationship by the "New Israel," led to the emergence of another widespread doctrine in patristic writings. I have in mind the so-called "perpetual wandering" theology which consigned Jews to a condition of permanent statelessness as a consequence of their displacement from the covenant as a punishment for murdering the Messiah. This condition of being permanently displaced persons was meant as an enduring sign of Jewish sinfulness and as a warning to others of what they could expect if they too failed to accept Christ. This theology became so deep-seated in popular culture that even a familiar houseplant—the "wandering Jew"—took on its name.

We can illustrate this theology of "perpetual wandering" with references from certain central figures in the patristic era. Eusebius of Caesarea (c. 265–339 C.E.), for example, speaks of how the royal metropolis of the

Jews would be destroyed by fire and the city would become inhabited no longer by Jews, "but by races of other stock, while they (i.e., the Jews) would be dispersed among the Gentiles throughout the whole world with never a hope of any cessation of evil or breathing space from troubles."[7] St. Cyprian of Carthage (c. 210–258 C.E.), relying on various prophetic texts, which suggest desolation and exile as a consequence of sin, envisioned Israel as having entered its final state of desolation and exile. Following in the same vein, St. Hippolytus of Rome, who was born around 170 C.E., insisted that, unlike the exilic experiences suffered by the Jews at the hands of the Egyptians and the Babylonians in earlier times, the post-biblical exile would continue throughout the course of human history. In the East, St. John Chrysostom (344–407 C.E.) clearly linked the now permanent exilic condition of the Jews with the "killing of Christ." And St. Augustine of Hippo (354–430 C.E.) in his classic work, *City of God,* speaks several times of the Jews as "having their back bend down always."

While the patristic writings were far more than an extended anti-Jewish treatise, Christians cannot ignore this "shadow side" of patristic theology, which in other aspects remains a continuing source of profound spiritual enrichment. The Jews are very well aware of the "shadow side" of this theology; unfortunately, Christians generally are not. It has been omitted from basic Christian texts far too often. Yet, we cannot understand the treatment of the Jews in subsequent centuries without some grasp of this theology. The history to which it gave rise is replete with persistent forms of social and religious discrimination and persecution, which brought upon the Jewish community continual humiliation as well as political and civil inequality. On occasion, this further degenerated into outright physical suffering and even death, especially in such periods as that of the Crusades.

The legacy of anti-Semitism, with its profoundly negative social consequences for Jews as individuals and for the Jewish community as a whole, remained the dominant social pattern in Western Christian lands until the twentieth century. While we can point to some notable breaks in this pattern in such countries as Spain and Poland, as well as for individual Jews in the liberal democracies created in parts of Europe and North America, the respite was something short-lived and, as in the

---

7. Eusebius of Caesarea, *Demonstration of the Gospel,* 1,1.

case of Spain, followed by even more flagrant forms of attack on the Jewish community.

At the dawn of the twentieth century the theology of perpetual divine judgment upon the Jewish people did not vanish overnight. Rather, it continued to exercise a decisive role in shaping Catholicism's initial reactions, for example, to the proposal for restoring a Jewish national homeland in Palestine. It also was of central importance in shaping popular Christian attitudes toward the Nazis and their stated goal of eliminating all Jews from Europe and beyond through deliberate extermination. While I will return to this question of classical anti-Semitism and its role during that period, there is little doubt that this persistent tradition provided an indispensable seed-bed for the Nazis' ability to succeed as far as they did in their master plan. They would not have secured the popular support they enjoyed were it not for the continuing influence of traditional Christian anti-Semitism on the masses of baptized believers in Europe.

Both Father Edward Flannery and the late Professor Uriel Tal have emphasized the significant impact of classical Christian anti-Semitism upon the development of Nazism, despite their shared conviction that the philosophy of the Third Reich resulted primarily from distinctly modern forces. Flannery argues that the architects of the *Shoah* found their Jewish targets well-primed for the formulation of their racist theories:

> The degraded state of the Jews, brought about by centuries of opprobrium and oppression, gave support to the invidious comparisons with which the racists built their theories. And in their evil design, they were able to draw moral support from traditional views of Jews and Judaism.[8]

Professor Tal offered an analysis very similar to that of Father Flannery's in this regard. He insisted that Nazi racial anti-Semitism was not totally original when subjected to careful scrutiny. Rather, traditional Christian stereotypes of Jews and Judaism were clothed in new pseudo-scientific jargon and applied to specific historical realities of the period. Tal insisted that:

---

8. Edward Flannery, "Anti-Zionism and the Christian Psyche," *Journal of Ecumenical Studies*, 6:2 (Spring 1969), 174 175.

. . . racial anti-Semitism and the subsequent Nazi movement were not the result of mass hysteria or the work of single propagandists. The racial anti-Semites, despite their antagonism toward traditional Christianity, learned much from it, and succeeded in producing a well-prepared, systematic ideology with a logic of its own that reached its culmination in the Third Reich.[9]

Contemporary Developments

Having traced the development of anti-Semitism within Christianity, we can turn to contemporary developments. In the three decades or so since the beginning of the Second Vatican Council, the negative theology of the Jewish people has lost its theological foundations. In chapter four of *Nostra Aetate,* the Council clearly asserted that there never existed a valid basis either for the charge of collective guilt against the Jewish community for supposedly "murdering the Messiah" or for the consequent theology of permanent Jewish suffering and displacement. With its positive affirmation of continued covenantal inclusion on the part of the Jewish People after the coming of Christ Jesus, following St. Paul in Romans 9–11, the Council permanently removed all basis for the long-held "perpetual wandering" theology and the social deprivation and suffering that flowed from it.

The Second Vatican Council's removal of the classical "displacement/perpetual wandering" theology from contemporary Catholic catechesis has been enhanced in subsequent documents from the Holy See and Pope John Paul II. The Holy See's 1985 *Notes on the Correct Way to Present the Jews and Judaism in Preaching and Catechesis in the Roman Catholic Church,* issued to commemorate the twentieth anniversary of Nostra Aetate, makes two very important constructive affirmations, especially when these are set over against the history of Catholicism's traditional approach to the question of Jewish existence. Both occur in paragraph 25 where the Notes maintain that "the history of Israel did not end in AD 70 (i.e., with the destruction of the Jerusalem Temple by the Romans). . . . It continued, especially in a numerous Diaspora which allowed Israel to carry to the whole world a witness . . . while preserving the memory of the land of their forefathers at the heart of

9. Urial Tal, *Christians and Jews in Germany: Religion, Politics and Ideology in the Second Reich, 1870-1914* (Ithaca, NY: Cornell University Press, 1975), 305.

their hope" and, subsequently, that " the permanence of Israel (while so many ancient peoples have disappeared without a trace) is a historic fact, and a sign to be interpreted within God's design."[10] Both these statements clearly repudiate a "displacement" theology.

Pope John Paul II, who has contributed significantly to the development of the Church's new theological outlook on Jews and Judaism,[11] wrote the following in his 1984 statement *Redemptionis Anno:*

> For the Jewish people who live in the State of Israel and who preserve in that land such precious testimonies of their history and their faith, we must ask for the desired security and due tranquility that is the prerogative of every nation and condition of life and of progress of every society.[12]

This statement clearly exhibits on the part of the Holy Father a sense of the deep intertwining of faith and continued attachment to the land on the part of the Jewish People, a sense that further draws out the profound implications of the renewed theology of the Christian-Jewish relationship put forth by the Second Vatican Council.

The two recent documents of the Holy See further seal the coffin of the biblically unfounded "displacement" theology. The first is the text of the new *Catechism of the Catholic Church,* which reaffirms the two major points on which the Council built its new theological approach to the Jewish People. In paragraph #57, the Catechism rejects any idea that all Jews then or now can be charged with the responsibility for Jesus's death. It reminds Christians that their sins were largely the reason why Jesus died on the cross. And paragraph #849 speaks of the distinctiveness of Jewish faith as an authentic response to God's original revelation and underlines the permanence of the divine promise made to the people Israel.[13]

The second document is the *Holy See-Israel Accords.* While this is fundamentally a political document that develops a framework for dealing with concrete issues, it has an underlying theological significance as well. Mindful of the long-standing theological approach to Jewish political sovereignty on the part of the Catholic tradition, the Preamble to

10. *Notes on the Correct Way to Present the Jews and Judaism in Preaching and Catechesis in the Roman Catholic Church*, (Vatican City: Libreria Editrice Vaticana, 1985), #25.

11. Cf. Eugene J. Fisher and Leon Klinicki, eds., *John Paul II on Jews and Judaism* (Washington, D.C., United States Catholic Conference, 1987).

12. Cf. *The Pope Speaks,* 29:3 (1984), 219–220.

13. Cf. *Catechism of the Catholic Church* (Collegeville, MN: The Liturgical Press, 1994), 597, 839.

the Accords has set this essentially political document within the over-all context of the process of Catholic-Jewish reconciliation underway in the Church since the Second Vatican Council:

> . . . aware of the unique nature of the relationship between the Catholic Church and the Jewish people, and the historic process of reconciliation and growth in mutual understanding and friendship between Catholics and Jews . . .

So reads the opening part of the Accords.

It is also well to note that article #2 of the Accords contains a very strong and unequivocal condemnation by the Holy See of "hatred, per-secution and all manifestations of anti-Semitism directed against the Jewish people and individual Jews. . . ." I welcome this forthright state-ment as well as the accompanying pledge by the Holy See and the State of Israel to cooperate in every possible way:

> in combating all forms of anti-Semitism and all kinds of racism and of religious intolerance, and in promoting mutual understanding among nations, tolerance among communities and respect for human life and dignity. (no. 1)

This statement makes concrete the renewed theological vision of the Christian-Jewish relationship developed at the Second Vatican Council. It also solidifies the notion that forms of racism, including anti-Semitism, are fundamentally sinful as the 1989 Holy See document and the papal statements I cited earlier make clear.

The Holy See's action in formally recognizing Israel through the Accords represents a final seal on the process begun at the Second Vatican Council to rid Catholicism of all vestiges of "displacement the-ology" and the implied notion of perpetual Jewish homelessness. The Accords represent the Catholic Church's full and final acknowledgment of Jews as a *people,* not merely as individuals. I recognize that for the vast majority of Jews, Israel signifies their ultimate tie to Jewish peoplehood, their central point of self-identity. And as the Holy See's 1974 Guidelines on Catholic-Jewish relations pointed out, authentic dialogue requires that all partners come to understand and respect one another as they define themselves. As Arthur Hertzberg has shown very well in his classic work,

The French Enlightenment and the Jews,[14] even democratic societies that were prepared to grant Jews a measure of personal freedom and political rights were unable to accept the idea of Jewish peoplehood.

Until now I have been speaking of developments that have already occurred. As we all know, much more needs to be done. In particular, there is need for continued scholarship and theological reflection, especially with regard to what many consider to be problematic New Testament texts. While it is not certain that any of these texts can be legitimately termed "anti-Semitic," or even "anti-Judaic," scholars differ significantly on this point and will likely do so for the foreseeable future. I am aware that some scholars doing important research on this topic, including people here in Jerusalem such as Malcolm Lowe, believe the problem is essentially one of mistranslation. Others interpret it primarily as an internal Jewish polemic, which was not an uncommon phenomenon in the period, as we know from certain Jewish documents, the Talmud included.[15] Retranslation (where scholarly consensus can be achieved) and reinterpretation certainly are to be included among the goals we pursue in the effort at eradicating anti-Semitism. But at this point, the requisite scholarly consensus on the especially problematic passages appears a long way off.

In the interim, as we await a scholarly resolution of the question of anti-Semitism in the New Testament, I would strongly urge that the Church adopt a pastoral approach. Father Raymond Brown, a renowned Catholic scholar on the Gospel of John, has suggested the basis of such a pastoral approach, at least with respect to the Fourth Gospel, which is generally considered among the most problematic of all New Testament books in its outlook toward Jews and Judaism. In commenting on John's use of the term, "the Jews," Brown expresses his conviction that, by deliberately using this generic term (where other gospel writers refer to the Jewish authorities or the various Second Temple Jewish parties), John meant to extend to the synagogue of his own day blame that an earlier tradition had attributed to the Jewish authorities. Although John was not the first to engage in such extension, he is the most insistent New

---

14. Arthur Hertzberg, *The French Enlightenment and the Jews: The Origins of Modern Anti-Semitism* (New York: Schocken, 1968).

15. Cf. John T. Pawlikowski, "New Testament Anti-Semitism: Fact or Fable?" in Michael Curtis (ed.), *Anti-Semitism in the Contemporary World* (Boulder and London: Westview Press, 1986), 107–127.

Testament author in this regard. Brown attributes this process in John to the persecution that Christians were experiencing during the time at the hands of the synagogue authorities. Jews who professed Jesus to be the Messiah had been officially expelled from Judaism, thus making them vulnerable to Roman investigation and punishment. Jews were tolerated by Rome, but who were these Christians whom the Jews disclaimed?

Father Raymond Brown maintains that this teaching of John about the Jews, which resulted from the historical conflict between the Church and synagogue in the latter part of the first century C.E., can no longer be taught as authentic doctrine or used as catechesis by contemporary Christianity. This is the key pastoral point. Christians today must come to see that such teachings, while an acknowledged part of their biblical heritage, can no longer be regarded as definitive teaching in light of our improved understanding of developments in the relationship between early Christianity and the Jewish community of the time. As Brown says in his book, *The Community of the Beloved Disciple,* "It would be incredible for a twentieth-century Christian to share or justify the Johannine contention that 'the Jews' are the children of the Devil, an affirmation which is placed on the lips of Jesus (Jn 8:44).[16]

Negative passages such as these must be re-evaluated in light of the Second Vatican Council's strong affirmation in its Declaration on the Relation of the Church to Non-Christian Religions *(Nostra Aetate)* that Jews remain a covenanted people, revered by God. The teaching of recent popes has also emphasized this. Pope John Paul II, in particular, has often highlighted the intimate bond that exists between Jews and Christians who are united in one ongoing covenant.

Nazism and Anti-Semitism

I would now like to return to the issue of Nazism and anti-Semitism, which continues to elicit considerable discussion today. I know it remains an important area of concern for this university, especially the Sassoon International Center for the Study of Anti-Semitism directed by Professor Yehuda Bauer. I am likewise aware of the many outstanding

---

16. Raymond P. Brown, *The Community of the Beloved Disciple* (New York: Paulist Press, 1979), 41–42. Cf. "The Passion According to John: Chapter 18 and 19," *Worship* 49 (March 1975), 130–131.

contributions made to our understanding of the *Shoah* by other members of your faculty, including Professors Israel Gutman and Emil Fackenheim.

During the past several decades, scholars throughout the world have advanced various perspectives on the relationship between the rise of Nazism and classical Christian hatred of the Jews. Some draw virtually a straight line from classical Christian thought regarding the Jewish people to the emergence of the *Shoah*. They point, for example, to Hitler's often-quoted remark to Church leaders, who came to see him to protest the treatment of the Jews that he was merely putting into practice what the Christian churches had preached for nearly two thousand years. These perspectives also highlight the close similarity between much of Nazi anti-Jewish legislation and laws against Jews in earlier Christian-dominated societies.

As I have already pointed out, relying on the research of Father Flannery and the late Professor Tal, there is little doubt that classical Christian presentations of Jews and Judaism were a central factor in generating popular support for the Nazi endeavor, along with economic greed, religious and political nationalism, and ordinary human fear. For many baptized Christians, traditional Christian beliefs about Jews and Judaism constituted the primary motivation for their support, active or tacit, of the Nazi movement. Some even went so far as to define the Nazi struggle against the Jews in explicitly religious and theological terms. In the Church today, we must not minimize the extent of Christian collaboration with Hitler and his associates. It remains a profound moral challenge that we must continue to confront for our own integrity as a religious community.

Nevertheless, in the final analysis, I must side with the perspective of those scholars such as Yosef Yerushalmi who have insisted that "the Holocaust was the work of a thoroughly modern, neo-pagan state," and not merely as "transformed" medieval anti-Semitism rooted in Christian teachings.[17] The *Shoah* cannot be seen as simply the final and most gruesome chapter in the long history of Christian anti-Semitism. Rather, it was a plan for the mass destruction of human lives, supposedly undertaken in the name of "healing" humanity, as the psychologist Robert J. Lifton has put it, rooted in modern theories of inherent biological and

---

17. Yosef Hayim Yerushalmi, "Response to Rosemary Ruether," in Eva Fleischner (ed.), *Auschwitz: Beginning of a New Era?* (New York: KTAV, the Cathedral Church of Saint John the Divine, and the Anti-Defamation League, 1977), 103.

racial inferiority, coupled with the escalation of bureaucratic and technological capacities. At its depth, it was profoundly as anti-Christian as it was anti-Jewish, evidenced by the fact that at least one of its theoreticians attempted to rewrite the New Testament totally based on Nazi concepts. It coalesced several important modern strains of thought into its master plan for human extermination.

To bring this plan to realization required, as the Nazis envisioned it, the elimination of the "dregs" of society. These they defined as first and foremost the Jewish people, but the category also was extended to embrace the disabled, Gypsies, the Polish leadership, homosexuals, and certain other designated groups. Proper distinctions need to be maintained between the wholesale attack on the Jewish people, for whom there was absolutely no escape from Nazi fury, and the others subjected to systematic Nazi attack. But there is also a linkage with the victimization of these other groups whose suffering and death were integral, not peripheral, to the overall Nazi plan. This is what makes the Holocaust *sui generis,* even though the fate of its primary victims, the Jews, has important ties to classical Christian teachings.

Future Possibilities

Let us turn now from the horrors of the past to the possibilities of the future. Confronting the legacy of anti-Semitism will not prove easy, but confront it we must. Allow me to discuss several ways in which this can be done.

1. The history of anti-Semitism and of anti-Judaic theology must be restored to our Catholic teaching materials. Innocence or ignorance is not a pathway to authentic virtue in this regard; courageous honesty is. In our religious education programs we should be prepared to tell the full story of the Church's treatment of Jews over the centuries, ending with a rejection of the shadow side of the history and theology at the Second Vatican Council. We can and should highlight moments of relative tranquility and constructive interaction when they occurred in such countries as Poland, Spain, and the United States, but these stories should never obscure the more pronounced history and subjection.

2. We also need an integral understanding of the Holocaust. In developing such an understanding, we have a responsibility to speak against

unwarranted and generalized accusations directed at the Church and Church leaders. We need to re-emphasize the protest statements and oppositional actions of Christian leaders and grassroots groups and individuals. The Fulda Declaration of the German Catholic Bishops, the Barmen Declaration of the Confessing Church (Lutheran) in Germany, the encyclical letter *Mit Brennender Sorge* issued in German by Pope Pius XI, the efforts of Archbishops Angelo Roncalli and Angelo Rotta, the Zegota movement in Poland, the many Catholic women religious whose communities hid Jews, the men and women of Le Chambon in France, Jan Karski of the Polish government-in-exile, the Austrian peasant Franz Jagerstatter—I could go on. To be sure, there were not enough. But these Christians preserved a measure of moral integrity in the Church during these years of Nazi darkness.

Nevertheless, the witness of these courageous Christian leaders, groups and individuals should never be used to argue against the need for a full scrutiny of Church activities by reputable scholars. We must be prepared to deal honestly and candidly with the genuine failures of some in the Christian churches during that critical period. To that end, I would repeat what I first said in my keynote address to those attending the meeting of the International Catholic-Jewish Liaison Committee held in Baltimore in May, 1992. The Catholic Church must be prepared to submit its World War II record to a thorough scrutiny by respected scholars. The detailed investigation of diocesan records from the Nazi era undertaken that same year in Lyons, France, with the support of the cardinal archbishop is a fine example of what I have in mind. Such efforts should avoid broad generalizations, but instead focus in depth on specific geographic regions, as do, for example, the recent work on Poland by Dr. Roland Modras[18] here at this university and the symposium papers collected by Professors Otto Dov Kulka and Paul Mendes-Flohr in the volume *Judaism and Christianity Under the Impact of National Socialism*.[19]

3. Education about the Holocaust should become a prominent feature in Catholic education at every level. To assist in realizing this goal, Seton

18. Cf. Ronald Modras, *The Catholic Church and Anti-Semitism Poland, 1933–1939* (Chur, Switzerland: Harwood Academic Publishers, 1994).

19. Otto Dov Kulka and Paul R. Mendes-Flohr (eds.), *Judaism and Christianity Under the Impact of National Socialism* (Jerusalem: The Historical Society of Israel and the Zalman Shazar Center for Jewish History, 1987).

Hill College near Pittsburgh has established a program explicitly designed for Catholic teachers that works closely with both Yad Vashem and the U.S. Holocaust Memorial Museum. And in Chicago, I have instructed the archdiocesan school system to comply with the state mandate on Holocaust education even though it does not technically apply to our institutions.

4. But we must go beyond merely teaching the failures of the past, as crucial as that task remains. *Nostra Aetate* and subsequent documents from the Holy See, as well as Pope John Paul II, have not merely removed the classical prejudices against Jews and Judaism from Catholic teaching. They have laid out the basis for a positive theology of reconciliation and bonding. This, too, must become part of our current effort in education.

In fact, several studies on Catholic religion materials undertaken by Sister Rose Thering at St. Louis University,[20] Dr. Eugene J. Fisher at New York University,[21] and most recently, Dr. Philip Cunningham at Boston College[22] have shown a steady development in the presentation of the Catholic-Jewish relationship, from one marked by classical stereotypes to one focused on the bonding of Christians and Jews within the one covenanted family. Not all problems have been resolved, but the progress has been remarkable. In this connection, I wish to add that it is my hope that, at the same time as we seek to develop a positive Christian understanding, Jewish educators will also be able to rethink the Jewish community's understanding of its relationship with the Church.

5. Liturgy and preaching are additional areas that require continued attention by the Church. In 1988, the U.S. Bishops' Committee on the Liturgy released a set of guidelines for the presentation of Jews and Judaism in Catholic preaching.[23] They offer directions for implementing the vision of *Nostra Aetate* and subsequent documents of the Holy See

---

20. For a description and analysis of the Thering study, cf. John T. Pawlikowski, OSM, *Catechetics & Prejudice: How Catholic Teaching Materials View Jews, Protestants and Racial Minorities* (New York/Paramus/Toronto: Paulist Press, 1973).

21. Eugene J. Fisher, *Faith Without Prejudice: Rebuilding Christian Attitudes Toward Judaism.* Revised and Expanded Edition (New York: The American Interfaith Institute and Crossroad, 1993).

22. Philip A. Cunningham, *Education for Shalom: Religion Textbooks and the Enhancement of the Catholic and Jewish Relationship* (Collegeville, MN: The Liturgical Press, 1995).

23. U.S. Catholic Bishops' Committee on the Liturgy, *God's Mercy Endures Forever: Guidelines on the Presentation of Jews and Judaism in Catholic Preaching* (Washington, DC: U.S. Catholic Conference, 1988).

in the Church's ministry of the Word during the various liturgical seasons. Especially highlighted are the seasons of Lent/Holy Week and Easter, whose texts can serve to reinforce classical Christian stereotypes of Jews and Judaism if not interpreted carefully. The great challenge of these liturgical seasons is that they become times of reconciliation between Jews and Christians rather than conflict and division, as they were in past centuries. Christians need to recognize their profound bonds with the Jewish people during these central periods of the liturgical year in accord with the vision expressed by the Second Vatican Council and Pope John Paul II.

6. But education and preaching will not prove completely effective unless we also have women and men of vision and reconciliation who embody the new spirit of Jewish-Christian bonding. I especially honor all those Christians in this land who have embodied *Nostra Aetate* in their lives and work for many years. In a particular way, I would like to congratulate Father Marcel Dubois of the Dominican community on this his seventy-fifth birthday. Through his many years of service as a member of the faculty here at Hebrew University, and through his painstaking efforts as a consultant to the Holy See's Commission for Religious Relations with the Jews, he has helped to shape the face of contemporary Catholic-Jewish relations.

7. Above all, in light of the history of the Holocaust, the Church needs to engage in public repentance. As I remembered the six million Jewish victims of the Shoah this morning at Yad Vashem, I was reminded of the Holy Father's call upon the Christian community, in preparation for the celebration of the third millennium of Christianity, to foster a genuine spirit of repentance for "the acquiescence given, especially in certain centuries, to intolerance and even the use of violence in the service of truth." The Church, he added, bears an obligation "to express profound regret for the weakness of so many of her sons and daughters who sullied her face, preventing her from fully mirroring the image of her crucified Lord, the supreme witness of patient love and of humble meekness."[24]

It is this spirit that my brother bishops in Germany, on the occasion of the fiftieth anniversary of the liberation of Auschwitz-Berkenau, issued a statement in which they took responsibility for the failure of the

---

24. Pope John Paul II, Apostolic Letter, *"As the Third Millennium Draws Near,"* Origins, 24:24 (November 24, 1994), 411.

Catholic community during the *Shoah*. While mindful of the exemplary behavior of certain individuals and groups, some of whom I have already named, the German bishops acknowledge that "Christians did not offer due resistance to racial anti-Semitism. Many times there was failure and guilt among Catholics." And they go on to add a point with which I wholeheartedly concur: "The practical sincerity of our will of renewal is also linked to the confession of this guilt and the willingness to painfully learn from this history of guilt. . . ."[25]

My friends, as I draw these reflections to a close, I cannot help but reflect on the fact that I have spoken to an often tragic past in the history of Christian-Jewish relations here in this city of Jerusalem, which both of our religious traditions have always envisioned as ultimately a city of peace. In this context, let me lift up the powerful words of the Nobel Prize winners, including Elie Wiesel, who gathered with President Lech Walesa of Poland at the fiftieth anniversary commemoration of Auschwitz-Birkenau. "To the victims of this crime, we owe a commitment to the memory both of their death and their life," they proclaimed in their *Appeal to the Nations of the World*.

> Their heritage must help mankind to build faith in a future free from racism, hatred and anti-Semitism. . . . In equal measure, we owe a duty to the living to safeguard peace, tolerance, and fundamental human rights. . . . Let instruments of governance be created which will guarantee the peaceful resolution of all conflicts.

As we reflect today on the legacy of anti-Semitism, Jews and Christians need to recommit themselves to counter its disturbing resurgence in North America, Latin America, and Europe, together with other forms of racism and inter-group violence. Here in Jerusalem, where the vision of peace may seem very far off at times, there is need to find ways to cooperate for the development of a genuine peace among Christians, Jews, and Muslims, Arabs and Israelis, that includes living faith communities with full opportunity for economic justice. Jerusalem, my brothers and sisters, cannot become a mere monument to peace. It must be a true city of living communities of peace, a true Neve Shalom. That is my prayer. That is my hope. That is my dream!

---

25. "Statement of the German Bishops on the Occasion of the 50th Anniversary of the Liberation of the Extermination Camp of Auschwitz," January 27, 1995, 1–2.

Jewish-Christian Relations after the Holocaust: Toward Post-Holocaust Theological Thought

Emil L. Fackenheim
April 17, 1990

After the success of Cardinal Bernardin's Dialogue Visit to Israel, the West Bank and Gaza, the staff of the sponsoring organizations asked the question of how to continue the progress of the Chicago dialogue. The Jerusalem Lecture had been the centerpiece of the visit to Israel. What was significant about the lecture was that it moved the Chicago dialogue away from the goal of good intergroup relations and firmly set before all parties the need to engage theology. Already in Chicago there was an effective Catholic-Jewish Scholars Dialogue, but what the Jerusalem Lecture had shown was the value of conducting the theological reflection in a more public forum. From these insights, the Jerusalem Lecture series was born. Cardinal Bernardin approved the idea and together with the American Jewish Committee, the Chicago Board of Rabbis, the Jewish Federation of Metropolitan Chicago and Spertus Institute of Jewish Studies, the Archdiocese of Chicago established an annual lecture series to study the theological issues affecting the relationship between Christians and Jews. To begin the project, the committee felt that it would be necessary for a Jewish scholar to respond to the themes raised by Cardinal Bernardin in the original Jerusalem Lecture. The two lectures would then serve as a foundation for what was to come later. Professor Emil L. Fackenheim was selected to deliver the first Chicago lecture.

*Professor Fackenheim is a Fellow of the Institute of Contemporary
Jewry of the Hebrew University of Jerusalem and of the Jewish
Institute of Public Affairs. He was born in Germany in 1916 and
ordained a rabbi in Berlin in 1939. Professor Fackenheim was a partici-
pant in the Dialogue Visit. He led a session of the dialogue at the
King David Hotel with the Cardinal and other members of the delega-
tion. His lecture builds on that exchange and is entitled "Jewish-
Christian Relations after the Holocaust: Toward Post-Holocaust
Theological Thought."*

I. Christmas in Sachsenhausen

In 1938, I took part in a memorable Christmas. Following the *Kristallnacht*
of November 9—they had burned down nearly three hundred synagogues,
smashed thousands of store windows, looted the stores, murdered
dozens of Jews, and arrested some thirty thousand—I was in a concentration camp. And here we were on Christmas Eve, in Sachsenhausen,
some sixty of us in our "block," Jews all except for three Christians. With
one, the head of the block, the *Blockaelteste,* I had no contact. The
second, Ernst Tillich, a nephew of theologian Paul [Tillich], belongs in
another story. Hans Ehrenberg belongs in this one. He was a cousin of
Franz Rosenweig, and a well-known theologian in his own right, but a
Christian, for he was a convert and a Protestant pastor.

The pastor looked depressed on Christmas Eve, and when I asked
him why, he said the he had a sermon but no parishioners. So I got him
three friends of mine, and the four of us, rabbinical students all, were
his congregation. Of these Karl Rautenberg, later Rabbi Charles Berg in
England, died some years ago. The other two are friends to this day:
Henry Fischel, a retired professor of Jewish studies at Indiana University,
and Hans Harf, a rabbi, also retired, in Buenos Aires.[1]

I have long forgotten what Ehrenberg said in that sermon of his, but
never the occasion. Gripped by the drama of a shared Christmas at this
time and place—the time: six weeks after Kristallnacht; the place:

---

1. Harf recently visited Jerusalem and corrected this: They had released him before Christmas.
But having thought of him as present all these years, I have let it stand.

Sachsenhausen—I was sure as only the young "existential" bent can be that this was an historic moment, a moment of truth: with this assault by the new pagans on both our faiths—the Jewish and the Christian—whatever had divided us for nearly two millennia just had come to an end. There just would have to be a new Jewish-Christian reality, a new bond between the two covenants, the Jewish and the Christian—between what, decades later, Protestant theologian Roy Eckardt would call "older" and "younger brother."[2]

It was young and naive of me to think of the new assailants as "pagans," an insult to any pagan who ever existed. (To consider them "barbarians," too, is to insult all whoever were that and nothing worse.) Yet other people, older and wiser, were naive also at the time. Indeed, to this day we may fail to grasp the apocalyptic horror—a Hitler victory—that the world has barely escaped: Humanity divided into sub-humans and supermen, both have ceased to be human, both enslaved—the first by others, the second to enslaving others, all born and bred to no other purpose, in turn breeding others to the same purpose, and these yet others, and so on, for the thousand years the Third Reich was to last.[3]

Some have forgotten, but others are obligated to remember, among them Jews and Christians, for while that victory never came, the Holocaust did; and—for serious theological thought—Jewish-Christian relations, afterward, cannot be what once they were. The regime had imposed a novum on that relation: the "Aryan/non-Aryan" distinction. Affirmed from the start, inescapable once made into law, it had a terrible climax in Auschwitz and Bergen-Belsen. It is over, thank God, but that fateful *novum,* the "Aryan/non-Aryan" distinction, still has an afterlife; hence I will, in this discourse, confirm my attention entirely to it. Winston Churchill has said that the world needs ridding, not only to Hitler but, also of his shadow.

Who was "non-Aryan"? There was some uncertainty about half-Jews, more about quarter-Jews, and ideological confusion about gypsies.

---

2. This image needs changing. A Christian is not a brother by blood, but can be a friend and ally by choice.

3. Before writing this sentence I read more than a thousand pages, especially, among recent works, Gerhard Weinberg, *A World at Arms* (Cambridge University Press 1995). According to Weinberg, Hitler planned bloody world conquest as early as in his 1928 secret book [Hitler's Secret Book (New York: Grove Press, 1983)] and later pursued that goal with frightening, increasingly ruthless consistency. I have also read or re-read early works, among them Bullock, Bracher, Fest, Jaeckel, Waite, even Irving and of course, Hitler himself, and ended with this, to me utterly scary sentence.

(Sometimes "good," "hard-working" gypsies—who played the violin—were distinguished from "bad," "shiftless," "thievish" ones—who didn't.) In contrast, the 1942 Wannsee conference (which planned the "combing" of Europe for "non-Aryans," including as-yet-unconquered Britain, Spain, Portugal, Sweden, and Switzerland) was unequivocal: Jews and they alone, were indisputably, inescapably "non-Aryan." And the goal, pursued with holy—or is it unholy?—zeal, was—for the time being—to make at least one continent *judenrein*.

Who were the "Aryans"? There was much latitude, for the Japanese wartime allies were honorary ones, as was the "Semitic" Mufti of Jerusalem, a guest in Nazi Berlin. And Christians? Unless converts from Judaism, they were "Aryans." Such was the division. Its crucial significance for Jewish-Christian relations concerns choicelessness and choice. *"Non-Aryans" were robbed of choice, for birth is choiceless. "Aryans," in contrast, in having that designation thrust upon them, had a choice thrust on them also: They could accept the designation or reject it.*

I need not, for the present, go beyond this aspect of Nazi theory and practice, for it quite suffices to demolish my starry-eyed view of our 1938 Christmas. In a concentration camp, four Jews and one Christian had been at one in worship? But just then the "Aryan/non-Aryan" dichotomy was driving them farther apart than ever. The history of Jewish-Christian coexistence is marked by much distance, with all too little bridging.[4] But the "Aryan/non-Aryan" dichotomy widened it into an abyss, with all bridges, or nearly all, burned and destroyed.[5]

Yet now, more than fifty years later, I find myself back with that Christmas in Sachsenhausen. The Holocaust has happened; the facts, for the most part, are in; and the survivors and their testimony are almost gone. *But the theological thought required by the catastrophe has hardly begun; and only one of its tasks is clear even yet: It must undo the twelve-year abyss so as to fashion a Jewish-Christian bond of shared purpose—a bond that is unbreakable.*

However, what is theologically necessary does not always come to pass empirically.

---

4. The best analogy on this subject known to me is Frank E. Talmage, ed., *Disputation and Dialogue* (New York: KTAV, 1975).

5. See further below, #5.

II. Theology Faces Up to the Past

In venturing into the mostly uncharted territory of a post-Holocaust theology, I am encouraged by two assertions made by Cardinal Bernardin when he spoke in Jerusalem. Christians, he contended, may no longer ignore—sweep under the rug—the anti-Semitism in their own past. They must confront and fight it. And, as well as in Christian life, they must confront it also in theological thought.[6] This second demand, it seems to me, is more significant even than the first. That the anti-Semitism, say, of the Oberammergau Passion Play can be blamed on "mere Christendom," that is on a popular Christianity without prejudice has not or not yet, penetrated.[7] But in demanding a critique of anti-Semitism in theological thought also, the cardinal touches Christianity as understood by the best, the most serious, the most saintly, the most authoritative.

What the cardinal now demands is all the more striking in that it is opposite to what, during the Nazi regime and for years after, most people of good will, on both sides of Jewish-Christian dialogue, considered appropriate. Think of the past as then it was. For Jews, the world was divided into enemies and friends. One part, the Nazi enemy, was murderous; the other, the democratic friend, lukewarm. When Jews were fleeing for their lives, the gates of that friend were not wide open; and when they could flee no more—the war was on, they could not escape—their rescue was not among their friend's priorities. Then what need was there, among Christians who were with Jews—clamoring for open gates, and for whatever rescue, even in war, was possible—to stress possibly lesser, certainly older forms of anti-Semitism that were, so to speak, in their own backyard? For Protestants in dialogue with Jews, was it not better to emphasize Luther on the liberty than his *The Jews and their Lies?*[8] For Catholics, rather than dwell on anti-Jewish texts that set Jews and Christians apart, did the times not call for a Thomas Aquinas, for whom "Rabbi Moises" (as he called Maimonides) was a fellow philosopher?

---

6. Joseph Cardinal Bernardin, *Antisemitism: The Historical Legacy and the Continuing challenge for Christians* (1995).

7. See Saul S. Friedman, *The Oberammergau Passion Play: A Lance Against Civilization* (Carbondale: Southern Illinois University Press, 1984).

8. When a colleague asked the Jewish philosopher Hermann Cohen (1842–1918) whether he would attend a Luther celebration, Cohen replied that if he didn't, who would? He thought of Luther as the theologian of the free conscience.

Just this was my view in 1942–43, a traumatic time for Jews and their Christian friends. As a graduate student at Toronto's Pontifical Institute for Medieval Studies, I studied Aquinas' *De Ente et Essentia,* privately, with Fr. Gerald B. Phelan, the institute's director. One day I noticed *St. Thomas and the Jews* on my teacher's desk, a French pamphlet by a Quebec cleric. I asked Fr. Phelan whether I could see it. He didn't want me to, so I guessed what was in it. Whatever anti-Semitism there was in Aquinas' writings, the obscure French-Canadian cleric had surely looked for it and found it. But Fr. Phelan didn't want me to see it. Maybe he didn't want to see it himself.

I studied Aquinas—attended the Pontifical Institute—in search of allies, philosophical and religious, against those "pagans" who just then were proving to be so much worse than real ones; and, in giving me a private seminar, Fr. Phelan was helping me find them. I did find some but, also, not only others. As an ally, Augustine survived my discovery— a shock—that he labeled Jews a collective Cain.[9] But Chrysostom, another Christian saint, didn't survive. I dutifully told my students what made him a saint: He preached about holiness "with a golden mouth." But about Jews, I once was forced to add, the preacher of the golden mouth was a preacher of the filthy mouth.[10]

But now, fifty years after the Holocaust, the cardinal is affirming that the time for the occasional outburst against Christian anti-Semitism— my Jewish one against Chrysostom, Christian ones against him and others—is past; that the time has come for a head-on Christian critique of anti-Semitism, the Christian included; and that, in view of what is at stake, the critique must not stop even at saints.

What is at stake? Nothing less, in my view, than for theology, Jewish and Christian—if necessary apart, when possible together[11]—to confront the Holocaust, no longer as shielded by theological armor but, as it were, nakedly, with brutal honesty; and hence, inevitably, as a threat to both Jewish and Christian faith: to theology, but also to faith itself. Traditionally, theology expounds the faith but also guards it; but it cannot guard it forever, if it is at the cost of truth.

---

9. *City of God* XV 7.

10. Chrysostom's attacks include the charge that Christian suffering is of martyrs, Jewish suffering, only of thieves; that Jews always act perversely, disobeying the Law when it is valid, and obeying it when it is superseded; and that the synagogue is a whorehouse.

11. See further below Nos. 5–7.

Let me illustrate from personal experience. The Israelite *Heilsgeschichte* begins with Abraham, then again with the Exodus from Egypt; and, for Jewish faith, divine salvation has never ended. The Passover Seder recalls the past: the Israelites were saved, then and there. But memory is also celebration, here and now, for we, their descendants, are saved here and now, if only because we exist to do the remembering.[12] Our survival may be precarious, and so, often enough in history, has been our Passover. (The feast is close in the calendar to Easter, often inspiring anti-Jewish violence).[13] But without divine salvation we would not be here at all.

"In every generation there are those who would exterminate us; but the Holy One, praised be He, saves us from their hands." This, taken from the liturgy, sums up the Seder, the home observance of the Exodus for the family, friends and strangers with no home of their own.

"The Holy One saves us . . ."—us, *but what of them?* For years no mention of the Holocaust marred our celebration, and what was true in our home was true also of many or most others. Was it too soon? It hadn't sunk in? It was too threatening? In spite or even because of what has happened, we must defy the murderers and have our celebration? Whatever explanation, this is the way it was.

Then one year I was sent a Ritual of Remembrance by a respected organization, decided to use it, and read the following: "And they slew the blameless and pure, men and women and little ones, with vapors of poison and burned them with fire." And right after: "But we abstain from dwelling on the deeds of the evil ones, lest we defame the image of God in which man was created."[14]

We defame the image of God by dwelling on what *they* did? They defame it by *doing* it!

For several years I carried on with the Ritual of Remembrance, but then no more. And now, after half a century, the time has come for honest thought, truthful thought. This cushioning of the Passover—this

---

12. On every festival the following blessing is recited: "Praised art Thou, Lord our God, King of the world, who hast kept us alive, preserved us, and let us reach this day."

13. The libel that Jews use Christian blood for Passover matzah is the theme of Heinrich Heine's *Rabbi of Bachrach*, a novel he never completed.

14. The text is reproduced in full in Azriel Eisenberg, *Witness to the Holocaust* (New York: Pilgrim Press, 1981), 624.

softening of the threat of the Holocaust to the Jewish faith—is no longer possible.[15] Nor is it necessary.

III. Implicating "Non-Aryans" in the Crime

The Holocaust Assault on Judaism

"If the prefect of a city orders a Jew to kill a certain person, he must refuse, even if in consequence he gets killed himself: Is his blood any redder than a stranger's?"[16]

When thinking of anti-Jewish violence—pogroms, expulsions, attacks resulting in deaths—Jewish thinkers have resorted to texts such as this one, for solace. *In extremis,* rather than commit murder, even of a stranger, Jews are to choose death for themselves. And the pious obey. Jews get killed but Judaism survives.

But this time it was different. The Third Reich was a criminal regime. It had a big and criminal job, Hitler's conquest of the world; hence, without second thought, it would implicate its subjects in its crimes—Latvians, Ukrainians, the Vichy police, and, of course, also and especially, its own people. So it was for the "Aryans." To implicating "non-Aryans," in contrast, they did not give just second thought but, as it were, third and fourth as well. With their well-known efficiency, why not run the ghettoes themselves, do their "selections" themselves? But it was better—more in line with the National Socialist *Weltanschauung*—to implicate the Jews. Not they but the *Judenraete* would select, not strangers but other Jews, their own people, for deportation and murder.

These Jewish councils have been maligned for collaboration, but what choice did they have?[17] As for the victims of what I have called the

---

15. Lawrence L. Langer's *Admitting the Holocaust* (Oxford: 1995) is outstanding among recent works in showing that we "admit" the Holocaust but shrink from admitting it was as it was. Wanting the "lesson" that the human spirit is always indestructible, we evade what unfortunately, is the real lesson of Auschwitz—that if perpetrators are powerful, cunning, evil, and above all, goal-directed enough, they can destroy that spirit, and at Auschwitz they did, countless times. An evasive theology is always worthless, of course. With the Holocaust it also ignores enormous tasks, among them addressing why the perpetrators wanted a *judenrein* world, how we must remember the victims and, in general, how to mend the rupture brought about by the Holocaust.

16. Talmud, Pessachim 25b, see also Sanhedrin 74a.

17. On this huge, much-discussed subject, see especially Isaiah Trunk's path-breaking *Judenrat* (New York: Macmillan, 1972).

"two-work-permit practice," they had not choice at all and had to finger their own families.

A work permit at Auschwitz meant the difference between life and death. Those denied a permit were murdered at once, while those given one would—for the time being—stay alive, and for later there was hope. But a father would sometimes be given two work permits: one, unexchangeable, for himself, and the other, at his discretion, for one member of his family—mother, father, wife, or one child. Could he refuse? Give his own permit to a son or daughter? Rather than make such a choice, kill himself? These options were all excluded. Unless he did the fingering—"select"—one for life, condemn the others to death—they would all be killed. At Auschwitz, that father was the "non-Aryan"—morally as well as physically choiceless—par excellence.

"Judaism *always* survives"? But at Auschwitz they crushed one pillar, Jewish ethics, fidelity to man. They also destroyed the other, fidelity to God.

Of this, the paradigm, in Judaism, is the "ten martyrs." Having defeated the *Bar Kochba* uprising (132–135 C.E.), Roman emperor Hadrian forbade Judaism on pain of death. Defying him by teaching Torah, ten rabbis, among them the famous Akiba, were caught, tortured, put to death. "Is this the Torah, and this its reward?" Thus in the legend, the angels are said to have cried. "Not another word," replied a voice from heaven. "Else the world will turn into the water of tears. You must accept this decree."[18]

After "the ten," others followed, in the Crusades in Germany in the eleventh century, during the Chmelnitzki massacres in Poland in the seventeenth.[19] And martyrdom was endorsed in the classical sources. "For thy sake are we murdered every day" (Ps 44:23). This refers to the martyrs, say the sages.

"No creature can reach the place of those murdered by the government, such as Rabbi Akiba and his colleagues." This is found in the Talmud (Pessachim 50a). And in Maimonides the following: "A human found worthy by God of dying *al kiddush ha-shem* (i.e., martyrdom, being killed for "the sanctification of the divine name") has reached the

---

18. See Talmud, Berakhot 61b, Menahot 29b. The story of the ten martyrs is part of the Yom Kippur Mussaf service.

19. Further on Jewish martyrdom, see Shalom Spiegel, *The Last Trial* (New York: Ramdom House, 1967).

highest rung of perfection possible for humans, and is destined for the world to come."[20]

But the Bible, Talmud, and Maimonides cope with Hadrian; they do not cope with Hitler. Hadrian *created* Jewish martyrs. In shifting the Jewish "crime" from the human will onto human birth, Hitler *murdered,* along with Jews, *Jewish martyrdom* itself. Defined as "non-Aryans," classified as such, isolated as such, ghettoized as such, Jews had the choice, not of whether to die but, at most, only of how—with the *Sh'ma Yisrael* on their lips[21]—and even this way was only for some. Others did not know this was death. They thought they were in showers. Others again died in terror—the screams, the curses, the dogs, the rifle butts. And of the death of still others Primo Levi has written:

> All the *Muselmaenner* who finished in the gas chambers have the same story or, more exactly, have no story; they followed the slope down to the bottom, like streams that run down to the sea. . . . Their life is short, but their number is endless; they, the *Muselmaenner,* the drowned, for the backbone of the camp, an anonymous mass, continuously renewed and always identical, of non-men who march and labour in silence, the divine spark dead within them, already too empty really to suffer. One hesitates to call them living; one hesitates to call their death death.[22]

They aimed to make the world rein of *Juden,* but also of *Judentum.*[23]

IV. Implicating "Aryans"

The Holocaust Assault on Christianity

"Christian Nazi": I once used that conjunction, in a lecture in Jerusalem. A Christian stormed forward afterwards. "A contradiction in terms," he protested. True, but it had been, empirically, real.

When Hitler came to power, the Christian faith was weak in Germany. It was divided within, by a self-styled "German Christianity—a Hitler-appointed *Reichbischof,* and "Aryan" Christ—best described as baptized Nazism. But Christian faith was also threatened from without,

20. Maimonides, *Letter on Destruction.*
21. Near death, Jews recite Deut. 6:4: "Hear, O Israel, the Lord our God, the Lord is one."
22. Primo Levi, *Survival in Auschwitz* (New York: Orion, 1959), 82.
23. On *Judentum* as a German term, see next section.

although not really at all, by half-baked attempts to revive the gods of Germany. This was not serous; it was even ludicrous. Nor was Christianity threatened by the regime's self-declared "positive Christianity": the fraud was too obvious. The real, deep threat was the drawing of Christianity itself into National Socialism, its crimes included; and—with the prime means to this end, the "Aryan/non-Aryan" dichotomy—the core were those against Jews.

From this point of view of enhancing Jew-hatred—its scope, its prestige—the concoction of the code-word "anti-Semitism," in late nineteenth-century Germany, was progress. The word preserved, nay, escalated the hatred, but covered it. "Christ-killer" or "his blood on us and our children" were not suitable for the platform of a respectable party in a modern state. In contrast, "anti-Semitism"—an antiseptic, quasi-scientific, even "philosophical" "anti" to "Semitism"—was. And having become respectable, it could spread and be spread. The old-fashioned Jew-hater, still with us even now, would be placed by us on the "extreme" "fundamentalist" "right." In contrast, the modern anti-Semite, on the "nationalist" right (for whom "Jews" are "communists") can have a counterpart on the "socialist" left (for whom even poverty-stricken Jews are "capitalists," "in love with money," or minimally, "in league with Rothchild.") Indeed, "nationalist" right and "socialist" left can make common cause against Jews—in case, "in league" means a plot using money and communism to rule and/or ruin the world.[24]

There is yet another easily overlooked aspect of this progress in Jew-hatred. The old Jew-hater is embarrassed by the fact that not all Jews are hateful, and protests that some of his best friends are Jews. For the new anti-Semite there is need for neither embarrassment nor protest. Richard Wagner, when he was young and unknown, got generous help from Giacomo Meyerbeer, but hated gratitude to Jews. Yet, since he was "anti" not Meyerbeer but his "Semitism," he could vent his hatred without restraint. "The Jew," he asserts in *Das Judentum in der Musik,* is uncreative, destructive of German music such as Wagner's own, and—he is not embarrassed to write it—is "the most heartless of all human

---

24. The allusion is to *The Protocols of the Elders of Zion,* a forgery that makes Jews into plotters against the world. In 1920, Hitler had already developed both his "socialist" and his "nationalist" anti-Semitism, now capable of what a contemporary called a "bottomless whipping up of the lowest anti-Semitic instincts." See Reginald H. Phelps, "Hitler's *'grundlegende' Rede ueber den Antisemitismus," Vierteljahrshefte fuer Zietgeschichte,* vol. 16, 1968, 390–419.

beings."[25] Is his "Semitic" character Meyerbeer's own fault? As little as a mouse is at fault in being a mouse and getting eaten by the cat. Thus Hitler, was on the same subject as Wagner. Hitler too had problems with Jew-hatred and gratitude, for Jews sold his pictures and (unlike a gentile) he suspected did so to cheat him; a Jewish doctor treated his mother (with Hitler on record as thanking him); and a man who probably was a Jewish officer got him his medal in the Great War. Hitler had been refused the Iron Cross, first class, several times. But Lieutenant of the Reserves Gutmann persisted and got it.

But after the loss of the Great War—the "November criminals," Jews and quasi-Jews, were responsible, with their stab in the back—twentieth-century Germany needed further progress in Jew-hatred. The "Aryan/non-Aryan" dichotomy provided it.

The old anti-Semitism, even if tough enough to use law, leaves room for exceptions and evasions. Thus if it outlawed *kashrut,* the ritual slaughter of animals, only Orthodox Jews were in trouble, and they could import meat from Sweden; and if a *numerus clausus* kept Jews out of one university, they could always try another. In contrast, the new "Aryan/non-Aryan" dichotomy ended evasions and exceptions. Right, left, rich, poor, Jewish, Christian, wicked, saintly—the "non-Aryan" was *born* Jewish. There were no exceptions or evasions. There was no way out. There was no escape. This is the core of the 1935 Nuremberg Race Laws.

For the SS periodical, the *Schwarze Korps,* these laws ended the worry about "impoverished German noblemen" marrying "daughters of rich Jewish department store owners." For the Jewish victims, the worry was not *Rassenschand,* now a crime, but that the laws distinguished between "Aryans" protected by the Law and "non-Aryans" who were not. These laws disenfranchised the German Jews, made them *vogelfrei.*

An outlaw has placed himself outside the law. A *vogelfrei* person is placed outside the Law by the Law itself. He has no protection. Any passerby can rob him, beat him, kill him, do to him what he likes. Nobody can come to his aid, least of all the police. In a photograph, all over Germany in 1935, a Jew is led through town by a multitude, cheering, jeering. He carries a sign. "I will never again complain to the police."

---

25. *Wagner on Music and Drama,* Albert Goldman and Evert Springhorn, eds. (London: Victor Gollancz, 1970), 53.

What happened in 1935 to Jews individually, happened during *Kristallnacht,* to all Jews collectively, or to all accessible at the time. The storm troopers acted, but the police looked on.

The action was against "non-Aryans," but the feelings motivating it were against *Juden,*—them, but also *das Judentum.*

I cannot convey what years of baiting, harassment, propaganda and—last but not least—the Fuehrer's very own *Weltanschauung* had done to the word *Jude.* The fear; the hatred; the nameless horror; the syphilis and/or poisoned blood "they" get into you; the slimy vermin that crawls at you; the wish to strike out, to grab a club and just hit.[26]

On *Kristallnacht* they did the hitting: *Juden*—smashing the stores, beating up Jews, arresting whomever they could grab—but also *das Judentum,* burning the synagogues. *"Judentum"* did not mean what "Judaism" means in English—the Ten Commandments, the Golden Rule, love your neighbor, studying Torah. Long before Nazism it meant something roughly translated as "what Jews are doing collectively." Wagner's pamphlet bears the title *Das Judentum in der Musik.* And Luther wanted the synagogues burned, four hundred years before it was done.

And—as the synagogues were burned while the police looked on— where was the *Church?*[27] Pastor Julius van Jan, of the tiny parish of Oberlenningen in Wuertemberg, denounced *Kristallnacht* from the pulpit, but was quickly taken away to a concentration camp. And a few in Baden-Baden compared the victims to their Christ, but behind closed windows.[28] (Probably there were also other expressions of whispered dissent.) The Church, in contrast, "kept a stunned and fearful silence," writes British scholar Richard Gutteridge.

---

26. This is the other sentence I could write only after much reading, with quite different feelings, however. Imagining a Hitler victory was scary. Imagining myself object of the hated Nazi hiss at Jews—innocent but without escape—feels like being naked in the "undressing room," with the gas chamber ahead.

27. See *Judaism and Christianity under the Impact of National Socialism, 1919–1945,* Otto Dov Kulka and Paul Mendes-Flohr, eds. (Jerusalem, 1987). My subject limits me to the German churches. Without the work and friendship of non-German Christians, I would have ventured on this essay, if at all, with much less hope. Franklin H. Littell in particular has been indefatigable in the work, and encouraging as a friend. See his "Inventing the Holocaust: A Christian's Retrospect," *Major changes within Jewish People in the Wake of the Holocaust,* Yisrael Gutman, ed. (Jerusalem: Yad Vashem, 1966), 613–634.

28. My first rabbinic assignment, for the High Holiday services in 1938, was in the Baden-Baden synagogue, just a month before they burned it down.

"No one ventured to take the initiative in organizing a protest." Just one bishop protested, Theophil Wurm of Wuertemberg, but even his Christian congregation and protest were weakened by his anti-Semitism.[29]

What could Christians have done? Soon, in the Minsk of 1942—when Reinhard Heydrich interpreted the Nuremberg Laws—it was too late for decisive Christian action, for the war was on, and the Holocaust was secret.[30] The right time had been in 1935, when the Nuremberg Laws bestowed the "Aryan" designation on all but "non-Aryan" Christians, when the Church could accept it only by abandoning the "non-Aryans" to their *vogelfrei* fate. Indeed—if the word *kairos* stand for Christian moments in which the faith is at stake—1935 was that very *kairos*. But the Church missed it.

Kristallnacht, then, was late, but was it too late? It was peacetime still; the crime, far from secret, had worldwide publicity; and large parts of that world, the Christian ones, were outraged. If 1935 was the *kairos* for the Church in Germany, 1938 was a chance, or at least could be seen as a chance. But, having played it safely "Aryan" with the Nuremberg Laws, the Church was now not just "Aryan" but not "non-Aryan," anything-but-"non-Aryan." It missed what turned out to be the last chance.

One Christian responded to *Kristallnacht*. Canon Bernhard Lichtenberg of the Berlin *Hedwigskirch* made a decision. "Now only prayer can help," he told himself. His prayer was public, for humanity as well as Divinity, and it contained *Jude,* the word that needed liberating from lies and hatred.

Lichtenberg prayed nightly, until August 29, 1941, when he was overheard, denounced, and arrested. He denied nothing, apologized for nothing, and stated in court that he would do it again. He applied to join his "non-Aryan" Catholic flock, due for deportation "East," but was sent

---

29. Kulka and Mendes-Flohr, ibid., 239. In his letter to Interior Minister Guertner, Bishop Wurm wrote: "I do not contest the right of the state to thwart the menace of Judaism. Since my youth I have recognized the truth of the statements by Heinrich von Treitschke and Adolf Stoeker concerning the corrosive influence which Judaism exerts in religious, moral, cultural, economic, and political spheres." For the complete text of van Jan's sermon and Bishop Wurm's letter, see Hartmut Metzger, *Kristallnacht* (Stuttgart, 1978), 33–36 and 49–52.

30. *Generalkommissar* Wihelm Kube of White Russia had belated scruples. Among the 7,300 Jews sent to him from Germany and Austria were two young women with "fully Aryan" features, as well as several men with Great War medals. Surely, he wrote to Reinhard Heydrich, these were exempt. Heydrich replied harshly, "I regret having to furnish this kind of justification, six and a half years after the decree of the Nuremberg Laws." They were all murdered. Gerald Fleming, *Hitler and the Final Solution* (Berkley: University of California Press, 1984), 117f.

to jail instead, and for two years of it, to Dachau. But Lichtenberg, well on in years and gravely ill, died on the way.

At the funeral, a non-Catholic walked over to a Catholic. "Today," he said, "they have buried a saint."[31]

Could Lichtenberg's prayer have helped more than it did? If the *Hedwigkirch* had been jammed with people, praying his prayer; if prayer meetings had been held all over Germany and Austria, in front of every burnt-out synagogue; if, moving overseas, the spirit had caught on, and climaxed with an Onward-Christian-Soldiers Battle Cry—"They say we are 'Aryans'? Abandon the 'non-Aryans'? Never! This is the *kairos* for us to be *Juden!*"—would the Evil Empire have collapsed? Perhaps, probably not. But the Church would be a great light today, dispersing Hitler's shadow.

But Bernhard Lichtenberg was alone.

V. Hitler's Shadow

Hitler has been dead for fifty years. His Reich, also, is dead; it survived him by just one week. Surely, the "Aryan/non-Aryan" abyss long has been bridgeable, has been bridged, and is being bridged! However, Hitler's shadow survives.

A bridging was tried in the Holocaust itself. *Juden* were shunned. "Stay away or their touch will poison you," said the powers that be, "or else we'll do the killing." Yet, "righteous gentiles" hid Jews, fed them, led a double life for them, risked their own lives and their children's lives. "We did nothing special," they protest when they are honored. "Anyone would have done the same." Not in Nazi Europe.

Yet Hitler's shadow is between even these, the closest of "Aryans" and "non-Aryans." If "righteous gentiles" failed, they were martyrs, and the Jew a victim; if they succeeded, they were heroes, and the Jew a survivor.

Hitler's shadow haunts the next and next-to-next generation also. Today, here and there young Jews and Christians share the Book, the

---

31. On Lichtenberg's desk was a hate sheet: Kindness to Jews is treason to the state. Lichtenberg was arrested before he could attack it from the pulpit; indeed, that was why he was arrested. His message, the report said—"Love your neighbor" as a "strict commandment of Christ"—was "dangerous." While the "Jewish problem" was being "regulated," it would have "disturbed the peace." Leon Poliankov and Josef Wuld, *Das Dritte Reich un die Juden—Dokumente und Aufsaetze,* 2nd ed. (Berlin: Arani, 1955), 432–437.

Book and also innocence, for birth is innocent. Yet despite this sharing, double though it is, Hitler's shadow comes between them, making one the heir of victims, while the other is the heir of those implicated in the victimizing.

"All who invoke the Lord will survive catastrophe," Jews and Christians read together. They read it in the "Old Testament," the prophet Joel (3:5, by Christian counting 2:30) but also, with the apostle Paul quoting Joel, in the "New" (Romans 10:13). But the Jew's grandparents never called on the Lord, yet they survived in America, while his uncle, staying behind, called in vain. The Christian, in turn, if German, finds his faith exists because he calls on the Lord; but he himself exists because his grandparents were "Aryans"; had they protested he would not be here.

VI. In Search of a Post-Holocaust Theology

Ridding the world of Hitler's shadow, wanted by Churchill, was wanted also by Jacques Maritain, and the Catholic philosopher, too, saw the need at an early time, when Hitler was alive, still heading for victory.

"The People of Christ," Maritain said then, "have become the Christ of the Peoples."

He did not spell out his statement, and even now, I think it needs spelling out. Clear even then was the fact that if *all* Jews are under attack—Jews simply because they are Jews—if Europe, nay, the world is to be *rein* of *Juden,* then the carpenter of Nazareth is one of them.

In 1940 this conclusion was reached also by Dietrich Bonhoffer. In 1979 I inquired of Eberhard Bethge, Bonhoffer's friend and biographer, whether Bonhoffer, had he lived, might have found his way to a post-Holocaust Christian theology. Bethge discovered the following in his friend's papers (It became the core of his subsequent *Bonhoffer und die Juden.*):

"For Christians the expulsion of the Jews from the West must be followed by the expulsion of Christ, for Christ was a Jew."[32]

---

32. Bethge's lecture was given in Oxford in 1980 (*Konsequenzen: Dietrich Bonhoeffers Kirchenverstaendnis Heute,* Ernst Feil and Ilse Toedt, eds. (Munich: Chr. Kaiser, 1980), 171–214. The subsequent *Ethik im Ernstfall: Dietrich Bonhoeffer Stellung zu den Juden und ihre Aktualitaet,* Wolfgang Huber and Ilse Toedt, eds. (Munich: Chr. Kaiser, 1982), responds to Bethge. William Jay Peck cites Bethge's "syllogism": If the *expulsion* of the Jews from the West means the expulsion

Bonhoffer knew about the expulsions but not in 1940, about the Holocaust; and Maritan, two years or so later, knew, but little except the fact. Filip Mueller knows everything. He was there.

The three SS officers in charge, he reports, Aumeir, Grabner, and Hoessler, were on the flat roof of the crematorium, making speeches intended to lull suspicions, to calm the victims. Have no fear, the officers said, these are just showers. There'll be jobs for everyone afterwards—electricians, mechanics, nurses. A tailor is told he is needed too. "Now get undressed quickly," is the last word before the victims, unsuspecting, walk in, and the door is shut, "otherwise your soup will get cold."

Mueller goes on: "Meanwhile, the *Unterfuehrers* on duty had gone onto the crematorium roof, from where the three SS officers had addressed the crowd. They removed the covers from the camouflaged openings. Then, protected by gas-masks, they poured the green-blue crystals of the deadly gas into the gas chamber.

> At Grabner's command the engines of the trucks still standing near were turned on. Their noise was to prevent anyone in the camp from hearing the shouting and the banging on the doors of the dying in the gas chamber. We, however, were spared nothing, but had to witness everything in close proximity. It was as though Judgment Day had come. We could clearly hear heart-rending weeping, cries for help, fervent prayers, violent banging and knocking, and, drowning everything, the noise of the truck engines running at top speed.

Aumeier, Grabnere, and Hoessler were checking by their watches the time it took for the noise inside the gas chamber to cease, cracking macabre jokes while they were waiting, like "The water in the showers must be very hot to make them scream so loudly."[33]

Why the "undressing room," "the showers," the victims in their nakedness? Earlier they had experimented without it, but undressing the dead had meant poor clothes, torn and blood-stained ones, hardly fit for further use. Reported here is the first undressing experiment, and

---

of Christ, what is the meaning of the *annihilation* of the Jews?" He goes on: "Here the syllogism breaks off, and we hear Bonhoffer speak of suffering with God His suffering in a godless world, just before he sealed his testimony with his death" (p. 29).

33. Filip Mueller, *Auschwitz Inferno: The Testimony of a Soderkommando* (London: Routledge and Kegan Paul, 1979), 37–39.

since it worked so well—the victims were naive, believed the believable—murdering them naked became routine, as Mueller puts it, in "monstrous proportions."

We call Auschwitz "hell" but say the sayable and mean the unsayable and—within a Jewish, Christian, "Judeo-Christian," or even any halfway decent context of good and evil, right and wrong, just and unjust—*unthinkable. "Hell" does not touch the innocent, but this place touched no one else; and the methods, perpetrators, and jokes all fit what was happening.*

Pulling out corpses and disposing of them—blood, maggots, feces, and all—was Mueller's job. That's why he was there. But would a *Sonderkommando* live? They wanted no witnesses. Would he *want* to live? The job "either made one insane the first day or else a robot ever after." Yet he reports that "the more menacing death grew, the stronger grew my will to survive, one minute, one hour, one day, one week. . . . I was obsessed and dominated by the determination that I must not die."[34] Filip Mueller's will to live was monumental.

But then it collapsed. One day, a group was brought into the "undressing room," and understood. They were stunned, of course. Then they sang the Czech National Anthem and the *ha-Tikvah*. "That moved me terribly," Mueller says in Claude Lantzmann's *Shoah*. "That was happening to my countrymen, and I realized that my life had become meaningless. Why go on living? For what? So I went onto the gas chamber with them, resolved to die. With them. Suddenly, some who recognized me came up to me. They looked at me and said, right there in the gas chamber . . ."

Lantzmann: *You were inside the gas chamber?*

Mueller: Yes. One of them said: "So you want to die. But that's senseless. Your death won't give us back our lives. That's no way. You must get out of here alive, you must bear witness to our suffering, and to the injustice done to us."[35]

VII. Against Trivializing

Why did they do it, dichotomizing "Aryans" and "non-Aryans," implicating both in their crimes, each in their way; and thereafter the

---

34. Ibid., 17.

35. Claude Lantzmann, *Shoah* (New York: Pantheon, 1985), 164–165.

Holocaust, the gas chambers, the *judenrein* Europe, a *judenrein* world? Perhaps this was the purpose, to kill God.

The God of the Jews and the Christians. By corrupting His witnesses, punishing them, making the world *rein* of them. Raul Hilberg has said that the "why" of the Holocaust is the "big" question, and warns against "small" answers. To kill God, at any rate, is not small.

But Jews stubbornly deny that God can be killed, even when they get killed themselves. And—for all the boldness of its parables, its Midrashic anthropomorphism—the theology of Judaism takes care not to trivialize God.

Dare we trivialize Mueller? The victims were to be *spurlos verschwunden,* to "vanish without a trace," and the last thought of the victims was that must not happen; their "suffering," the "injustice done to them" must be known. Thus they pushed Mueller out, and he let them, and here he is, the only human being to have been inside a gas chamber, and with us, alive. *Dare we trivialize him?* Or even, God forbid, entertain, if but for the furtive moment, the wish—he disturbs our sleep and our theology—that he had never returned?

He has returned to the Jews, a surviving remnant, but also to whomever else listens, can listen, cannot not listen.

"We Christians must begin again at the beginning, with the first two questions of the Bible: 'Where are you, Man?' and 'Where is your brother?'"[36]

"Christian anti-Judaism will never end until Christians relate positively to Jews, not despite their non-acceptance of Christ, but because of it."

"We Christians will never again get behind Auschwitz, and [we can get] beyond it no longer alone, but only with the victims of Auschwitz."[37]

---

36. Midrash, the deepest theology in Judaism, is in parables taken seriously but not literally. My *To Mend the World: Foundations for a Post-Holocaust Jewish Thought* (Bloomington: Indiana, 1994) ends with this Midrash: "You are My witnesses, says the Lord"—that is, if you are My witnesses, I am God, and if you are not my witnesses, I am, as it were, not God" (Midrash Psalms, on Ps 123:1). The *k'b'yachol* ("as it were") indicates that, whereas a God uninvolved with His witnesses is not the Scriptural God, to make Him dependent on them would be to trivialize Him. In first citing that Midrash, nearly thirty years earlier, I had thought of a world without Jewish witnesses. In citing it again in *To Mend,* I had to think—as a threat too close—of a world without Jews.

37. The first two statements I heard at a Jewish-Christian conference, held in Pabst Johannes Haus, Krefeld, Germany, in 1983. For the third, see *"Oekumene nach Auschwitz," Gott nach Auschwitz* (Freiburg: Herder, 1979), 124. Stoehr's rethinking of Christianity, not just to Christian but to pre-Christian origins, would seem to make him replace Christian supersessionism—The "Old"

These statements, by authors who cannot not listen, reflect traces of a post-Holocaust Christian theology. Martin Stoehr's statement came after a long, sad litany of Christian "teaching of contempt" for Jews and Judaism, and marks a new beginning radically purged of that teaching by harking back beyond Christian origins, to pre-Christian ones—to the "Old" Testament, old only in time and now widely called "First." Hanns Hermann Henrix goes on with a call for Jewish otherness, a Christian need of it, this in place of conversion. And the implicit post-Holocaust theology in both these statements is explicit when Johann Baptist Metz writes: "We can pray after Auschwitz because there was prayer in Auschwitz itself."[38] But how do Jews pray after Auschwitz? They too need a post-Holocaust theology.

"I was young, and now am old, but I have never seen the righteous forsaken, or their children begging for bread."

This passage is in the Bible (Ps 37:25), but although evidently false, it was included by the rabbis in Jewish thanksgiving after meals, and this—the rabbis were not stupid—in deliberate, pious stubbornness. My father never said that verse, always skipped it, for he would not lie to the Holy One, blessed by He. Then, why, after Auschwitz, do I find myself saying it?

Perhaps the answer is this. Jews after Auschwitz are a remnant of catastrophe. For them to exist at all is, as it were, to hold a fort. Perhaps Jewish prayer is part of that effort, an indispensable part, sustained by the kabalistic hope that an effort below calls forth a response from above.

Testament," read correctly only in the light of the New, must be taken from the Jews—with a Jewish-Christian sharing of the Book. For my view on the subject, see my *The Jewish Bible After the Holocaust—A Re-reading* (Bloomington, Indiana: 1990), chapter IV.

38. Metz, op. cit.

3 Catholic-Jewish Relations: A New Agenda

Edward Cardinal Cassidy
April 30, 1997

The second Jerusalem Lecture was delivered in Chicago on April 30, 1997, by Edward Cardinal Cassidy, President of the Pontifical Council for Promoting Christian Unity and the Pontifical Commission for Religious Relations with the Jews. For many years, Cardinal Cassidy served in the diplomatic service of the Holy See. He was Undersecretary of State for the Holy See until Pope John Paul II named him to the presidency of the Pontifical Council in 1989. He was created cardinal in 1991.

Cardinal Cassidy had a close relationship with the Archdiocese of Chicago because of its prominence in the field of ecumenical affairs and Catholic-Jewish relations. He had made a number of visits to Chicago and followed the progress of the local dialogues from Rome.

In his lecture, in which he addresses some of the issues raised by Cardinal Bernardin, he calls for renewed commitment to a better future for relations between Christians and Jews.

Introduction

It is indeed a special privilege for me to have been asked by the late Archbishop of Chicago, His Eminence, Joseph Cardinal Bernardin, to give this 1997 Jerusalem Lecture, the second in a series that His Eminence wished to take place annually as a follow up to his important lecture in Jerusalem on March 13, 1995.

At the beginning of my reflections, I should like to pay tribute to Cardinal Bernardin, not only for that lecture and the present follow-up, but for all he did over many years to promote a new spirit of understanding and cooperation between Jews and Catholics—in the Archdiocese of Chicago, elsewhere in the United States, and far beyond the borders of this country. I recall in particular his opening address in Baltimore, in 1992, to the meeting of the International Liaison Committee between the Holy See's Commission for Religious Relations with the Jews and the International Jewish Committee for Interreligious Consultations (IJCIC), and the initiatives taken here in Chicago after the fall of communism to heal memories adversely affecting Jewish-Catholic relations in those countries of Central and Eastern Europe that had been victims of communist oppression.

In the Jerusalem Lecture of 1995, Cardinal Bernardin spoke of the development of Christian thought on anti-Semitism and called upon Jews and Christians to recommit themselves to counter the resurgence of this and other forms of racial and ethnic violence. He also suggested several ways, in which he believed Christians and Jews could, together and separately, build a better future for their relationship.

My address this evening will seek to take up some of the issues raised in this latter connection by Cardinal Bernardin and develop them in the light of the experience of the Holy See's Commission on Religious Relations with the Jews and my own personal reflections. Having in mind the progress made in our relationship and the present healthy state of our relations, I believe the time has come to ask ourselves: Where do we go now? Do we continue along the path that we have been treading for the past 30-odd years? Or should we already be preparing a new agenda for the years ahead?

The Old Agenda Fulfilled

I do not intend to go back over the ground covered in our relations in the period since the Second Vatican Council. Most if not all of you will be well aware of the principal events that marked our progress or presented difficulties for that progress as we sought to absorb into the life of our communities the consequences of the teaching of that Council in the Decree *Nostra Aetate,* no. 4.

At the same time, I must admit that it is interesting to look back through the book published by the Holy See's Commission for Religious Relations with the Jews in 1988, entitled *Fifteen Years of Catholic-Jewish*

Dialogue, 1970–1985.[1] There we have an account of the work accomplished by the International Catholic-Jewish Liaison Committee and we are able to appreciate just how real the progress in our relations has been. But we also find there a reflection of the difficulties encountered along the way, and the great effort that was required on both sides to overcome those obstacles.

In fact, when, shortly after the publication of that book, I was appointed as president of the Holy See's Commission for Religious Relations with the Jews, at the close of 1989, our relations were at an extremely low level. One could well speak of crisis. The International Catholic-Jewish Liaison Committee was unable to meet, and much of the good work done in previous years was threatened, mainly as a result of the presence of a Carmelite convent on the limits of the camp at Auschwitz and the failure of attempts to overcome this problem.

There was also the delicate question of diplomatic relations between the Vatican and the State of Israel: delicate for my Commission because this was for us exclusively a matter for the Secretariat of State of the Holy See, while for our Jewish partners it was a question of deep religious significance.

The years since 1990 have seen these outstanding questions brought to a satisfactory conclusion. I must give due credit to Pope John Paul II for his outstanding leadership and personal example in achieving these results, while at the same time acknowledging the vital role played by many Jewish friends who, despite the difficulties faced and the criticism they themselves had to bear, never gave up the attempt to overcome these problems and remained firmly convinced that a solution could be found through ongoing contacts and dialogue.

The Present Situation

The signing of the Fundamental Agreement Between the Holy See and the State of Israel on December 30, 1993, and the establishment soon after of official diplomatic relations between these two international bodies, brought to a close this first period of 30 years following the

---

1. *Fifteen Years of Catholic-Jewish Dialogue, 1970-1985,* selected papers, published by the *Libreria Editrice Vaticana* and the *Librerie Editrice Lateranense, Theologia e Filosofia XI,* 1988.

Second Vatican Council. In his Jerusalem Lecture of 1995, Cardinal Bernardin stated:

> The Holy See's action in formally recognizing Israel through the Accords represents a final seal on the process begun at the Second Vatican Council to rid Catholicism of all vestiges of "displacement theology" and the implied notion of perpetual Jewish homelessness. The Accords represent the Catholic Church's full and final acknowledgment of Jews as a people, not merely as individuals.

The signing of the Accord had been preceded, in September 1990, by a meeting of the International Catholic-Jewish Liaison Committee in Prague, which had opened up a new vision of Catholic-Jewish relations. At the close of that meeting, the very representative Jewish and Catholic Committee members present committed themselves to promoting "a new spirit in Catholic-Jewish relations, a spirit which emphasizes cooperation, mutual understanding and reconciliation, goodwill and common goals, to replace the past spirit of suspicion, resentment, and distrust."[2]

When the same International Catholic-Jewish Liaison Committee met in Jerusalem in May 1994, there was clearly a feeling that the time had come for us to live out more fully that commitment. We should finally stop acting simply as a meeting place to deal with problems and seek rather to discover new ways of responding to the challenge placed before us in the Prague declaration to which I have just referred.

We were not unaware, of course, of the fact that several important questions from the former agenda would continue to require our constant attention. Anti-Semitism, for example, was by no means a thing of the past. Only recently, in fact, the Catholic Bishops of Switzerland felt the need to repeat in the strongest terms that "anti-Semitism is incompatible with Christian faith."[3] Moreover, some of that suspicion, resentment, and distrust of the past remains in the collective consciousness of our respective communities. Not all Catholics have absorbed the teaching of the Second Vatican Council: not all Jews are aware of the changes that have taken place in Catholic thinking and practice over the past 30 years.

---

2. Declaration of the International Catholic-Jewish Liaison Committee, Prague 1990, *Information Service of the Pontifical Council for Promoting Christian Unity*; No. 75 (1990), 176.

3. *L'Osservatore Romano,* March 15, 1997.

I have been concerned on many occasions, when addressing Catholic or Jewish audiences, at the lack of knowledge of what has been happening in recent years in Jewish-Catholic relations. The documents published, the initiatives undertaken, and the common statements issued so often remain unknown. I shall come back to this problem later on; let me return now to the 1994 Jerusalem meeting of the International Catholic-Jewish Liaison Committee.

The Prague Declaration had suggested that the way to overcome anti-Semitism and to remove suspicion, resentment, and distrust from within our communities was cooperation, mutual understanding and reconciliation, goodwill, and common goals; in other words, by working together with a common agenda.

Hence, in Jerusalem, we asked ourselves: Who are we, Catholics and Jews that are called to work together? In what way can we, and should we, work together? What would be this new agenda? I believe that on that occasion and in subsequent contacts some basic principles upon which to build our future cooperation have been established.

The first such principle is the fact that we are speaking in this context of joint action in favor of the moral values which as *faith communities* we share. We are not two humanitarian societies, far less are we two debating clubs. We are two faith communities and as such we are being called to respond to a common challenge. Let me quote a Jewish affirmation of this claim:

> Christians and Jews are encountering each other by facing God in new historical conditions. This is a response to God's call beyond Christian-Jewish voluntary or forced alienation. It is a time of joint response to the evils of the world.[4]

I was able to make a similar statement during the Jerusalem 1994 meeting of the International Liaison Committee, when I pointed out that:

> . . . both in Prague 1990 and in Baltimore 1992, we saw ourselves as representing *faith communities*. It is on the basis of our separate identities, but frequently common vision as religious communities, that we can and

---

4. "The Once and Future Dialogue: Christian-Jewish Relations at the Turning Point," in *PACE* (Issues), May 1993, 15.

should be able to respond together to some of the needs and evils of the world in which we live together.[5]

This same basic understanding of our relationship is to be found in the Preamble to the Fundamental Agreement Between the Holy See and the State of Israel itself, which states:

> Aware of the unique nature of the relationship between the Catholic Church and the Jewish people, and the historic process of reconciliation and growth in mutual understanding and friendship between Catholics and Jews. . . .[6]

Pope John Paul II, during his visit to the Great Synagogue of Rome on April 13, 1986, referred to his Jewish hosts as "our elder brothers" and pointed out that "with Judaism therefore we have a relationship we do not have with other religions."[7] His Holiness called for cooperation for the well-being of humankind and common reflection on how to help men and women today to achieve true justice and freedom in truth.[8]

It is important, I think, for us to keep this "unique" aspect of our relationship in mind, especially when we enter into a wider interfaith dialogue. Christians and Jews have an agenda based on what John Paul II has described elsewhere as being "linked together at the very level of their identity."[9] With no other faith community, not even Islam, do Christians have such a relationship.

When the first ambassador of Israel presented his credential letters to Pope John Paul II, in September 1994, he made the following statement:

> The establishment of diplomatic relations between the Holy See and the State of Israel is not the point of arrival, but, on the contrary, a starting point, a new constructive dimension in which to bring together in dialogue the Catholic Church and the Jewish people. We must all seek greater mutual understanding with patience and persistence.[10]

---

5. Address to the Jerusalem meeting of the International Liaison Committee, May 1994, *Information Service PCPCU*, No. 87 (1994), 233.

6. Fundamental Agreement, Preamble.

7. *Attività della Santa Sede 1986*, 309.

8. Ibid., 310.

9. *Attività della Santa Sede 1982*, 184–185.

10. *Attività della Santa Sede 1994*, 670–674.

I agree fully with Ambassador Samuel Hadas that the great progress achieved in our relationship has not led to a situation with which we can be satisfied, "a point of arrival." Much has still to be done: our journey must continue.

But let us turn now to the second question that I asked: In what way can we, and should we, work together in this new situation? What is to be the agenda of the future?

Dialogue between Christians and Jews

At the basis of any future agenda for fostering better relations between Catholics and Jews there must, of course, be dialogue, a constant dialogue at all appropriate levels. Indeed, much of the progress achieved so far has been the result of dialogue, but now the time has come for us to reflect on the nature of our dialogue and on possible ways of deepening and expanding it.

Let me say at once that I do not wish to take away anything from the dialogue that has been carried on so fruitfully between the Holy See's Commission for Religious Relations with the Jews and the International Jewish Committee on Interreligious Consultation (IJCIC), through the International Catholic-Jewish Liaison Committee. The regular meetings of this body over the past 25 years have been irreplaceable in promoting the spirit of cooperation and reconciliation between Jews and Catholics. Other joint organizations have also played an essential role in this process. The International Council of Christians and Jews is just one such organization whose work deserves our appreciation and praise, while at the national level the dialogue here in Chicago has made invaluable contributions to this relationship. But at this stage there are questions that we must ask about the nature of our dialogue. For many, including several leading rabbis who have approached me in this connection, it seems strange that often the representatives on one side of the dialogue are hierarchs, clergy, or theologians, while those on the other side are lay representatives of their community organizations. Yet, the questions dealt with in our dialogue have primarily a religious significance and, we are meeting as communities of faith.

Maybe as a consequence of this, our dialogue has tended to remain on a rather superficial level. We have faced practical problems and have sought practical answers. But when, in 1994 in Jerusalem, we began to seek ways of taking up the challenge of Prague, the two topics that were selected for discussion, while eminently practical in their consequences, went beyond such superficial considerations to touch the basis of our respective faiths. The Jerusalem meeting issued a common statement on how Jews and Catholics understand the family and began a study on ecology. At once it was evident that we have entered into a new phase of dialogue, based on our understanding of these questions *in light of our religious or faith principles.*

And so we must now ask the question: Could not, and should not, then, our dialogue be able to envisage an even wider field of discussion? When Catholics raise this issue, there is often an immediate negative response within some sectors of the Jewish community. I believe, nevertheless, that we must open this question for reflection and study if we are to leave aside the superficial and move ahead in a significant way in giving a common witness to the religious values that we share to a world that is becoming more and more secularized and bereft of such values.

There is, unfortunately, much misunderstanding about the type of theological reflection that I am proposing. Let me make it clear that there is a real and important distinction between theological dialogue and Christian mission. When I speak of theological dialogue with Jewish representatives, I am not speaking of discussions leading to unity in faith, but of a dialogue that helps the partners to understand and accept each other as they really are, in order to be what God wants them to be in their societies today, despite their basic differences. I am truly amazed at times to read Catholic teaching and doctrine explained in Jewish publications in such a way that no Catholic would recognize them as part of his or her faith. It is likely that Jews would have a similar reaction to some Catholic understandings of their faith.

An essential element in our relationship is, therefore, that we begin to see each other as the other sees himself. In an exchange with Rabbi Leon Klenicki, published in April 1996, Padraic O'Hare, associate professor of religious studies at Merrimack College in North Andover, Mass., expressed disappointment "that none of my Jewish friends and professional partners in conversation and common action show much interest in the evolution of Catholic theological self-understanding; many are ersatz ultra-modernist for the simple reason that the Vatican

can be so influential in helping to promote peaceful relations among Jews and others around the globe."[11]

> For his part, Rabbi Leon Klenicki expressed the following opinion: We have to ask ourselves, "What are our missions?" This is more than an academic search. It should be a joint reflection on God's essence for our time, and very specifically the meaning of God for all of us after the total experience of evil as personified by Auschwitz and the Gulag."[12]

If we are not willing to engage in a theological thought or dialogue, how are we to enter into a more profound reflection on anti-Semitism, as Cardinal Bernardin called for his lecture at the Hebrew University of Jerusalem in March 1995? How are we ever going to respond to the challenge placed before us by Professor Emil L. Fackenheim in his 1996 Jerusalem Lecture "to confront the Holocaust no longer as shielded by theological armor but, as it were, nakedly, with brutal honesty and hence, inevitably, as a threat to both Jewish and Christian faith?"[13] How to respond to Fackenheim's troubling question: "What was the purpose of the Holocaust? To kill God. The God of the Jews and the Christians?"[14]

We must throw off all fear of the truth. Why should we be afraid of the truth? It is the truth that makes us free! What harm can come to us from a dialogue that goes beyond the discussion about problems and enters into the heart of what constitutes our identities as faith communities, in order to allow us to proceed along the path of common action?

In a book published in March of 1997, the British Chief Rabbi Sir Jonathan Sacks reflects upon the failure of right-wing libertarianism on the one side of the political aisle and the politics of collectivism on the other, to create a truly just and free social order. Speaking the language of hope, he calls upon Christians and Jews to work together to restore the Judeo-Christian tradition to the center of British national life, by promoting a liberal society rooted in communal and family values. Are we, Christians and Jews, ready to enter into a dialogue that will allow us to promote such a society? We have the answer, given to us in the same

---

11. *Foundations,* April 1996, 25.

12. Ibid., Rabbi Leon Klenicki.

13. In "Jewish-Christian Relations after the Holocaust: Toward Post-Holocaust Theological Thought," the 1996 Jerusalem Lecture by Professor Emil L. Fackenheim.

14. Ibid.

Holy Books that we, Jews and Christians, have in common; but are we ready to commit ourselves to this kind of common witness?

To go back for a moment to our ILC Common Declaration on the Family and our preparations for a similar document on ecology, I have been greatly encouraged by the success achieved in these initiatives. When the proposal to prepare a statement on the family was first discussed, we were warned that nothing would come of it, that it would be better to avoid this type of project. Yet we came to a good declaration with a little difficulty and no significant negative reaction.

As I have already mentioned, already in Jerusalem in 1994, two introductory papers were presented on ecology, one by a Catholic religious sister deeply involved in questions of justice, peace, and the protection of the environment, the other by a well-known Jewish rabbi. No previous consultation took place between the two speakers, yet their papers were almost identical in approach, biblical citations, and conclusions. In his presentation, Rabbi Norman Soloman explained:

> As well as common interest, Jews and Catholics share a biblical tradition on creation and can jointly affirm a wide range of values relating to the created world. Our methodologies, superficially at least, differ. Catholics are apt to draw on the principles of moral theology: whereas Jews are apt to draw on the specific provision of the *Halakha*. Yet this difference is more apparent than real.[15]

I was also encouraged when, at a meeting in the Vatican on February 18, 1993, Catholics and Jews explored together the possibility of a common approach to the questions on the agenda of a United Nations World Conference on Human Rights, which was to take place shortly afterwards in Vienna, Austria. The concerns expressed by the Jewish organizations represented there proved to be very similar to those of the Holy See. In particular, strong convergence was manifested on the following issues: the universality of human rights; the recognition of the collectivity (the group) as the subject of rights; the importance of freedom of religion; the need for effective procedures for dealing with the violation of human rights.[16]

---

15. In a paper presented to the ILC meeting (Jerusalem, May 1994), cf. *Information Service PCPCU*, No. 87 (1994), 231.

16. *SIDIC*, Vol. XXIX, No. 2–3, 1996 English edition, 44.

From April 7–11 1997, the Pontifical Biblical Commission met in Rome to study the relationship between the First and Second Testaments, and the influence of this on the relationship between Christianity and Judaism. Addressing the participants, Pope John Paul II noted that "it is not possible fully to express the mystery of Christ without having recourse to the Old Testament." At the same time His Holiness stated that we cannot ignore that the New Testament preserves traces of clear tensions that existed between the early Christian communities and some groups of non-Christian Jews. And he observed that if a Christian, by his adhesion to Christ, is convinced that he has become a "descendent of Abraham," "he will never be able to accept that Jews be scorned, or much worse, badly treated, just for being Jews."[17] This is a subject full of promise, but up to now it is being done exclusively by a Catholic Commission.[18] My hope is for a joint study in the not-too-distant future.

I made a suggestion similar to my present proposals at a symposium in Jerusalem on February 10 this year. In a paper presented on the same occasion, Rabbi David Rosen of the Anti-Defamation League, himself an Orthodox Jew, explained that the reluctance of many Orthodox Jews to engage in dialogue reflects an ignorance of the "revolution" that Church theology regarding Jews has undergone in recent years. He pointed out that the rabbinical world, unlike the Catholic Church, is an inherently decentralized structure, in which there is no dominant hierarchy. Catholics, he said, should not therefore be unduly disturbed by the fact that leaders of various Orthodox groups have so far been unwilling to join the circle of theological discussion. For Rabbi Rosen, "there are plenty of good rabbis with whom to dialogue."[19] On this positive and optimistic note, let me move on to consider some less controversial items on my proposed agenda for the future.

Information, Formation, and Education

Dialogue is of its very nature the work of those who have the necessary preparation and bear a particular responsibility for Catholic-Jewish

---

17. *L'Osservatore Romano*, April 12, 1997.

18. *Radio Vaticana radiogiornale, Anno XLI*, n. 93, April 3, 1997.

19. Unpublished papers of a symposium on the Future of Jewish-Catholic Relations in the World and in Israel/The Holy Land (February 10-11, 1997), in the Van Leer Institute, Jerusalem.

relations. The danger is that it will not therefore widely influence the thinking of a great number of those who make up the two faith communities. To ensure the future development of our relationship and bury in oblivion, once and for all, every form of Catholic-Jewish hostility and suspicion, it is necessary that mentalities change and that a new collective consciousness be created.

Hence the future agenda for Catholic-Jewish relations must include a greater emphasis on local contracts and activities between the two communities. If we wish to consolidate the work done so far and build a new future, much more attention will have to be paid to information, formation, and education.

As I mentioned earlier, so much of what has already been accomplished is not widely known. During the 1994 Jerusalem meeting of the Catholic-Jewish International Liaison Committee, the president of IJCIC, Geoffrey Wigoder, pointed out:

> We well know the abyss of ignorance in both our communities concerning the other which includes dangerous myths, stereotypes, and prejudices.[20]

We cannot expect much help in this from the media, which unfortunately are always ready to give prominence to new difficulties that may arise, but rarely find newsworthy the progress that we make. It is up to us to use all the means at our disposal to inform our communities of the good things that are taking place and seek to interest the media also in this aspect of the life of our communities.

Hand-in-hand with efforts to have our communities better informed, attempts need to be made also to extend further our work in the field of formation. I am well aware of the initiatives in seminaries and the training schools for future rabbis to form these future leaders of the two faith communities in the new spirit of Catholic-Jewish relations, to have them study the results of our dialogues, to bring them into contact with responsible teachers from the other religion. Excellent work has been done and is being done in this context here in the United States; each year there are visiting rabbis lecturing in Roman Catholic universities[21]; the Archdiocese of Chicago has sponsored valuable initiatives in

---

20. *Information Service PCPCU,* No. 87 (1994), 233.

21. Rabbi L. Klenicki lectured on "Saint Paul and Judaism" in the spring 1997 semester at the Seminary of the Immaculate Conception, Huntington, N.Y. There are special courses at Seton

exchanges with Polish seminaries; there is the special faculty for Jewish Studies at Sacred Heart University, Bridgeport, Conn. Roman universities have invited leading Jewish scholars to give lectures and courses to their students in recent years. Courses are available in Jewish and Christian Institutes in Jerusalem. Much more is needed in this field, however, if we really wish to dismiss once and for all the old prejudices and stereotypes from our societies. In this connection, I can only endorse wholeheartedly Cardinal Bernardin's reflections on this aspect of Catholic-Jewish relations in his Jerusalem Lecture of 1995.[22] The question of formation is one that affects both our communities and perhaps is less developed in Jewish formation centers than in Catholic seminaries and universities.

Thirdly, attention must be directed to the field of education in general. Again, in the United States there are examples of rabbis being invited to Catholic schools to address the children attending these institutions. Cardinal Bernardin has mentioned in his Jerusalem Lecture, programs about the Holocaust in Seton Hall College near Pittsburgh and in the Archdiocese of Chicago. But as he rightly points out, "we must go beyond merely teaching the failures of the past" and make known to our younger generations the basis that recent teaching has given us for a positive theology of reconciliation and bonding.[23] This for me is one of the main concerns and issues facing us today: how to prepare future generations and in particular their leaders, in the new spirit of cooperation, mutual understanding and reconciliation, goodwill, and common goals of which the ILC spoke in Prague in 1990.

Practical Cooperation

The final entry on my new agenda would go hand-in-hand with the other items: dialogue, information, formation, and education. It would profit from these, but at the same time contribute to them. It is something that is already underway, but which is so far greatly limited in its extension. I refer to practical cooperation, especially at the local level.

Hall University, N.J., and in other similar Catholic centers of higher study.

22. Pages 14–18, this volume.

23. Page 15, this volume.

Practical cooperation is itself a kind of school for learning about each other; it is a way of living out that new spirit of mutual understanding, reconciliation, and goodwill that we wish to promote. Let me give you some examples of what is actually taking place in this regard, in the hope that they may serve as an inspiration for others to do something similar within their own communities.

I was pleasantly surprised to learn, during a visit to our Commission in Rome of a group of Conservative Jewish rabbis from several parts of the United States, of the various forms of cooperation that exist between some of their communities and the corresponding Catholic parishes. They spoke of study groups and of a variety of practical working groups, which are creating a whole new relationship between these communities.

Another Jewish rabbi, visiting my office, strongly recommended such initiatives and spoke of the deep effect that the presence of a priest or rabbi at the events in the life of the other community can have. He claimed that the embrace of a rabbi and priest, in front of either congregation, can change radically the collective consciousness of that community.

The Agreement between the Rochester Board of Rabbis, the Jewish Community Federation of Rochester, and the Roman Catholic Diocese of Rochester, signed on May 8, 1996, is a more official, but highly visible act of reconciliation and cooperation. This Rochester Agreement brings much of what I have been speaking about to the institutional level, as you will realize from the following brief outline of its recommended provisions:

• To combat and respond publically to "all forms of anti-Semitism, racism, anti-Catholicism, and religious intolerance";

• To promote richer and more frequent communication that "will serve to instruct, enlighten, and heal";

• To initiate efforts "to ensure appropriate and accurate curricula when teaching about each other's faith tradition";

• To explore areas in which resources or parallel services, such as in family services, might benefit from cooperation between the two communities;

- To strive to enlighten and become more sensitive to each other in areas of particular concern, such as the link with the State of Israel for Jewish people and issues of sacredness of human life for Catholics.[24]

It is the hope of both the Catholic and Jewish communities in Rochester that the Rochester Agreement will be taken up and serve as a model for communities in other places. By being adapted to local needs and possibilities, such action could help to make Catholic-Jewish dialogue, a reality in the life of these local communities, affecting positively not only the members of the communities themselves but the community at large.

I should like to add a final word in this context on cooperation within the context of the coming Christian Jubilee year 2000. This will of course be a Christian celebration, but Pope John Paul II in his Apostolic Letter *Tertio Millennio Adveniente* expressed the hope that the Jubilee year might provide also "a great opportunity for interreligious dialogue," in which "the Jews and the Muslims ought to have a pre-eminent place." He was careful, however, to emphasize that "care will always have to be taken not to cause harmful misunderstandings."[25] I understand that a representative body of Jewish leaders here in the United States is already discussing with the United States Conference of Catholic Bishops possibilities for promoting such dialogue. An essential element of this Jubilee celebration will be the fostering of a genuine spirit of repentance within the Catholic Church for "the acquiescence given, especially in certain centuries, to intolerance and even the use of violence in the service of truth."[26] At the same time, it is the Holy Father's fervent wish that in the present circumstances it may be possible for Jews to be associated with a family feast of their friends, the Christian community.

Conclusion

As will be obvious from these thoughts that I have shared with you in this presentation, Catholics and Jews are not at this time struggling with

---

24. The text of the Rochester Agreement and comments on it are available in a publication of the Anti-Defamation League (1996).

25. *Tertio Milennio Adveniente*, No. 53.

26. Ibid., No. 35.

questions that call for urgent solutions. We are fortunately not passing through a period of tension or divisive debate.

The issues before us at this time are directed to consolidating the new situation that has been achieved since the Second Vatican Council and building on it in such a way as to ensure that the future will not be darkened by events which threaten this relationship. I believe that it is precisely through common action, greater mutual understanding, and continued dialogue that we can do this. Moreover, I am convinced that such cooperation on the part of Jews and Catholics can contribute greatly to the well-being of our societies. In the words of Pope John Paul II, addressed to the Jewish community in Poland on the occasion of the 50th anniversary of the Warsaw Ghetto Uprising:

> As Christians and Jews, following the example of the faith of Abraham, we are called to be a blessing for the world (cf. Genesis 12:2ff.). This is a common task awaiting us. It is therefore necessary for us, Christians and Jews, to be first a blessing to one another.[27]

---

27. Published in *L'Osservatore Romano*, August 17, 1993.

4 The Theological Significance of Israel

David Hartman
March 17, 1998

The third Jerusalem Lecture was delivered in Chicago on March 7, 1998, by Rabbi Dr. David Hartman, the founder and director of the Shalom Hartman Institute in Jerusalem, a center for higher Jewish learning and a think-tank for research on issues facing the Jewish people today. Among Dr. Hartman's widely known writings in Jewish philosophy, Maimonides: Torah and Philosophic Quest *(1976) and* A Living Covenant *(1986), received the National Jewish Book Award. Rabbi Hartman's lecture, "The Theological Significance of Israel," approaches its topic from a biblical, rabbinic, and philosophical perspective. Dr. Hartman explores the implications of this subject for the future of Judaism and discusses the implications of the perspective he offers for relationships between Judaism, Christianity, and world religions.*

I would like to deal, in this presentation, with two themes. The first is the biblical, rabbinic and philosophical foundations of my perception of the theological significance of Israel and its implications for the future of Judaism. In the second half of my talk I shall discuss the implications of this perspective for the relationships between Judaism and Christianity and Islam and other world religions. What is the significance of the Jewish return to Jerusalem for the future of religious pluralism, in general, and for biblical faiths nurtured on a theology of a Lord of history, in particular?

One of the most important questions you face when you decide to cast your lot with the people of Israel is: how did this people develop the human resources and strength to choose to be visible and vulnerable in history given the conditions of modern Western culture and Jewish history? The trauma of the Holocaust, which follows us continuously, should have produced people who wanted to leave history, to withdraw to the "coffeehouses" of Western culture and to say to the world: "I prefer to remain invisible and unexposed; I no longer wish to be part of Western civilization." This would have been an understandable response of Jews to the decimation of European Jewry and civilization.

Hermann Cohen, the eminent German-Jewish philosopher of the nineteenth and twentieth centuries, spoke of Germany as the carrier of human idealism and of the greatest values Western culture had to offer. He was profoundly anti-Zionist, for he considered himself a deeply rooted German, and he was grateful that German Jews could imbibe the best of Western culture. In "A Reply to Dr. Martin Buber's Open Letter" (1916), Hemann Cohen wrote:

> We love Germany and all it stands for not merely because we love our homeland as the bird loves its nest; nor do we love it merely because we draw our spiritual sustenance largely from the treasure-troves of the German mind (and surely not from the Bible or Talmud alone). Weighty though these motivations for our love may be, they lose some of their significance when compared to our awareness of that innermost accord existing between the German spirit and our Messianic religiosity. The German spirit is the spirit of classical humanism and true universalism. . . . What other people possess such unity of classical poetry and philosophy! All these German thinkers are prophets of the one humanity. Therefore, it is only natural that we German Jews should feel at one with ourselves, as Jews and as Germans. And the Jews of other countries, whose religious life has been fructified by the science of Judaism (which has its roots in Germany), should learn to acknowledge and appreciate Germany's central significance for moral culture. . . . While the Zionist believes that Judaism can be preserved only by an all-encompassing Jewish nationalism, we are of the opposite view, believing that only a universal, mankind-oriented Judaism can preserve the Jewish religion.

The Holocaust involved not only the decimation of millions of people and the loss of whole societies and civilizations, but also the loss of faith in Western humanism. You can't understand the reactionary repudiation by many Jews of Western civilization or the refusal of religious fundamentalists to relate to the secular world unless you appreciate the trauma that destroyed the credibility of Western culture as a serious option for many Jews. The question, therefore, that must be answered is: where did we get the strength to choose to be visible despite all of this?

Israel, in the deepest sense, represents the choice of visibility, the choice not to hide. Once you choose to build a Jewish state, you cannot hide. Time magazine and CNN follow you wherever you go, whatever you do. Everything becomes exposed to public scrutiny.

Furthermore, Jewish statehood should not be understood as a people's defiant leap into absolute self-reliance. To describe our choice of sovereignty and statehood in terms of independence from others and dependence on our own resources is only partly correct, because Israel's survival continues to depend on the goodwill of the world. Israel's choice is less one of independence—of "going it alone"—than of dependence on the good faith and cooperation of people of goodwill throughout the world. The establishment of the State of Israel represents, therefore, the choice both of independence and of interdependence with the world community. There is a double, dialectical movement involved in our choice of sovereignty. Israel means that our survival depends on our own strength and initiative; yet, at the same time, it represents a move toward human interdependency and a deep faith in human decency.

Interdependency and visibility thus reflect what Israel is really about. The question we must now ask is: what are the roots of this choice? My claim is that these roots lie deep within the biblical foundations of Judaism. Let us look, therefore, at some of the central metaphors and categories of this tradition.

The first category is the fundamental notion of creation, which, as distinct from Aristotle's doctrine of eternal necessity, indicates the mystery of God's creation of that which is other than God. The essence of biblical creation—to rephrase the language of Genesis—is: Let there be an "other." The "other" stands in opposition to God; it stands there as an "other." In an Aristotelian universe, the world is co-eternal with God. God is essentially self-sufficient. The primary conception of human perfection in Aristotle as well as in the Stoics is self-sufficiency and independence from external conditions and other people. Aristotle's God has no need or interest in the world or human history.

The biblical God however, is deeply involved in the world and human history. As Professor Yochanan Muffs, a great biblical teacher and scholar, once said, God is the most tragic figure in the Bible. The

Biblical God, the Lord of history, has an interest in creation. God has needs. God is hungry to be accepted, to be loved, to be worshiped. The most characteristic mode of behavior of God in the Bible is that of reacting. God is forever in need of human allegiance and submission to the divine will. One of the functions of biblical prophets is to pacify and calm God's rage. This often leads to a situation where both God and the prophet try to calm each other down. Yochanan Muffs presents a brilliant analysis of the psychological dynamics of the relationship between the prophet and God in the Bible in his essay, "Who Will Stand in the Breach?: A Study of Prophetic Intercession," in his book *Love and Joy: Law, Language and Religion in Ancient Israel* (Cambridge, MA: Harvard University Press, 1992).

If you look closely at the dialogue between Moses and God in the incident of the Golden Calf (Ex 32), you get the impression that each one is doing therapy on the other. Moses says to God, "Sorry, God, you can't lose your temper anymore. If the Egyptians find out or it gets reported in the world press that you, God, took the Jews out of Egypt and abandoned them or wiped them out in the desert, your reputation is finished! You will never 'make it' as the Lord of history."

What an argument to address to God! Can you imagine speaking to the God of Aristotle in this manner? "Listen, You, the self-contemplating First Cause of being, cannot behave this way if you expect to make it in this world!" Aristotle's God simply has no interest whatsoever in human history or, for that matter, in anything else other than His own perfection. This God can't even think about human beings, because to think about imperfection is itself an imperfection. The divine being only thinks that which is perfect and, therefore, God only thinks God.

The notion of a God that is thought on thought reflects a totally different conception of perfection than that which we find in the Judaic tradition. The greatness and perfection of the biblical God involves divine vulnerability. God is perfect but is prepared to suffer. And God suffers in the Bible because of God's great expectations of human beings and of history.

The stories in the book of Genesis can be described as a series of divine experiments and failures. The Garden of Eden—an experiment that failed; Noah—a failure; the Tower of Babel—a failure. But then, with Abraham, God decides that this time He's going to make it work. He will try doing it differently and so he decides . . . (I use the word "decides" because, in reading the Bible, I imagine that God "thinks" and "decides" the way human beings do. After all, the Bible was not embarrassed to portray God very humanly. So why should I, an ordinary mortal, be embarrassed to do so?)

Now, God creates human beings in His image, and they are expected to mediate God's presence in the world. After relating the failure I mentioned previously, the Bible describes Abraham's becoming God's elect by introducing the new idea of a covenant between God and human beings. In contrast to Von Raad, I claim (in my essay "Fundamentals of a Covenantal Anthropology" in my book *A Living Covenant,* Woodstock, VT: Jewish Lights Publishing, 1998) that the covenant of Noah is really between God and nature. It is a unilateral statement by God not to destroy the world. A genuine covenantal relationship with human beings only begins with Abraham when God realizes that without human responsibility and active cooperation, the world will not turn out the way God would like. This covenant reflects the new theological idea that God needs the cooperation of human beings to achieve the divine vision for history.

The principle of election thus grows out of God's choice to become dependent on human beings as co-partners in the creation of a human world. The rabbis remark with reference to God's statement, "Shall I hide from Abraham what I am about to do?" (Gn 18:32), that God, as it were, had to ask Abraham's permission to destroy the city of Sodom. God didn't ask for Noah's permission before bringing about the flood, because Noah did not have a covenantal relationship with God. God did not feel responsible to Noah.

The biblical narrative in Genesis describes this dramatic theological transformation from God's self-congratulatory excitement at having created the universe to God's gradual realization that unless human beings cooperate, even divine omnipotence cannot bring a perfect world into being. Human beings are essentially co-partners with God in building a just world because divine fiat alone failed to achieve this. This idea points to the theological notion of a self-limitation that makes room for the human—the "other"—in the creation of history. Covenantal consciousness begins with the awareness that God has burdened human beings—Abraham and the elect people of Israel—to be the carriers of God's vision for human history.

And so the history of Israel begins with the awareness that the Lord of history is not self-sufficient. The Lord requires human beings to mediate in their personal and collective lives the principles of justice, love, and truth. As the Midrash says with reference to Abraham's use of the phrase "the God of heaven and the God of the earth" (Gn 24:3): "Before Abraham came into the world, God was king of the heavens alone—*Elokei hashamyim* (the God of heavens)—but after Abraham, God also became the God of the earth." Human beings, in the person of Abraham, extend God's majesty to include the earth.

To be part of the covenantal community of Israel is to carry the burden of God's vision for history. It is significant, therefore, that the first experience the Bible relates about Israel is their enslavement in Egypt. This is the first time that the biblical narrative describes a person or community suffering without any moral justification. There is no sin that precedes their suffering. This is surprising, since the biblical prophets interpret every situation in history with reference to the providential principle that suffering is the result of a moral cause. The prophetic logic is: You are suffering, therefore, you have sinned. But here, in Egypt, Israel begins its history with suffering but without any description of previous sin or moral failure.

The experience of slavery signifies the inception of a people within the womb of Egypt. It is the moment of Israel's birth as a people, the moment when we move from family—to national—consciousness. The only "sin" in the story—the cause of Israel's suffering—is the threat of revolt that Pharaoh fears. Their "sin" is their being thought of as dangerous outsiders who bring suffering upon themselves by their very otherness. Israel's destiny arouses the suspicion and fear of tyrannical rulers in history who seek absolute control and obedience. This account is the first reference to Israel's role in history as the stranger, as the "other."

"A new king arose over Egypt, who did not know Joseph" (Ex 1:8). What does "who did not know Joseph" mean? How could he not know Joseph? asked the Rabbis. Did Joseph not rescue the Egyptian economy from disaster? Was this not recorded in Egyptian archives? The Midrash answers by reading the frightening logic of human tyranny into the text as follows: "A new king arose over Egypt, who made himself into a person who did not know Joseph." We have here the beginning of a process of dehumanization by which a whole community is isolated, humiliated, and exploited.

And he (Pharaoh) said to his people, "Look, the Israelite people are much too numerous for us. Let us deal shrewdly with them, so that they may not increase; otherwise in the event of war they may join our enemies in fighting against us and rise from the ground (gain ascendancy over the country). So they set taskmasters over them to oppress them with forced labor; and they built garrison cities for Pharaoh; Pithom and Raamses. But the more they were oppressed, the more they increased and spread out, so that the [Egyptians] came to dread the Israelites" (Ex 1:8–12).

The biblical narrative thus reveals the capacity of a society to dehumanize the "other," to actively forget the humanity of people, to objectify and quantify human life, to turn people into commodities. The slave is essentially a commodity, the object of the master's will—a social entity without the power of freedom and self-determination. And this is the beginning of Israel's covenantal history—Israel as the stranger, as the "other," as one who is vulnerable because one is different.

Because the Torah had not yet been given, the rabbis had to explain the source of Israel's difference. The Midrash explains: "*Shelo shinu et shmam, shelo shinu et Ishonam,* v'lo shinu et amlbusheihem (Because they didn't change their names, and they didn't change their language)." Their language, dress, and names were sufficiently distinctive to create animosity and fear in the dominant culture. Even before the Torah of Moses with all its distinctive dietary and ritual practices, these people were sufficiently different to be recognized and labeled as dangerous "others." And this, ultimately, was their "sin," the source of their vulnerability and the reason why they suffered for hundreds of years.

In other words, Israel is cast into history as the carrier of the divine concern to be present in history. Israel is the eternal opponent of the pharaohs of history who cannot succeed as long as Israel exists. Israel inspires terror in the hearts of political tyrants who long for absolute power and control.

The classical biblical description of Israel in Egypt is *ger,* stranger, the vulnerable minority, the disenfranchised "other." "You shall not oppress a stranger, for you know the feelings of the stranger, having yourselves been strangers *(gerim)* in the land of Egypt" (Ex 23:9); "The stranger who resides with you shall be to you as one of your citizens; you shall love him as yourself, for you were strangers *(gerim)* in the land of Egypt" (Dt 10:19). I can safely say that one of the definitions of Israel is *ger,* in the sense of the stranger, the "other." As the Midrash says with regard to the Bible's description of Abraham as *ha-ivri* (translated as "the Hebrew") (Gn 14:13): "The whole world lives on one side (ever) and Abraham lives on the other side *(ever)*." According to this Midrash, the term "hav-ivri" derives from Abraham's other-ness with respect to his cultural/religious environment.

What this means is that this lonely people of faith must carry God's loneliness in history until God's dream of justice is realized. As long as history is unredeemed, Israel will remain a lonely people destined to carry the burden of God's loneliness and God's yearning for justice. Their suffering testifies to the failure of the world to acknowledge the humanity of the "other."

So far we have introduced the biblical categories of covenant, stranger, Egypt, the "other," which are fundamental to understanding the idea of Sinai. It is important for me to make a point I wrote about recently in a paper on Sinai and Auschwitz. I believe strongly that it is a serious mistake to make Auschwitz the organizing image of Jewish self-understanding in the modern world. In contrast to what has been understood from the writing of Emil Fackenheim and others, I maintain that I am a Jew not because of Hitler's nightmare but because of Moses' hope and promise. I am not a Jew because of Hitler; I am a Jew because of Moses. My people fell in love with Moses' dream. "*Ve'atem tihyu li mamlechet kohanim v'goi kadosh* (And you shall be to Me a kingdom of priests and a holy nation)" (Ex 19:6). It is Moses' aspiration for this slave people that is ultimately responsible for Jewish history.

Even though biblical scholars like to make a distinction between the Exodus and the Sinai traditions, the Jewish tradition viewed them as one unified whole. The Exodus festival of Passover is conceptually and experientially linked to Shavuot (The Festival of Weeks, "Pentecost"), which, in the rabbinic tradition, are merged together by the counting of the Omer (49 days between the second day of Passover and Shavuot) and by the reference to Shavuot as *"Atzeret shel Pesach"* (the conclusion of Passover).

Let us try to understand the significance of joining together these two moments of the Jewish calendar. If we only celebrated Egypt, then perhaps the Jewish story would have been told as follows: "Oy! ("oy" is a Jewish metaphor) was it ever hot! Oy! Our slavery, our persecution, lasted two hundred years!" We would tell stories of our victimization, of what they did to us. In other periods of history, we would tell other

Egypt stories, other victim stories. In other words, we would walk through history as victims. But Sinai came and liberated us from building our self-definition solely in terms of our suffering and helplessness. Sinai gave us a vision of hope, an aspiration of holiness, a way of life informed by value and sanctity, an abiding belief that something new is possible in human history. The covenant of Sinai was not addressed to Israel the eternal victim but to Israel the eternal believer in the possibilities of the future.

The Sinai moment is realized when the future rather than the past defines one's identity. "And you shall be to Me a kingdom of priests and a holy nation." It is interesting to note that although Sinai retains the memory of the past, it turns this memory into a normative catalyst. We don't remember suffering for its own sake. We remember suffering because it has a normative effect on our lives. "For you were strangers in the land of Egypt" is mentioned in connection with not oppressing the stranger (Ex 23:9), but with loving the stranger (Lv 19:33; Dt 10:19), observing the Sabbath and treating servants with dignity and fairness (Dt 5:12–15; 15:14; 16:12). The liberation from Egypt is also cited in support of the commandments to keep honest weights and balances (Lev 19:35), to release slaves in the jubilee year (Lev 25:55), and so on. Rather than wallowing in the memory of past injustices and victimization, the Bible uses the memory of Egypt to support the *halakhic* (legal) significance of the commandments.

We now come to the categories of the desert and the land, which conclude my analysis of the basic foundational categories or metaphors of the biblical narrative. The land, as opposed to the desert, represents Israel's entry into normal life, with all its problems and seductions, carrying the message of covenantal politics into a world that doesn't always understand it. From a theological perspective, the land is God's desire to be revealed not only within the privacy of individual life—in the leap of "the alone to the Alone"—but also in the collective frameworks of community and history.

It is extremely important to understand the land as a symbol of God's concern with becoming present in human history by being mirrored in the collective life of a nation. The totality of life is brought under the judgment of God—its social, political, and economic structures, its understanding and implementation of social justice, social welfare, and so on. This is the theological meaning of "the land." In other words, it is not only the kitchen that must be placed under the judgment of God. I have nothing against *kashrut* (dietary laws) but I must emphasize that the category of the land means that God wants more than the kitchen and the synagogue. God wants the totality of life, the fullness of human concerns and activities—that is the biblical message.

Now, if you read the Bible seriously, you will meet the all-inclusive divine concern with being mediated in every aspect of life. We may choose to reinterpret many aspects of the Bible, but one thing remains permanent and fundamental: the seriousness and all-inclusive nature of the divine demand. God is the energy, the driving force of moral demand. And therefore, Moses repeatedly reminds the people of Sinai, "The Lord spoke to you out of the fire; you heard the sound of words but perceived no shape—nothing but a voice" (Dt 4:12). God is the word. God is present not in the symbol nor in the image but in the normative force of the word. God is present in our lives when we become conscious of our covenantal responsibilities.

After hearing the word at Sinai, Israel enters the land, but once again the experiment fails. The prophets scream out at the failure of Israel's attempt—its first attempt—at living by the covenantal vision.

Given these biblical foundations, there is, I believe, one more category that becomes especially significant during the second commonwealth. Ezra returns after the destruction of the first commonwealth and the exile. Although Jeremiah had predicted seventy years in exile followed by a glorious return, the return from exile was less dramatic than anticipated. The king of Persia sent troops to accompany some of the returning exiles, who were broken and fragmented as a community and forced to start again under imperfect, incomplete conditions—a far cry from the drama of Joshua's conquest of the land and the grandeur of the prophetic promise.

This is a very important point and, as I shall explain, it is the basis of my criticism of the messianic politics found in Israel today. Ezra returned to an imperfect reality, to a world that did not reflect the dramatic involvement of God in history, yet he succeeded in reconstructing the community and, thus, in laying the groundwork for the development of the Talmudic tradition. The biblical prophetic world was gradually replaced by the very different ethos of the second commonwealth and of the rabbinic civilization that followed it.

The new ethos that set this period off from its biblical predecessor involved a radical change in theological descriptions of God and religious sensibilities. A new theological metaphor enters into religious discourse, as can be seen in the *gemara* (Talmudic discussion) in Yoma and Sanhedrin and throughout the *Mechilta* (rabbinic commentary to Exodus). When Israel crossed the sea, God was hailed as *"ish milchama"* (a man of war)—as the conquering hero, the triumphant Lord of history. After witnessing God's power in defeating the Egyptians, in splitting the sea, and in leading a powerless group of slaves to freedom, the prophet Moses leads Israel in a spontaneous victory song celebrating God's omnipotence. "Who is like You, O Lord, among the mighty?" (*"mi kamocha ba-elim"* (elim = mighty) (Ex 15:11). Who can be compared to God, to the triumphant mighty Lord of history? The Midrash, however, offers a very different reading of these biblical words of praise. In place of *mi kamocha ba-elim hashem* it reads *mi kamocha ba-ilmin hashem*—Who is like You, O Lord, among the silent ones? (*ilmim* = the mute, the voiceless) Who can be compared to You, the mute, silent God, the God who is blasphemed and disgraced yet remains quiet and impassive?

This motif recurs in the following discussion in Yoma:

In the West [Palestine] they taught it thus: R. Gidda said: [And Ezra praised . . . the] great [God], that is, he magnified Him by pronouncing the Ineffable Name. R. Mattena said: He said: "The great, the mighty and the awesome God" *(hael hagadol, hagibor, vehanorah).* The interpretation of R. Mattena seems to agree with what R. Joshua b. Levi said. For R. Joshua b. Levi said: "Why are they called men of the Great Assembly? Because they restored the crown of the divine attributes to its ancient completeness. [For] Moses had come and said: "The great God, the mighty and the awesome God." Then Jeremiah came and said: "Aliens are destroying His temple. Where, then, are His awesome deeds?" Hence he omitted [the attribute] "awesome." Daniel came and said: Aliens are enslaving His sons. Where are His mighty deeds? Hence he omitted the word "mighty." But they came and said: On the contrary! Therein lie His mighty deeds, that He suppresses His wrath, that He extends long-suffering to the wicked. Therein lie His awesome powers: For but for the fear of Him, how could one [single] nation persist among the [many] nations! But how could [the earlier] rabbis abolish something established by Moses? R. Eleazer said: Since they knew that the Holy One, blessed by He, insists on truth, they would not ascribe false [things] to Him. (Yoma 69b).

Although Moses referred to God as "the great, the mighty and the awesome," the rabbis asked: "Where is God's might when Rome is in control of Israel? Where is God's might when Israel is subject to the powers of the world? But, the Talmud says, Ezra gave a new interpretation of "might" when he said, *"shenoten erech apayim l'reshayim"* (who extends long-suffering to the wicked).

A new image of the Lord of history now emerges. God waits silently, showing patience with evil doers and not immediately striking them down as He did with Pharaoh and his armies. The triumphal God of the Bible undergoes a radical transformation. The Lord is no longer seen in the triumphant events of history, but, instead, in the everyday events of life of the community. Study and learning becomes the community's new form of prayer. The community learns to meditate on God through study and learning. The word of the Torah scholar replaces the word of the prophet in mediating God's presence.

The Talmud says: "When two people study Torah, *the shechinah,* the divine presence, is in their midst." God's everlasting love and presence are experienced where Torah is learned. In Talmudic academies learning often takes the form of worship. People sway while rhythmically repeating the words of a difficult Talmudic passage. Intricate logical arguments are analyzed to the melody of a *nigum* (song). Nothing typifies the ambience of a yeshiva (Talmudic academy) more than the song of learning, the song of reading God's love letter in the form of the Talmudic text.

Rabbi Akiva was noted for his ingenious interpretations not only of the meaning of the words of the biblical text, but also of the *tagim* (crownlets atop the Hebrew letters) and the *ethim* (particles of speech). Rabbi Akiva read the Bible as the intimate love letter. He read and re-read the words; he examined the handwriting, the shape of the letter, the marks on the page, always looking for signs and clues to hidden meanings and secret messages. Rabbinic Judaism thus gave new meaning to the divine presence. The word of God that I studied and that I felt in everyday life replaced God's victory over the enemy on the battlefield in mediating the immediacy of God's presence for the rabbinic Jew.

Now, giving these categories, let us move from the theological/philosophical plane to an analysis of modern Israel. What do these categories have to do with modern Israel?

Jews returned to history and chose visibility because they were burdened with the covenantal message that Jews must remain in history as a community. Instead of defining themselves as Auschwitz victims, they defined themselves as pioneers building a new history and a new reality. There is something here of the experience of the resurrection of the dead, of Ezekiel's vision of the dry bones. The experience you have in Israel is, on one level, of people in whom you see the horrors of the Holocaust and, on another level, of a proud people building a nation. In some way, the impulse to build and to defy despair reflects a deeply rooted religious refusal to abandon history. One way or another, it expresses the biblical demand to carry the Lord of history into the totality of life, into the concrete reality of history where the divine presence seeks to become visible.

I recall my enthusiasm in the aftermath of the Six-Day War. People were convinced that this was the beginning of the messianic era. Rabbis were writing, "The footsteps of the Messiah can be heard in the distance; the land is opening up before us; the covenant of the Bible is being revealed; God confirms the wisdom of the Zionist revolution and we are now witnessing the unfolding of the process of redemption."

The Greater Land of Israel movement gained unprecedented support. I am not referring to political arguments for retaining control of the land because of security reasons: that's a different issue that should not be dismissed lightly. I am talking about the concept of the land as a symbol of the messianic vision, as a sign that Israel's triumph is the Lord's providential way of vindicating our exilic history.

I too was caught up in the enthusiasm of the Six-Day War. I felt I had to be in Israel because, in some way, the fate of history was going to be decided by whether and how the Jewish people would rebuild itself in Israel.

I remember my congregation in Montreal saying to me: "Rabbi, how can the captain of the ship leave now? You're supposed to leave last." I remember so many people crying when I left. It was so moving to discover the love of a whole community, but it was equally shocking to discover the loneliness you could feel among your own people in Israel. It was far from simple. When I left America, I was a Jew; but when I arrived in Israel, I was an American. *"Atah Amerikai"* (You're an American) was all I heard. It took a while before I could find a way of communicating my ideas about pluralism, about the American experience and about a live-and-let-live way of relating to others.

I learned about pluralism from Professor Robert Pollock, at Fordham University, who had a profound spiritual influence on my life in his teaching of American philosophy. I played basketball in Lincoln Terrace Park with African Americans and Italians. In other words, I knew about and believed in pluralism in America, but when I came to Israel and I spoke about pluralism I soon discovered that not all Jews had read John Stewart Mill's *On Liberty*. So I decided that it was my masochistic destiny to explain to my people that the Jewish experience in America had produced some important values worth considering.

I remember the incredible stories people were telling about miracles after the Six-Day War. A grenade was thrown into a synagogue but failed to go off. There were only ten Israeli soldiers facing thousands of Egyptians attacking in the Negev desert when suddenly the Egyptians began to retreat. When asked why they had retreated the Egyptians said they had seen someone with a white beard—Elijah the prophet was over there.

The problem, I understood, was that Jews had lived as victims for so long. They were taught to say: "Who is as silent as you, God?" But they also remembered the original words of the prayer: "Who is as mighty as you, God?" This tension kept alive a deep longing for the day when God would say to the world: "Listen, Israel is my people. They are my children. They have returned home. And I shall now vindicate their suffering and their waiting by giving them a mighty victory." I can understand why a people who are taught to wait for two thousand years could fall victim to the belief that something radically new was now taking place. Something extraordinary was happening. The Lord was speaking.

I remember going to Rav Joseph B. Soloveitchik after the Six-Day War and saying to him: "Declare a holiday. I don't want to celebrate only festivals that give me memories of what God did in the past. God did something new! Please, my teacher, declare a holiday." But he answered: "David, I appreciate what you feel, but the Talmud says"—I knew I was going to get a Talmudic answer!—"that after the Maccabean victory they waited a year before declaring the holiday of Hanukkah." So as a good sober-minded Lithuanian, he told me that you don't react ecstatically to events in history. You wait to see the implications.

At the moment, I felt I couldn't any more be his student and I left him. I was on fire and felt spiritually alienated from him. I was caught up in an electrifying moment when all Jews felt as one for the first time in history. Many of us felt that a great drama was unfolding. Israel was not just another community. It was the carrier of what Jewish history was about. And if it were to go, then it would be all over.

So, although I can understand messianic politics and explain it in a sympathetic manner, I believe it is fundamentally mistaken, because triumph is not a form of divine vindication. God does not speak through victory. During most of our history we were the defeated ones. We were lonely figures without power and we argued against triumphal theologies that saw in our exile proof of divine rejection.

St. Augustine and the early Church Fathers argued that the destruction of the Temple and the exile of Israel were signs of God's rejection of Israel and of the validity of the New Testament as opposed to the Old Testament. Israel's homelessness and wandering, Israel's suffering and vulnerability were cited as proof of this theological position, a position that was based on theological dogma that today, I am happy to say, is being seriously rethought and will hopefully be revised. Nevertheless, I have to be honest and acknowledge that this theme was a dominant theological motif in Christian history. (We can only rethink the past if we are prepared to look at it honestly.)

I understand how this theological position developed out of Christianity's view of itself as a radical revolution. Christianity at a time of the early Church Fathers made the decision to see itself as the continuity of Israel, as the new Israel, and, therefore, it had to explain and justify itself in relation to the old Israel. How do you justify your claim to inheriting the biblical faith as the children of Abraham, yet you repudiate the Law of Moses? How do you explain people who stubbornly refuse to give up the Law and their allegiance to the old covenant that, you claim, was superseded? The answer of many Christians was that Jews were either ill-willed or spiritually blind. Augustine, for example, disavowed excessive persecution of Jews because he wanted Jews to suffer just enough to enable them to go through history bearing the mark of Cain for having rejected the Good News, in other words, to suffer continuously but without disappearing form history, so as to bear witness to the biblical prophetic foundations of Christianity.

Jews, however, didn't buy into this understanding of history, because they rejected triumphal theologies. We rejected the idea that God always belonged to the victor. It is ironic that although the idea of the suffering God is of the essence of Christianity, it nevertheless became a triumphal faith. I am, therefore, grateful to those voices in the Church that wish to recapture the essential meaning of Christianity and to reinterpret Paul's treatment of the law in various ways. The field of modern scholarship on Pauline theology is amazingly rich and interesting.

I applaud this new spirit in Christianity and I am open to what it has to say, because I no longer am a victim in history. The Jewish exile is over. Even Jews who live in the Diaspora don't regard America as exile. Christianity must know that the Jewish exile is over. We have returned home. Israel is not any more a homeless people and, therefore, Christians cannot use our exile to validate their theological dogma. Israel thus forces a whole new perception of itself on Christianity. The papacy can now recognize Jerusalem and establish diplomatic ties with the Jewish state because of the stubborn refusal of the Jewish people to perceive itself a victim and to step out of history.

We have returned home and the wandering *galut* (exilic) Jew is no longer the defining metaphor of our history. Israel bears living testimony to the fact that triumphal theologies have ended in history. The weakness and homelessness of the Jewish People can no longer serve as proof of the victory of other monotheistic faiths. Islam too must rethink its classification of the people of the Book—both Christians and Jews—as second-class citizens. Moslems too have difficulty accepting a strong Israel, for they too claim to be the sole authentic carriers of the biblical message. So again, Israel becomes a problem when it can no longer play the role of the suffering victim.

Because of this, I believe there is a different way of creating a new spirit of Jewish/Christian relations. When Christian theologians and pilgrims come to Jerusalem, I welcome them with love. I had a marvelous dialogue with Cardinal Bernardin and many of those who visited the [Shalom Hartman] Institute in Jerusalem. We have a center for religious interfaith relations, where leading Catholic and Protestant theologians will be visiting with us next week. Dean Gilpin and David Tracy of the University of Chicago Divinity School will present papers on the theme of the Trinity. Many people in Israel wrote to me saying: "Do you really want to advertise the fact that the Shalom Hartman Institute is having Father Tracy give a lecture on the Trinity with David Hartman responding? Do you realize what kind of reaction you are inviting?" I answered: "One has to live with risks. This is the meaning of being visible and not being a helpless victim." (Listen, if you hear any stones coming my way, please prepare a city of refuge for me here in Chicago.

Cardinal, I'll be welcome here, won't I? Okay. Now I feel a bit more secure going back home.)

It is important to understand the significance of Israel without having to make it the precursor of messianic redemption. History can have significance without a grand teleological scheme, a la Hegel or Marx or anyone who insists on turning history into a progressive eschatological drama leading toward redemption. My claim is that redemption is God's. Whatever has to do with the messianic reality—when it will be, what it will be like, and so on—I hand over totally to God. When people say to me: "There are many Christian fundamentalists who think that Israel's rebirth is the forefunner of the new messianic reality. Doesn't this make you feel undignified?" I say: "No, I don't feel undignified. I am even willing to say to these people: 'I'll sign an agreement of mutual respect and support with you as long as you agree to support Israel until the Second Coming.' If they say yes, then I say: 'Okay, we have a deal.'"

My primary interest is in being alive and in finding significance in everyday reality. History has holiness not because it points to the messianic kingdom. History has holiness when it provides opportunities to live in a covenantal relationship with God. History has significance when we can bring God into everyday life.

In my chapter on the celebration of finitude in my book *A Living Covenant,* I argue against those who see creation, revelation, and redemption as essential categories of our religious consciousness. I argue, contrary to Franz Rosenzweig, for the possibility of creation and revelation having significance without necessarily pointing to the redemptive moment. For me, God is present in the world when human love and human justice exist.

Israel, therefore, does not have to be the harbinger of the messiah. It does, however, have to provide conditions for building a total society where the strangers of history can feel at home. Jerusalem must stand firm, together with Christianity and Islam, and say: "We are not leaving history. We are here. Our voice will be heard." I live near the Old City and I love to hear the church bells on Sunday, the muezzin calling Moslems to prayer on Friday, and Jews singing on the Sabbath eve: *"L'Cha dodi likrat kalah pnei Shabbat n'kablah"* (Come, my beloved, to greet the bride, let us welcome the Sabbath).

When I hear these different faiths singing their songs, I ask myself: Can we sing our songs without dehumanizing the "other"? Can we sing our song and not feel that the "other" is a threat to our religious beliefs and integrity?

When I see passionate love expressed within a Christian context, I do not feel threatened or intimidated as a Jew. On the contrary, my five years at Fordham University brought me closer to the God of Israel. My awareness that Von Hildebrand, Quentin Lauer, and especially Robert C. Pollack could spiritually enrich me convinced me of the value and importance of genuine dialogue with people of other faith traditions. When I went back to my yeshiva, I prayed differently because something in their experience had touched me deeply. I feel the presence of the living God when I meet decent people of faith. Listening to other traditions doesn't have to destroy our own voice. Listening to the "other" can enrich your own voice.

And that's my dream for Jerusalem. Jews have returned home to Jerusalem to teach the world to give up the belief in one universal faith that includes everybody. We've come home—we've returned to our particularity—to teach the world about the meaning of the dignity of particularity. And this is my prayer and my hope for the future: May God's scheme for history be realized in radical diversity.

Israel is not the embodiment of the universal. Israel is an expression of the dignity of particularity. In the eighteenth century, Jews felt that in order to speak ethically, you had to embody the universality of Kantian ethics. In order to be dignified, you had to embrace universality and reject particularity, which many of them did by giving up their particular traditions. Jews assimilated in droves because they believed mistakenly that you became universal by discarding the particular.

The reborn State of Israel is an intensified expression of a people's particular identity. And it is this very particularity that can teach us the meaning of universalism as an outgrowth of a commitment to particularities. Intense particularity can be a blessing if Israel welcomes all the voices of goodwill in the world, if it welcomes all people of faith in all their diversity, if it can sing together with Moslems and Christians. I would love to witness the flourishing of Islam. (I did work in Maimonides, and when President Sadat made peace I secretly hoped I would be invited to Egypt to discuss Maimonides and Ibn Bajja and al-Farabi. But that never happened.)

I still look forward to a Jewish/Islamic dialogue that will begin and flourish. From Israel will go forth a truth that says: No one has an exclusive monopoly on truth. The key to truth is to live with the "other" without feeling threatened.

People often say that the greatest biblical commandment is: Love your neighbor as yourself. I claim the greatest biblical commandment is: Love the stranger. Loving your neighbor is loving someone who is like you. It is not that difficult to love those who are like you or who can become like you. But can you love an "other" who remains an "other" to you? Can you respect the dignity of a tradition that is not digestible in your own categories or framework of experience?

Israel says to the world: We proudly choose to be the stranger in history, the "other." And we commit ourselves to making sure that every "other" who lives in this country will feel dignity and love.

This is my prayer for Israel. And this is my prayer for the future of Jewish/Christian relations.

5
Christian Anti-Judaism: The First Century Speaks to the Twenty-first Century

Anthony J. Saldarini
April 14, 1999

The fourth Jerusalem Lecture was delivered in Chicago on April 14, 1999, by Professor Anthony J. Saldarini, Professor of Biblical Studies in the Department of Theology at Boston College. Professor Saldarini specializes in Second Temple and early Rabbinic Judaism and the New Testament. Among his eight books on these topics are Scholastic Rabbinism *(1982) and* Matthew's Christian-Jewish Community *(1994). Professor Saldarini has also published over fifty articles, and for over a decade he has served as the founding scholar of the Abrahamic Accord, a group which initiates conversations on the theological tensions and links between Jews and Christians. Professor Saldarini's lecture addressed "Christian Anti-Judaism: The First Century Speaks to the Twenty-First Century."*

PERHAPS we are wasting our time here. History teaches us that Jews and Christians have been fighting since the late first century and experience has demonstrated again and again that the Christian tradition readily generates anti-Jewish and anti-Semitic attitudes and actions. Since the second century the Christian "teaching of contempt"[1] concerning the Jews has dominated our theological, communal and political relationships. Christians, who read the New Testament seriously, frequently learn to despise Jews because of the anti-Jewish polemics there. Twenty-five years ago the theologian and scholar, Rosemary Radford Ruether of this city, warned that "possibly anti-Judaism is too deeply embedded in

---

1. The phrase comes from Jules Isaac, *The Teaching of Contempt: Christian Roots of Anti-Semitism* (New York: Holt, 1964).

75

the foundation of Christianity to be rooted out entirely without destroying the whole structure."[2]

How might Christians correct anti-Judaism in the New Testament? Some have suggested excising anti-Jewish statements from the text, but Christians can no more do that than Jews edit the Torah. We can correct the biases in translations, but in the end many New Testament passages still attack Jewish leaders, practices, or views.

Perhaps Christians could just leave the Jews alone. This is an attractive idea, but impossible. Christians have received revelation about God from and within the Jewish community and constructed their very way of life and thought from the Bible and early Jewish traditions. Christians have to study Judaism; Jesus the Jewish teacher and his early Jewish followers began as a Jewish reform movement or sect, so Christians have to say something about Jews. To this day Jews and Christians remain historically linked for better or worse. Safe to say after three thousand years, Judaism is here to stay and after two thousand years, Christianity as well. So, despite the shameful history of Christian anti-Semitism, we need to get on with our lives.

What then are we to do? Christians need to rethink and reform their theological tradition. A negative evaluation of Judaism has dominated Christian theology since the second century. This authoritative theological tradition goes by the names supersessionism, substitution, fulfillment, and replacement. The Christian Church, according to this view, is the new people of God and the true Israel founded by a new covenant. Most Christians understand this view in a fairly crass fashion. Christians have superseded Jews, that is, Christians have set aside or forced out Jews as inferior or taken the place of Jews. The old covenant is no longer valid because it has been replaced by a new covenant. The new covenant has completed, fulfilled, or perfected the preparatory, preliminary, temporary, imperfect, limited, defective old covenant. Consequently, Jews are no longer the "Israel" of the Bible. As early as the mid-second century the Christian writer Justin Martyr informed his astonished literary dialogue partner, Trypho the Jew, that Jews had been replaced by gentile Christians as God's "true Israel."

---

2. *Faith and Fratricide: The Theological Roots of Anti-Semitism* (New York: Seabury/Crossroad, 1974), 228.

I am sure that some of this language I have just used sounds familiar and comfortable to many Christians here. Really? Turn to the Jews nearest you and tell them that you are the true Israel and they are not. Tell all the Jews in this room frankly and clearly what the Christian theological tradition has said for nineteen hundred years: that their way of life and relationship with God, their covenant, ended two thousand years ago. No? Why not? This theology is impeccably traditional and orthodox.

I concede immediately that this Christian supersessionist outlook has been seriously criticized by many Christian writers and teachers since World War II. But I emphasize to you that replacement theology has not been replaced. Despite thousands of dialogues, uncounted pages of criticism and frequent ecclesiastical pronouncement, Pharisees are still hypocrites to most Christians because Matthew says so (Mt 23) and Jews are still legalistic because Paul criticized the law. For most Christians and in most educational textbooks and ecclesiastical documents, including the recent *Catechism of the Catholic Church,* Israel has value only insofar as it has provided the foundations for the Christian Church. In the view of most Christians what is good in Jewish teachings and practices has been absorbed by, integrated into, and subsumed under the new, final, and fully adequate revelation from God in Jesus Christ. To put the manner bluntly, for most Christians Judaism doesn't matter after Jesus Christ.

Christian preachers and teachers who have been informed and sensitized by Jewish-Christian dialogue avoid articulating the insulting claims that I have reviewed. But a tactful and prudent silence will not cure the tradition and cannot endure. Christians must proclaim what they know and act accordingly. So, we Christians must correct the underlying theology which replaces Israel with the Church and thus denies the integrity and legitimacy of the Jewish people as the people of God. If we do not, anti-Judaism and anti-Semitism will continue to arise. If we can make a little progress on this problem, we will not have wasted our time here this evening.

Let me make four connected statements about Jews and Christians which underlie what I will say here about Jesus and the New Testament.

1.   History matters in theology and in our relationships with God. God teaches us through history, we learn from history and our religious traditions change in history.

2.   After nineteen hundred years of vigorous religious life in intersecting communities, both Jews and Christians may safely conclude that theologically speaking God remains faithful to Israel as his people and that God has called the nations to worship and obey him through Jesus Christ.

3.   Both the Jewish and Christian communities are here to stay.

4.   God has called the Jewish and Christian communities to be his people in some sort of relationship with one another.

But what about two millennia of anti-Judaism? At this point you may be thinking, with British understatement, "Stoutly said, Saldarini, but there is this little matter of two millennia of anti-Semitism and violence." Or you may be recalling the gently ironic Irish joke about the two women conversing outside church after Sunday Mass: "Ah, didn't Father preach a fine sermon on marriage." "Indeed he did: I only wish I knew as little about marriage as Father!" We need not close our eyes to anti-Judaism to appreciate and accept one another, and we need not to be naive to hope for change. We who are here today cannot escape history, but we are not totally determined by it either. We make history because our one God is a living, revealing, active God who has changed us and our two communities over the course of human history. We have in our hands the means to reverse our traditions of mutual denigration.

Since I am a teacher of early Christianity and its relationships with early Judaism, I will contribute to a new relationship between Jews and Christians by drawing an extended analogy between the first century world and the post-World War II United States. In both periods Jews and followers of Jesus regularly lived and worked closely together with a growing understanding of one another and freely disagreed with little institutional oppression. In the first century the boundaries between Jewish followers of Jesus and the majority of the Jewish community had not yet hardened and in the twentieth century the hostile walls which estranged us for one another have been somewhat lowered.

How have these changes in historical interpretation altered Christian views of Jesus? At St. Kevin's Parish in Uphams Corner, in the Dorchester section of Boston, Massachusetts in the 1940s and 1950s when I was boy, Jesus was a Christian. In many places he still is. Even more strangely in the 1930s and 1940s in Germany, Jesus was an Aryan

Christian. How could a first-century Galilean Jew become a Christian and for some an Aryan, non-Jewish Christian at that?

Let me make three preliminary points which will begin to explain conflicting points of view concerning Jesus and the New Testament.

1.   First, we have four late first-century interpretations of Jesus in each of the four gospels. We have not a word written by Jesus and no contemporary accounts of his activities.

2.   Second, Christians must in each generation interpret Jesus for themselves just as the first-century gospel authors did.

3.   Third, though the risk of misinterpreting Jesus is great, no single interpretation is valid to the exclusion of all others.

This last point should not trouble us. Both Jews and Christians love to interpret their traditions, to argue about their interpretations and to reinterpret once again. Look, at the books and commentaries on our shelves and the gusto with which we discuss them and produce even more. We like to think that what we believe is the way it always was and that the truths of our religions are eternal and unchanging, but two hours of reading and reflection will show that this is not true.

We necessarily interpret as we read, listen, and try to understand, but not all interpretations are created equal, despite the claims of some post-modern interpreters. History has the vocation of criticizing and limiting interpretations to the rationally probable. Historically a Christian Jesus is a parochial, self-serving myth and an Aryan Jesus perverse. If Jesus is a Jew, how can we understand that reality and how can it help Jewish-Christian relations and a renewed Christian theology of Judaism today?

Jesus and His Jewish Followers in the First Century

Jesus came from a little village called Nazareth in central lower Galilee. Lower Galilee is the Esdraelon Valley which runs from the Mediterranean Sea to the Sea of Galilee for about twenty-five miles east-west by twenty miles north-south. It is a region smaller than a daily commute in many metropolitan areas. As a young man Jesus moved to Capernaum, a medium-sized town (10,000 to 20,000 people) in the north-eastern corner of the Esdraelon Valley on the north-west shore of the Sea of Galilee. Although Jesus has become an internationally known Christian religious figure and Christians revere Jesus as the savior of the world, during his lifetime he was a strictly local teacher who worked within a twenty mile radius of Capernaum, teaching and healing farmers and artisans from his own social class in villages, which probably numbered a few hundred at most. Jesus never worked in the two large Galilean cities, Tiberias the capital on the shore of the Sea of Galilee and Sepphoris three miles north of Nazareth, nor did he go into the large cities of the Decapolis in the Jordan River area nor those along the Mediterranean coast.

Jesus was a non-institutional, "popular" teacher and worker of powerful deeds who attracted wide local interest but only a small group of dedicated followers. He was one of those holy men, like the Biblical prophets and wise men, who had a special relationship with God. Some people accepted Jesus's relationship with God as authentic but most distrusted his claims, as we would expect. After all how many of you have been moved by modern spiritual teachers, faith healers, or mystics? What would you think if a family member became a follower of the messiah, Sun Myung Moon, of the Unification Church?

Jesus was a Jewish reformer, one of many in the Greco-Roman period. He and his disciples promoted renewed social relationships based on the Biblical tradition, a program communicated by the metaphor of the kingdom of God. Other Jewish movements and sects emphasized other themes and aspects of the Jewish tradition. The Pharisees had their own program for creating a law-observant Jewish society with special stress on purity, tithing, and sabbath rest. The Dead Sea community committed itself to a renewal of the covenant and it, along with other groups of priests, argued over sacrificial law, holiness, and priestly purity. The Sadducees exhorted the ruling class to remain faithful to Biblical law traditionally interpreted. They all drew from the same Biblical sources, but emphasized distinctive themes and practices. They were so similar that they constantly disagreed with one another.

Jesus the Jew in Christian Theology

As interesting as all this first-century practice, thought, and sociology may be in itself, what does it matter for believing Christians and for

Jewish-Christian relations? Does Jesus the Jew precisely as a Jew have any impact on Christian theology and on Jewish-Christian relations? Or is Jesus's life as a Jew just accidental? After all, he had to be born something: Inca or Ethiopian, Mongolian, or whatever. Is Jesus's Jewishness superseded by his role as Christ, the anointed one, the Messiah sent by God to save all nations? For Christians the Christ is universal, a God-man for all humans. So is Jesus "Everyman" for everyone? Has Jesus become an abstracted, allegorical character in a morality play?

Any human being, even the Son of God incarnated as Jesus of Nazareth, must live concretely in a place, time, society, and culture. To wrench Jesus out of his Jewish world would destroy Jesus as he really is and destroy Christianity, the religion which grew out of his teachings. Even Jesus's most familiar role as Christ or Messiah (the Hebrew for "anointed one") is a Jewish role. Christians may respond that Jesus is the Son of God, the second person of the one triune God. But the term "Son of God," is a Biblical Hebrew idiom for kings and prophets and others chosen by God. And the very term "God" and the way Christians conceived of God rests on the Jewish Bible and dissolves without it. If we Christians leave the concrete realities of Jesus life and of the history of Israel behind in favor of a mythic, universal, spiritual Christian Church and an otherworldly kingdom of God, we deny our origins in Israel, our history, and with that, God who has loved and protected Israel and our Church. We cease to interpret the actual Jesus's sent by God and make him over into our own image and likeness. Finally, to move from theology to the brutalities of life, if Christians violently wrench Jesus out of his natural, ethnic, and historical place within the people of Israel, they open the way to destroying Israel, the place and people of Jesus, with equal violence. This is a lesson of history which haunts us all at the end of the twentieth century.

If, however, Jesus the Christ and the Son of God is as radically Jewish as are his titles, if the core symbol of Christianity is permanently Jewish, then Jesus and his followers remain permanently related to Israel. An old joke about a priest, minister, and rabbi captures the irony of this situation well. The priest and minister arrived at the heavenly gates where St. Peter welcomed them, but put off their entry due to Jesus's busy schedule. A while later a rabbi arrived and was immediately sent in. When the priest and minister protested, Peter shrugged and explained, "A relative of the boss."

Matthew's Community

Even if Jesus was a Jew living in Galilee, by the last third of the first century, when the four gospels were most probably written, the majority of Jesus's followers were gentiles living in the eastern Mediterranean. Many people think that Jews and Christians were sharply divided from one another by this time and that a new Christian religion was fighting its Jewish parent for independence and supremacy. But for most places in the Mediterranean world this view is inaccurate. Most people still could not clearly distinguish the followers of Jesus from Jews. A large number of Jesus's followers were ethnic Jews and still lived as Jews. Non-Jewish converts from Greco-Roman gods to the God of the Bible lived and thought substantially like Jews. For their part followers of Jesus did not call themselves Christians (the word only appears in the New Testament three times, always in the mouths of outsiders) and the word does not appear widely in literature. The assemblies of believers in Jesus may have had their conflicts with the Jewish community, but they were for the most part not yet self-consciously opposed to the Jewish community. The clear boundaries that divided us today had not yet been drawn.

Among the many Jewish groups in the late first century, such as the early rabbis, the priests who survived the destruction of the Temple and local villagers faithful to their ancestral customs, was a group of Jewish followers of Jesus who were addressed and instructed by the Jewish author of the Gospel of Matthew. They probably lived in the vicinity of Galilee or in southern Syria-Lebanon. By becoming followers of Jesus neither the author nor his audience ceased to be Jews. People did not change the ethnic group into which they were born, and Christianity did not yet exist as a separate religion which they could join. Many first-century Jews probably viewed the author of Matthew as deviant, mis-guided or strange, but he was precisely a strange Jew. Think of the variety of Jews in the United States and Israel today and what they think of one another. Christians in the Appalachian mountains who handle snakes and drink poison because the longer ending of Mark says God will protect them (Mark 16:18) are in my judgment seriously mistaken in their practice and orientation, but they are still Christians.

In what ways is the Gospel of Matthew Jewish and what can we learn from it?[3] The narrative implies that the author of Matthew around 90 C.E. hoped to attract members of the larger Jewish community to Jesus's new interpretation of the Jewish tradition. He cites the Bible frequently, using Hebrew and Greek versions, in order to authenticate his view of Jesus and his teaching. Matthew's Jesus fits comfortably within first-century Jewish understandings of how God guides human affairs and acts through divinely empowered agents. Typological associations of Jesus with Moses, personified Wisdom, and the prophets resonate deeply with the first-century Jewish understandings of history and its heroes.

The author of Matthew is an informed participant in a number of first-century Jewish legal debates. Second Temple Jewish documents, such as the Book of Jubilees, the Temple Scroll, and the Covenant of Damascus as well as the early strata of the *Mishna,* finally edited about 200 C.E., argued over tithing, the validity of oath and vows, the conditions for divorce, the exact requirements of Sabbath, the conditions of purity, and dietary laws. The Pharisee, Sadducees, and priestly factions clashed over these items before the Temple was destroyed, and their heirs continued the disputes afterwards. Matthew joins in this debate as a serious defender of his group's understanding of how one should live as a Jew according to the teachings of Jesus. He accepts the Jewish Bible and bases his arguments on it, using the types of reasoning found in first-century Jewish literature. But he sees the whole tradition through the eyes of Jesus as he understands him.

Many argue that Matthew's polemics against Jews proved that he has left the Jewish community. But his harsh attacks against his opponents and their positions are typical of inner Jewish sectarian conflict. In fact, vilification of one's rivals and opponents appears in modern political campaigns in the United States and in Israel and in ancient Jewish, Greco-Roman, and Christian literature. Bare-knuckle power struggles among rival groups go back as far as we have writing. Matthew's accusations of hypocrisy and blindness against his opponents, the "scribes and Pharisees" in chapter twenty-three, communicate the same message as the epithets "Wicked Priest," "Scoffer," "man of the Lie,"

---

3. The interpretation of the Gospel Matthew as coming from a community of Jesus's followers who still considered themselves Jewish comes from my book, *Matthew's Christian-Jewish Community* (Chicago: University of Chicago Press, 1994). This book was published in the series "Chicago Studies in the History of Judaism."

"violent One," and "Seekers After Smooth Things" that lace the Dead Sea Scrolls. Significantly, the author of Matthew, like the authors of the Dead Sea Scrolls, attacks only the leader of the Jewish community who, in his judgment, culpably rejected Jesus and misled the people away from him. He does not attack the Jewish people in general. In the gospel narrative the crowds of Jewish people remain for the author of Matthew fertile ground for sowing the teachings of Jesus concerning Judaism. In Matthew's late first-century setting he directs his polemics against rival leaders and their competing programs for understanding and living Judaism in the light of the loss of the Temple.

What can we learn from Matthew and the historical Jesus?

1.   First, neither in the first century nor in the late twentieth for that matter have the relationships between the followers of Jesus and the Jewish community as a whole been completely peaceful or trouble free. Prejudices, stereotypes, polemics, and conflicts have caused social discord in the first century and today. We must recognize that even though everyone "does it," everyone engages in social, religious, political, and cultural conflicts, they are destructive within each of our communities and between them.

2.   Second, in the first century and in our half of the twentieth century both the positive and the negative relationship between Jews and Christians have for the most part been real, experienced, lived relationships and the conflicts real, face-to-face conflicts. We have not engaged in elaborate, traditional set-pieces based on Jewish conspiracies to take over the world. I acknowledge that many people carry around stereotypes in their heads and emotions, but rubbing shoulders continually challenges those imaginary figures. Real conflicts can be solved and real relationships can be worked out in contrast to universal, eternal prejudices which resist reason and experience.

3.   Third, the New Testament, read in context, may subvert the anti-Jewish theology which it spawned and suggested new avenues of thought.

Now, can we put these experiences from the first century to work at the beginning of a new millennium?

The Need for a New Christian Theology of Israel

In contrast to the Gospel of Matthew, the traditional Christian theology which replaces Israel with the Church and condemns the Jews for rejecting Jesus does not reflects a real relationship between Christians and Jews today. It does not apply to the contemporary Jewish community in any recognizable fashion or to the first-century communities of Jews and followers of Jesus which I have described here. The New Testament documents reflect a time when followers of Jesus sincerely and creatively struggled to understand God's will for Israel. The New Testament does not have a clear answer to the problem because its authors' views vary greatly and are underdeveloped. But the flexibility and openness of the New Testament has the potential to shake Christians loose from the over determined traditions, attitudes, and institutions which subordinate or annihilate the Jews. We need a robust, nuanced theology for Jews and Christians which grapples with the tensions and anguish of our history without the first-century polemics and the nineteen hundred years of theological anti-Judaism and social anti-Semitism.

But a new theology, a new understanding of God, of our traditions, and thus of our relationship is easier proposed than developed. We have come to like orthodoxy. Even the liberals among us like a nice, stable, reliable, liberal doctrine criticizing the traditional teaching. Orthodoxies seek oneness and unity in response to our experience of plurality. But orthodoxies tend to subsume, subordinate, modify, or obliterate that which does not fit. In contrast, our historical experience strongly suggests that after two thousand years God has called and formed our communities as intersecting, but not as one; as related to one another but not identical; as differently but authentically faithful to God. Our separateness is normative, not sinful, and our relationship with one another is normal and necessary. God calls us to similar but distinct ways of life in our world.

Christians may think that goodwill, repentance, and a firm purpose of amendment will end anti-Semitism. Good intentions and a change of heart are essential, but not enough. The Second Vatican Council told Catholics to stop persecuting and discriminating against Jews and to reform their anti-Semitic attitudes. Vatican II succeeded, but only partly. Catholics have stopped teaching that the Jews killed Jesus and that God repudiated or cursed the Jews. But the Council did not correct the theology which underlay anti-Judaism and anti-Semitism. It said "the Church is the new people of God"[4] and linked the value to Judaism to its fulfillment in Christianity. The recent *Catechism of the Catholic Church* has not gone beyond Vatican II.[5] Both documents affirm the traditional replacement theology, even if more circumspectly and tactfully than in the past.

Some conferences of Catholic bishops and analogous Protestant bodies have done better. For example, in 1973 the French Catholic bishops recognized the living and permanent relationship of Israel to God and of Christians to the Jewish people.[6] Responding implicitly to the Holocaust, to Christian persecution of the Jews and to Christian theology which sought to supersede Israel, the French bishops began with the historical fact that the Jewish people survived and began to develop a theological thesis that this was God's will. They acknowledged that the theological problem has not been worked out when they said that the Church "perceives in the uninterrupted existence of this [Jewish] people through the centuries a sign that she [the Church] would wish to fully comprehend."[7] The bishops affirmed a permanent, enduring divine call to Israel, even though they could not fully explain it.

> Even though in Jesus Christ the Covenant was renewed for Christendom, the Jewish people must not be looked upon by Christians as a mere social and historical reality but most of all as a religious one; not as the relic of a venerable and finished past but as a reality alive through the ages. The principal features of this vitality of the Jewish people are its collective faithfulness to the One God; its fervor in studying the Scriptures to discover, in the light of Revelation, the meaning of human life; its search for an identity amidst other men; its constant efforts to re-assemble other men; its constant efforts to re-assemble as a new, unified community. Their signs pose questions to us Christians which touch on the heart of our faith: What is the proper mission of the Jews in the divine plan? What expectations

---

4. *Nostra Aetate*, 4.

5. Mary Boys, "How Shall We Christians Understand Jews and Judaism? Questions about the New Catechism," *Theology Today* 53 (1996) 165–170.

6. "Statement by the French Bishops' Committee for Relations with Jews," in Helga Croner, ed., *Stepping Stones to Further Jewish-Christian Relations: An Unabridged Collection of Documents,"* (New York: Paulist, 1977) 60–65. The statement was issued in April, 1973.

7. "Statement by the French Bishops' Committee for Relations with Jews," 60.

animate them, and in what respect are these expectations different from or similar to our own?[8]

Answers satisfy more than questions, but questions at least acknowledge the problem.

The French bishops laid down two of the foundation stones of a new Christian theology of Israel when they affirmed that the "First Covenant was not made invalid by the Second" and that "the Jews as people have been the object of an 'eternal Covenant' without which the 'new Covenant' would not even exist."[9] Translated into the language of this lecture, Jesus as a Jew does matter for Christian theology and Christians do have a permanent relationship with the real, living Jewish community.

So far so good, but the tensions between the reigning tradition of replacement theology and post-Holocaust attempts to understand our relationship so muddle the French bishops' forthright stand in favor of the Jewish community. They correctly instruct Christians to understand the Old Testament/Hebrew Bible in itself, but they quickly add that "the Old Testament renders its *ultimate* meaning to us [presumably, gentile Christians] *only* in the light of the New" (emphasis mine).[10] Their theological language is still weighted against Jews. Less sophisticated and enlightened preachers, teachers and people still put Jews down or outside in some sense and treat them as incomplete or as an appendage or as part of the foundation of the Christian church, rather than as a chosen community of God's people.

Only if Christians thoroughly think out a new doctrine, as the French bishops began to do, a new way of teaching and speaking to replace the old, only then will they change their story and their interpretations and affirm the integrity, vocation, and value of the Jewish community in itself, under God. If Christian theological teaching does not change, then Christian thought and attitudes will not change and inevitably, the traditional anti-Jewish teachings will reappear in new ways and anti-Semitism will go on and on. The problem of anti-Semitism in the Christian community and of anti-Judaism in Christian theology is rooted in the New Testament, has flourished in almost all Christian theologies and societies for centuries, and is alive and well today despite

---

8. Ibid., 61.

9. Ibid., 62, 64.

10. Ibid., 62.

massive efforts by Jews and Christians since World War II. Radical intervention is required.

Creating a New Theology of Christians and Jews

So how shall Christians speak of God, Jesus Christ, Israel, and the Church? Christians have favored grand schemes which somehow encompass the history of Israel and Christianity's goal to convert all people to faith in the Biblical God through Jesus Christ. Ironically, such theological and historical schemes (covenantal theology, dispensationalism, salvation history, theologies of history, and so forth) have frequently ignored history, oversimplified the realities of our communities and prejudiced theology against all non-Christians. The very popular concept of "salvation history" is an ineffective dodge in the face of science and historicism. God does not work in some ethereal dimension of salvation history or spirituality or grace. Grace is God's self-gift to us. Spirit is incarnate in matter. Either God acts in history on and with us as we are, here and now, in this room and in the city and suburbs of Chicago where people are watching TV, playing, fighting and talking, or God does not act at all. No special sphere of "salvation history" will preserve God from modern criticism of religion. Covenantal theology, too, is an ineffective abstraction in the face of Christians' uncertainties about their relationship with Israel and with other nations.

We may make more progress by speaking of the actual relationships of our communities in the first century as well as in the twentieth. Recent interpretations of the letters of the apostle Paul have argued that Paul did not create a new religion, as late nineteenth century liberal Protestant theologians argued, but that Paul, in Romans 9–11, sought to bring the nations, the gentiles, into Israel as worshipers of the one Biblical God. Perhaps Paul the Jew who believed in Jesus and reached out to the nations, can be a model for us Christians today. He affirms God's choice for Israel, the twists and turns of Israel's history; God's freedom to judge and show mercy to both the nations and Israel; God's will to save all humans; the dependence of gentiles on Israel for their relationship with God; and God's enduring faithfulness to Israel. Paul expects God to resolve everything soon, at the end of the world which he expected during his lifetime. He does not know exactly how it will happen because he concludes Romans 9:11 with a hymn of praise to the inscrutability of God's wisdom and judgments—a sure sign of confusion.

Neither Paul's expectation of the end of the world in his lifetime nor our neat schemes of covenants and salvation history work very well. We live concretely in a messy, unfinished world. If the stories about God in the Bible are to be believed, that is, really accepted as revelatory of God, God works in this messy world, not in an antiseptic salvation history nor with one pristine, clearly outlined covenant. The creation of humans did not go smoothly in the early chapters of Genesis. The Hebrews' march through the desert was less than a triumphal celebration of God's power. The anxieties of Jeremiah, the agonies of Job, the "necessity" of Jesus's death, all these human experiences authoritatively recorded in the Jewish and Christian Bibles, inscribe for Jews and Christians a God who responds to human needs in the vagaries of history. Thus we must accept God and each other even if we do not fully understand our troubled relationship. We must humbly defer to God and leave room for each other because God has called both our communities, has kept us both alive and vigorous and has forgiven our sins.

What I will say at the end of this lecture may seem strange to some Christians, but it is a return to the tradition. At the most fundamental level of theology, Christians need to emphasize God more than they have and Jesus Christ as savior within the context of God's relationship to humanity. Christians too frequently center everything on Jesus to the determent of the God who sent him, guided him, and sustained him. Jesus subordinated himself to God's will to rule, conserve, care for, and bring to fulfillment humanity and the universe in which humanity lives. The kingdom, that is, the rule of God should rule theology. God rules over and loves and cares for Israel, the Church, and all nations.

This may sound as if I am pushing Jesus to the side in order to solve the relationship between Israel and the Church. But when I speak of God, I speak of God specifically and precisely as a Christian. The triune Christian God is one reality with inner relations among three subsistents: the begetter, the begotten, and the spirated one, or more familiarly, the Father, Son, and Holy Spirit. In all else, in all activity, in all relationships with humans, God is, acts, loves, and saves as one, indivisibly. To say that God saves humans means that the Father saves as do the Son and the Spirit. To say that Jesus the Son of God saves is to say that God saves. When God saves Israel, in the Christian understanding of God, the Spirit of God and the Son of God as well as God the Father, save Israel. God has acted and acts today in and for Israel and the Church.

Why these word games about God and Jesus? Because the game is very serious and often deadly. Christians have often said that because Jews did not accept Jesus, they are damned and rejected by God. But Jews have always accepted God, even when sinning, suffering and repenting. Let me put this in Christian language for Christians. Jews accept and faithfully follow the God of the Bible. The God of the Bible is the God whom we Christians believe sent Jesus Christ to save us. So Jews accept the same God we Christians worship, even though we understand God differently. If Christian Trinitarian theology is to be actively believed and not ignored, God as Father, Son, and Spirit is there for Israel, faithfully fulfilling the covenant made centuries ago. When we Christians say that God loves Israel and God cares for Israel and God saves Israel we mean that God as Father and God as Son and God as Spirit does all these things as one. And so Jesus is implicitly involved even if not explicitly invoked. Christians need not try to take over for God in running the universe. God does not need the Church or the nations to attack, denigrate, or coerce Israel concerning faith in Jesus Christ. God in God's fullness is with Israel already.

For Christians the corollary to God's love for Israel is clear: what Jesus Christ did and was, what Jesus Christ does and is in his Church today takes place within Israel. We see this in the life of Jesus, in the history of our two communities and in the deeply Jewish roots of the Christian traditions which sustains us every day. The Israel on which the Church depends and with which it lives is not some abstraction found in books, not a historically obsolete religion, nor a purely spiritual entity which transcends this world. Israel is the actual, living community of Jews which whom Christians live in a permanent relationship to this very day. Now let us live this relationship and speak of it appropriately.

6 Bethsaida: Home of the Apostles and the Rabbis

Richard A. Freund
April 10, 2000

The Fifth Jerusalem Lecture was delivered in Chicago on April 10, 2000, by Rabbi Dr. Richard A. Freund, Maurice Greenberg Professor of Jewish History and Director of the Maurice Greenberg Center for Judaic Studies at the University of Hartford, Connecticut. He is the director of the Bethsaida Archaeological Excavations Project and director of the Dead Sea Cave of Letters Archeological Project.
Dr. Freund has appeared in many documentaries on sites associated with the origins of Christianity in Galilee. In addition to many articles and other books, he is the co-author with Dr. Ravi Arav of Bethsaida: A City by the North Shore of the Sea of Galilee, Volume I and II.
Dr. Freund's lecture, "Bethsaida: Home of the Apostles and Rabbis," addressed the historical and symbolic connections between the authority of Pope John Paul II and the ancient Jewish Apostle, Peter of Bethsaida.

HOW appropriate that just over two weeks after my meeting with Pope John Paul II on the shores of the Sea of Galilee, I am here in Chicago to deliver the Cardinal Bernardin lecture. Since we arranged this lecture nearly a year ago, it is really remarkable how timely it is for me to stand before you and show you a replica of the antiquity from Bethsaida, a key to the first-century Fisherman's House at Bethsaida, which I presented to the Pope that evening. It is a symbol for the Church, and especially the authority of the Church, but it also is a symbol of the connection which binds us, as Jews and Christians, to a site in Israel in this Jubilee Year and the Millennium. On Friday, March 24, 2000, after completing his meeting with Prime Minister Ehud Barak of Israel, Pope John Paul II arrived at the Tabgha Monastery (which is associated by Church tradition with the Miracle of the Multiplication of Loaves and Fishes) to pray at the Byzantine altar and receive a replica of an iron door key found at the Bethsaida excavation. The key was discovered in 1994 in a house directly adjacent to the large courtyard of the Fisherman's House at the site. I was able to present the key to the Pope and explain to him the significance of the key in our short meeting and tell him a little about our excavations, in the presence of a group of university presidents and officials from the Bethsaida Excavations who came with me and the cardinals, bishops and priests, gathered with us in the Tabgha church that evening.

The ceremony sparked great interest amongst the worshipers, including cardinals and bishops from many world locations, and the world press who were there for the Pope's visit to the monastery. Many of the faithful passed by the key (or better: replica of the key), kissed or touched the glass of the protective presentation case created to protect it, and proclaimed it as "Peter's Key" (although the legend underneath the key which we gave him states simply: "Bethsaida: Key, Roman Period," Bethsaida Excavations Project, 2000). When the Pope finished listening to my explanation, he blessed the key replica he would receive and the second replica, which I am displaying this evening in Chicago.

The place of the meeting in Israel was not accidental nor was the timing of the ceremony. Tabgha is a very appropriate location for a presentation of this kind since Bethsaida is specifically linked with the "feeding of the multitudes" tradition in the Gospel of Luke and the monastery commemorates the miracle. Since Bethsaida was missing from sacred geography for nearly 2000 years and was so important to the history of the Church, a place of remembrance of these crucial events was established nearly 1,500 years ago to commemorate the miracles. Since Peter (according to the Gospel of John) was from Bethsaida and since the "key" is a symbol of authority of the papacy on flags and objects associated with the papacy, having a key from first-century Bethsaida was seen as particularly meaningful for Pope John Paul II's Jubilee celebrations in Galilee. Following the ceremony the Pope was flown in his helicopter over Bethsaida (which is located some six miles away on the northeast shore of the Sea of Galilee). The site was specially lit that evening for the occasion, and the proud excavators from Bethsaida gathered at the site to wave at the helicopter as it passed overhead.

It is a tribute to the power of our two traditions and how intertwined they are that I show you this key this evening and explain to you the power of symbols both real and imagined which bind us and often divide us. It is a very long journey of one single artifact (but also this site, which has only recently been rediscovered) and now stands as a testament to our shared and common symbols and especially this one, which has taken on enormous importance and which is now in the Vatican archives and is on its way to becoming a "relic," as is the site of Bethsaida. For those of you who have never heard of Bethsaida or never knew that it had only recently been recovered, I refer you to our two books and the scores of articles which have been written about its recovery by the Bethsaida Excavations Project. For those who are hearing about it this evening for the first time, here is a short overview of Bethsaida which reveals an authentic ancient village where the major apostles and Jesus as well as rabbis and kings trod. It is an appropriate topic to remember the legacy of Cardinal Bernardin and his work.

Bethsaida: A City by the North Shore of the Sea of Galilee

Et-Tell, a large, artificial mound located in the Jordan Park (Park Hayarden) at a distance of 2.5 kilometers from the present shore of the Sea of Galilee and a few hundred meters from the Jordan River, has been designated as Bethsaida on maps of the State of Israel since 1989. This identification followed a series of probe excavations in 1987 and 1988, initiated by Dr. Ravi Arav on behalf of the Golan Research Institute and Haifa University, which eliminated other reasonable proposals. The identification was based, in part, upon the absence of a large settlement in the Late Hellenistic–Early Roman level in the probe excavations of other sites proposed as Bethsaida; on the presence of an extensive Late Hellenistic-Early Roman level at et-Tell; and on a reasonable geological hypothesis initially confirmed by Israeli and American geologists as to why a fishing village was located so far from the present coast of the Sea of Galilee.[1] Since 1991, the Bethsaida Excavations Project continues

---

1. See reports of earlier seasons: R. Arav, "Et-Tell and el_Araj," IEJ, 38, 3 (1988), 187–188. R. Arav, "Et-Tell, 1988," IEJ, 39, 1–2 (1989), 99–100. R. Arav, "Bethsaida, 1989," IEJ, 41, 1–3 (1991), 184–185. R. Arav, "Bethsaid, 1992," and R. Arav, "The Bethsaida Excavations, Historical and Archeological

under the direction of Dr. Rami Arav on behalf of an international consortium housed at the University of Nebraska at Omaha and the University of Hartford. The three major goals of this consortium are to more fully excavate the geological phenomena which affected the life (and demise) of the site and to compare and contrast these findings with the extensive literary information extant on the site. The findings were first published in the first volume of an original study of Bethsaida and the Bethsaida Plain in 1995, with the second volume published in 2000.[2]

The mound of Bethsaida is situated (as mentioned above) near the north shore of the Sea of Galilee, at the northern center of an alluvial plain known as *Beteiha*.[3] Oval in shape, the mound was created as an extension of the lava flow that formed the Golan Heights. The size of the mound, 400 meters in length and 200 meters in width, makes it one of the largest sites around the Sea of Galilee. At its highest point, the mound is 165.91 meters below sea level, and it rises approximately 30 meters above its surroundings and 45 meters above the Sea of Galilee. On a clear day there is a commanding view of the entire Sea of Galilee. One can see sites designated as Capernaum, Chorazin, Magdala, Kursi, Dalmanutha, Hippos, and Tiberias in the south from atop the mound. A beautiful lookout/chapel, which was financed by the Papal Nuncio at Notre Dame in Jerusalem, shows all of these sites from atop the mound of Bethsaida. It was here that we had hoped the Pope would celebrate Mass, since the shore line is now 2.5 km away and a large plain or natural amphitheater has been created to the south of the mound. This view is an outstanding feature of the site in relation to the Sea of Galilee, but it is the plain in front of the mound which led the geological team to suspect that it was not always as dry as it currently appears, and which began the new quest for the recovery of the ancient site of Bethsaida.

Approaches," in *The Future of Early Christianity, Essays in honor of Helmut Koester,* B. A. Pearson, ed., (Minneapolis: Fortress, 1991), 77–106.

2. R. Arav and R. A. Freund, *Bethsaida: A City by the North Shore of the Sea of Gallilee* (Kirksville, MO: Thomas Jefferson University Press, 1995), Vol. I and Vol. II in 2000.

3. According to M. Jastrow, A *Dictionary of the Targumim, the Talmud Babli and Yerushalmi, and the Midrashic Literature* (Jerusalem reprint 1972), 156, the root *Betah* can indicate a hollow, column-like receptacle for collecting rainwater kept near the house.

Bethsaida: The House of the Fisherman

Bethsaida, (literally: "the house of the fisherman") is a significant archaeological site for a number of reasons. The material culture suggests that during the Early Bronze Age, a strong fortified city was established there on a basalt mound, which later became the biblical Iron Age city of Bethsaida. The Iron Age city is quite extensive. Since the name "Bethsaida" does not appear in the Hebrew Bible (or any other ancient Near Eastern text for that matter), it is much more difficult to relate the Iron Age material culture of the site to any literary traditions. Bethsaida was apparently known by another name in the Iron Age.[4] During the Iron Age the site may also have served as a major center in an area which is sometimes called the Biblical Land of Geshur. A large complex with includes an extensive city wall, a four-chamber gate (which is preserved in an unprecedented state and which is being restored), and a temple and palace complex, has been discovered. Some of the discoveries from this period will be discussed later in this article. The pottery and architecture at the site are consistent with other sites in the general region which have been identified as Geshurite.[5]

Since the Geshurites were, as the name implies (*Gesher* in Hebrew is "bridge"), a "bridge" people between the ancient Israelites and the Mesopotamians to the east, the presence of Bethsaida as the largest and most extensive city ever discovered in this area is significant to the history of ancient Israel as well as the ancient Near East. According to the Hebrew Bible, King David married the daughter of the King of Geshur, Maachah, and as a symbol of how important this union is. Their son, Absalom, would surely have been king after David, had events in the royal court been different. As it turns out, this capital city of Geshur located at Bethsaida may have ended up playing a key role in the planning and construction of an ancient Israelite capital in Jerusalem both as a political and religious site. The architecture must have been an excellent model for the creation of palaces and gates of Jerusalem (which

---

4. R. Arav and R. A. Freund, *Bethsaida: A City by the North Shore of the Sea of Galilee,* 193–202.

5. See the article by M. Kochavi et al., "The Land of Geshur Project: Regional Archaeology of the Southern Golan," in the *IEJ* 39, (1089) and a more popular version of this in "Rediscovered! The Land of Geshur," *BAB,* (1992), 30-44; 84–85. On the relationship between the Maacanthites and the Geshurites, see: B. Mazar, "Geshur and Maacah" in: *Cities and Districts in Eretz Israel,* (Jerusalem, 1975), 190–202.

at the time was a small, backwater on top of an obscure mountain off the beaten track); and so while it is difficult today to see the ancient Israelite capital of David in Jerusalem, at Bethsaida it stands in enormous grandeur.

During the Hellenistic period the Iron Age town was apparently re-established as Bethsaida and then re-founded again by Philip Herod in the first century as Bethsaida Julias. Pliny the Elder, who lived in the period of the first century C.E., actually describes the location of Julias in relation to the Jordan in his *Natural History:* ". . . it widens out into a lake usually called Genesara. This is 16 miles long and 6 broad,[6] and is skirted by the pleasant towns of Julias and Hippo on the east . . ."[7]

Josephus, the prominent first century C.E. Jewish historian, complements and completes important details found in New Testament and rabbinic literature about the city. Philip, the son of Herod the Great, inherited from his father (4 B.C.E.) the tetrarchy of Iturea (Lk 3:1), which included the Golan and Bethsaida. Philip elevated Bethsaida to the status of a *polis* because of its large population and strength. According to Josephus, Philip renamed the city "Julias" in honor of Julia Augustus' daughter (Ant 18:22) even though it was probably renamed for the honored mother and quasi co-regent of Tiberius, Livia-Julia, and not Julia, Augustus' daughter.[8] According to our present study of the information, the *polis* Bethsaida-Julias may have been re-founded in the year 30 C.E.[9]

Strategically, however, Bethsaida-Julias did play a role in the military maneuvers of the Jewish Revolt. Josephus, the Jewish historian, reports that in 67 C.E. Gamla, the rockbound fortress overlooking the Valley of Daliyot and the Plain of Bethsaida, along with Seleucia, on the shore of Lake Hula, were the only towns left unconquered by the Romans. The area around Julias was at the western limit of King Agrippa II's kingdom (War, III, 3, 5/57) and marked the northern limit of the mountain range running parallel to the Jordan down to Moab (War, 4, 8.2/454). In *Life*

---

6. In Josephus' *Jewish Wars*, 3.10.7, the Sea of Galilee was described as 140 furlongs by 40 (16 miles by 4½). See H. St. J. Thackeray translation in the Loeb Classical Library (LCL-Cambridge: Harvard University Press, 1976) 718 footnote a. There are 606 3/4 English feet in a Greek furlong. The present dimensions of the Sea of Galilee are only 12.5 miles by 7 miles!

7. M. Stern, *Greek and Latin Authors on Jews and Judaism,* Vol. I. (Jerusalem: Monson Press, 1976), 468ff.

8. See F. Strickert, "The Coins of Philip," in *Bethsaida: A City by the North Shore of the Sea of Galilee,* 165–192.

9. Ibid.

71–73, he describes his indecisive battle against Sylla, the commander of the pro-Roman Agrippa II's army. Sylla prepared a siege of the town. At the outset of the siege Sylla was sent to cut off the supply routes from the Galilee to Gamla. In order to do so, Sylla pitched camp in the vicinity of Bethsaida controlling the traffic in the plain. His enemy, Josephus, commander of the Jewish forces in the Galilee, sent a contingent of 2,000 men under a certain Jeremias from his headquarters at Taricheae-Magdala (the hometown of Mary Magdalene) to the plain. Two important facts are related in this account in Josephus' *Life* 71:

1.   That Bethsaida could be reached by boat and that it was on a main supply route.

2.   In addition, Josephus himself relates that in an apparently marshy territory around Bethsaida he fell off his horse and wrenched his wrist; and his troops did not succeed, and the battle at Bethsaida was a crushing defeat which could have been a significant victory.

These literary facts became increasingly important in light of our geographic/ geographical studies of the area.

The importance of Bethsaida, however, for the general public lies in its prominence in the New Testament and the lack of consensus among medieval pilgrims over its location. Next to Jerusalem and Capernaum, one of the towns most frequently mentioned in the Gospels is Bethsaida— the birthplace of the Apostles Peter and Andrew and the home of the Apostle Philip according to the Fourth Gospel. Theodosius (530 C.E.) reports an early Church tradition that Bethsaida was also the home of the fisherman Zebedee and his sons James and John. In later medieval studies, conflations and exaggerations about the importance of Bethsaida persisted, perhaps because of the mystery of its location. Other medieval traditions include James, the son of Alphaeus as well. A total of six of the twelve Apostles from one city!

As a part of the "evangelical triangle" (Tabgha, Chorazin, and Bethsaida with Capernaum at the midpoint of the triangle's base), Bethsaida was situated in the northern area bordering the Sea of Galilee where Jesus was most active (Matthew 11:20–24, Luke 10:13–15). Bethsaida is mentioned by name twice in the Gospel of Mark (6:45 and 8:22), once in Matthew (11:21), twice in Luke (9:10 and 10:13) and twice in John (1:44 and 12:21). Some of the most significant accounts of the New Testament occur at Bethsaida: the healing of the blind man, the feeding of the multitudes, and the walking on the water to name just a few. This, of course, will affect the site's importance for later pilgrimage accounts. The references in the New Testament leave us in no doubt that Bethsaida was a fishing village. John's gospel tells us that Philip, Andrew and Peter, who were fishermen, came from this town (1:22). Mark states, "As soon as it was over he made his disciples embark and cross to Bethsaida ahead of him" (6:45). As a fishing town it would have been situated on the Sea of Galilee. Josephus tells us that Bethsaida was "situated on the lake of Gennesareth."[10]

But the pilgrimage accounts and the Gospel and Josephus writings are separated by hundreds of years. The Christian pilgrimage sites in Nazareth, Jerusalem, Capernaum, and so forth, are the product of the fourth and fifth century C.E. when spiritual journeys of informed Christian leaders searched for sites which represented the life and times of Jesus. By the fourth century, Eusebius suggested that Bethsaida was no longer on the shore at that time: "Bethsaida, city of the apostles, Andrew, Peter, and Philip, is in Galilee *near* the lake of Gennesareth."[11]

Jerome, writing directly after the period of Eusebius, states: ". . . the lake of Gennesareth on the shore of which are situated Capernaum, Tiberias, Bethsaida, and Chorazin."[12] The cities of Tiberias and Capernaum are today situated on the shore *of* the Sea of Galilee but Chorazin is and has always been set back far from the water. By the fourth and fifth century C.E., the idea of being *on* the Sea of Galilee may not have been a geographical term but rather a spiritual term. By this period, almost every site associated with Jesus's ministry had been identified by the early Church (and those that had not been conclusively located still had pilgrimage sites!) and churches were built for pilgrimage visitors and places of prayer and study. Unlike most of the other important locations, Bethsaida could not be definitively identified. Although Bethsaida is mentioned hundreds of times in medieval pilgrimage accounts, a controversy developed over whether it was located on the east or the west

---

10. Antiquities, 18, 2.

11. A full assessment of the medieval citations in a chapter by E. McNamera in Arav/Freund, *Bethsaida*, Vol. II. Erich Klosterman, *Eusebius of Caesarea*, Leipzig: J. D. Hinrichs, 1902. *Eusebius of Caesarea* (Leipzig: J. C. Hinrichs, 1902), 58.

12. Jerome, *Commentary of Isaiah* 9.1.

shore of the Sea of Galilee and whether it was on or near the shore. The controversy has continued to the present with some of the most famous names in archeology making pronouncements one way and the other.

A New Holy Site in the Modern Period: The Modern Search for Bethsaida

When I was a student I was taught that Bethsaida was a myth. An ancient myth which was created to inspire early readers of the New Testament. My teachers said: "How could a city as big as Bethsaida in an area as small as the Sea of Galilee not be found?" They had ample reason to see it as a myth. The ancient myth was of grand proportions. The place where Christianity "began." The place where most of the major miracles took place, where the historical Jesus had healed and where the seminal figures met and created the main images for early Christians: Fishers of Men, healing and faith of the main disciples, and so forth. The scores of pilgrims in hundreds of years were all in search of the site and could not find it. How could we in the end of the twentieth century resolve this mystery? In fact, it is not that others in early, modern archeology did not try to resolve this before us.

The modern quest for the site of ancient Bethsaida began with the rise of modern biblical research. During the mid-nineteenth century Edward Robinson, a prominent biblical scholar, visited the area and reassessed the literary sources, based on his personal impression of the site. He suggested identifying Bethsaida with a large mound, named et-Tell, situated at the northern corner of the Beteiha Plain. A few decades later, Gottlieb Schumacher, a scholar from the German colony at Haifa, maintained that it was implausible that a fishermen's village should be located over two kilometers away from the Sea. He proposed two sites located on the shore of the Galilee, one by the name of el-Araj, a few hundred yards away from the mouth of the Jordan River, and the second a small ruin named el-Mesadiyeh located further southeast. Since these two proposals were made, no significant change in the possible identification of the town has occurred.

Following the Six Day War in 1967, the northeastern region of the Sea of Galilee and the Golan have become more accessible to researchers. Construction of new roads and bridges over the Jordan River, has facilitated considerable progress in the scientific investigations of the region.

Through the 1980s three sites continued to be considered as possible candidates for the location of Bethsaida: el-Araj on the present day shore of the Sea of Galilee; el-Mesadiyeh, on kilometer southeast of el-Araj, two hundred meters away from the Sea; and the mound et-Tell some two kilometers north of the Sea of Galilee. In 1987, the excavations began in an attempt to resolve the confusion. The probes of el-Araj uncovered a single level of occupation, dating from the sixth century C.E., a period when the settlement on et-Tell had been entirely abandoned. No significant finds from the Hellenistic and Roman periods were discovered, although a few shards from these periods were found at the site. Ruins of a Byzantine monumental building were scattered around the house of the former Damascene proprietor. The latter probably reused the foundations of the ancient building to construct his own house.

A third mound, et-Tell, some two and a half kilometers north of the Sea of Galilee and some 20 acres large, yielded clear and systematic evidence of a Hellenistic/early Roman fishing village including fishing equipment and anchors. The problem remained as to why Bethsaida, a supposed fishing village, was located so far from the Sea. That is the way that good science begins, with a question and a hypothesis. We had the question, now we would propose a hypothesis and a method for testing the hypothesis.

Geology and Geography First: The Implications for Bethsaida's Recovery

Unlike other searches by competent archaeologists, we started with the geology and geography of the region first, and then assembled a variety of pieces of evidence starting with the geology and geography. The present identification was initially based upon cumulative evidence that included among other elements:

1.   The presence of large-scale and extensive Hellenistic and Roman structures and finds on the largest artificial mound in the area (over 20 acres of et-Tell versus one- to two-acre locations of other contenders) and the absence of any other traditionally/historically validated site (with or without a medieval church/synagogue building) with extensive fishing

artifacts, dock facilities, and remains of an imperial Roman period "polis," and the lack thereof at the other proposed sites.[13]

2.   The absence of (and impossibility for) a Late Hellenistic-Early Roman settlement in the other sites proposed as Bethsaida (namely at el-Araj and el-Mesadiyeh).

Work began on the geographical and geographic questions surrounding the Beteiha Plain and Bethsaida starting in 1992. Professors John F. Shroder Jr. and Michael Bishop of the University of Nebraska at Omaha's geology and geography department together with Professor Moshe Inbar and M. Shoshani of the department of geography at Haifa University have already arrived at preliminary results. Work continued through 1995 on the Beteicha plain, Jordan River gorge, el-Araj and el-Mesadiyah with a follow-up work in 1999. Work was conducted during drought and in lush years to gain a full perspective of the Sea of Galilee. Israeli and American geologists, geographers, hydrologists, and their students were employed in the task of investigating whether el-Araj or el-Mesadiyeh could or did support a settlement in the Greco-Roman period when Bethsaida was known from literary sources to have flourished.

This type of geoarchaeology demands rigorous science and scientists and extensive testing. U-series and Carbon 14 tests were run on organic matter found in the course of investigations in the Beteiha Plain. Microorganisms and core samples were sent to two separate labs to confirm many of the results. In addition to 26 backhoe trenches and two boreholes dug from the bottom of the et-Tell mound to the Sea of Galilee, extensive field surveys, and finally Ground Penetrating Radar were used on the research area. In short, one of the more extensive and long-term

---

13. Having recently reviewed the original reports made after the 1967 war at "el-Araj, el-Hasel, and Beth ha-Beq" and "el-Mesadiyeh" (1968–1972) from the archives of the Israel Antiquities Authority, it is clear that nothing found before the probes of Dr. Arav suggests any systematic and extensive Hellenistic-Roman settlement at any other site on the northeast shore of the Sea of Galilee. In fact, the random Hellenistic and Roman shards, high lake levels and periodic flooding in the area (all mentioned in the earlier surveys), all suggest what the geologists in our studies state: other sites closer to the Sea of Galilee were created as a result of the catastrophic flooding and sedimentation and the random Hellenistic-Roman shards found there are the result of "float" from sites upstream. R. Arav, "Et-Tell and el-Araj," *IEJ*, 38, 3 (1988), 187–188. R. Arav, "Et-Tell, 1998," *IEJ*, 39, 1–2 (1989), 99–100. R. Arav, "Bethsaida, 1989," *IEJ*, 41, 1–3 (1991), 184–185. R. Arav, "Bethsaida, 1992," *IEJ*, 42, 3–4 (1992), 252–254. H.-W. Kuhn and R. Arav, "The Bethsaida Excavations, Historical and Archaeological Approaches," in *The Future of Early Christianity: Essay in honor of Helmut Koester;* B.A. Pearson, editor, (Minneapolis: Fortress, 1991), 77–106.

investigations ever conducted of the north shore of the Sea of Galilee was undertaken by the Bethsaida Excavations Project Consortium in the course of our excavations at el-Tell. Considerable resources were invested in dispelling any lingering suspicions about the possibility of el-Araj or el-Mesadiyeh being the original Greco-Roman period Bethsaida site, using the most sophisticated data-gathering equipment available.

All of this has been documented since 1993 in articles and papers presented at meeting of the American Schools of Oriental Research (ASOR), geological and geographic professional societies, in scientific journals, our own two volumes of research and in a documentary produced by Nebraska public television entitled *The Lost City of Bethsaida*, which premiered in 1997. According to the present status of information gained from the geological and geographic investigations, Bethsaida had full boat and fishing access to the Sea of Galilee during the Iron Age through the Roman period. Some 1,600 years ago only indirect boat and fishing access was available to the site, and presently at Bethsaida there is no direct access to the Sea of Galilee.

Evidence now suggests that the Sea of Galilee and Beteicha plain have been affected by shoreline progradation southward for thousands of years. Episodic sediment increments from the Jordan River provided a new land, which slowly emerged from the Sea of Galilee as the land rose and the water level declined in these same areas due to the sediment build-up. At some point, perhaps 1600 years ago, a serious flood down the Jordan River probably from the breaking of an earthquake-generated landslide and lake, filled the entire lower Jordan grade and swept gravel all across the western Beteiha Plain. Such gravels contained a well-mixed stew of artifacts, of wide age ranges, from upstream, with absolutely no reliable stratigraphic or archaeological context. Then, in a period following this catastrophic event the beach ridge of el-Araj and el-Mesadiyeh was sufficiently dry enough for long enough to attract some minimal habitation, the remains of which exist now as the ruins of the present-day site.

The fact that the entire area of the Bethsaida and Beteiha Plain is located on the Dead Sea-Jordan Rift fault system, has made the area prone to fault creep, subsidence, upwarping, catastrophic flooding, and earthquakes. Minor and major recorded earthquakes which affected the region occurred in 1927, 1896, 1837, 1759, 1546, 1457, 1303, 1202, 1157,

1114/5, 1033/34, 859, 756, 749, 551, 363, 306, 115, first century C.E.,[14] and the first century B.C.E.[15] Other forms of land changes, *tsunami* (lake "tidal waves") and sediment buildup along the Jordan River (immediately adjacent to el-Tell) are well known and historically documented over the past 2,000 years. The slow disintegration of the fishing industry at Bethsaida probably began in the second century C.E. and ended when there were no outlets to the sea by the end of the fourth century C.E.

What was not known was how important this information could be for the understanding of other archaeological sites located in the northern Upper Galilee and Golan region. The combination of fault slippage, catastrophic flooding, tectonic uplift, and sediment discharges from the Jordan River may have quickened the pace of the natural processes present in this unique geological area. These geological phenomena have contributed to the disappearance of other ancient ports which existed in antiquity such as Troy, Ephesus, and Miletus. Similarly, ports have been isolated by decline of water level in inland seas such as the modern Aral Sea of central Asia, or abandoned habitations around ancient Lake Seistan, now Dasht-Margo or "Desert of Death" in Afghanistan.

These geological factors help to explain the mysterious disappearance of Bethsaida in antiquity. In addition, it is not surprising that when Byzantine Christian pilgrims were searching for a fishing village on the northern shore of the Sea of Galilee and did not find it, they may have established small relics to commemorate their search of Bethsaida at new areas along the sea, such as Tabgha, el-Araj, and el-Mesaidyah, despite the lack of any Roman settlements at the site.

Kings, Apostles, Rabbis, and Relics: The Finds

Damage to the site which was inflicted in the recent past (and in medieval secondary use) has made the detailed analysis of the small finds crucial to the identification of the site. The finds are generally from

---

14. The most recent review is "Earthquakes in Israel and Adjacent Areas: Macroseismic Observations since 100 B.C.E." by D. H. K. Amiran, e. Arieh, and T. Turcotte, in *IEJ,* Vol. 44. 3–4 (1994), 260 ff. The original article by D. H. K. Amiran is "A Revised Earthquake Catalogue of Palestine," *IEJ,* 1 (1950-1951), 225ff. Also, E. Netzer, ed., "Greater Herodium," *Qedem* 13 (Jerusalem: Israel Exploration Society, 1981), 28 134 n. 22.

15. R. G. Boling, *Joshua: A New Translation with Notes and Commentary,* The Anchor Bible Series, Vol. 6, (New York: Doubleday, 1984), 169–170.

two periods: The Iron Age (1200 B.C.E.–586 B.C.E.) and the Hellenistic (333 B.C.E.–325 C.E.) and Roman periods, although there are random finds from other periods as well. It seems that after the Roman period Bethsaida disappeared from the world stage until the present period.

During the Iron Age the site may also have served as a major center in an area which is sometimes called the Biblical Land of Geshur. The most impressive discovery from the period is the city gate complex of the Iron Age Bethsaida. Although we have not excavated the gate in its entirety, the main features and scope are visible. The approach to the gate was made at the eastern city wall, and the city wall and gate complex is one of the best preserved in Israel today. At points the city wall is nearly 20 feet thick and indicates the importance of the city in this period. In the northern corner of the gate a small so-called "high place" (religious site) and shrine were discovered. Three steps lead to the top of the high place where a carved shallow basalt basin was discovered with what appear to be incense burners. Patches of white plaster found on the steps of the high place and on the walls testify to a white coating. In an area directly adjacent to the high place a bench-like area built into the wall is found. This is where the city elders would have gathered in judgment "by the city gate," illustrating a clear biblical custom.

A stele was found smashed into several pieces at the bottom of the high place and shrine. The top of the stele was found, upside down at the foot of the steps. The positioning of the discovery indicated a deliberate act of violence. The stele measures nearly 4 feet high, one and a half feet wide and nearly a foot thick. The artist who created this stele chose a rough basalt stone with many bubbles, as opposed to the more condensed basalt stones used for many of the other standing stones found at the site. The top of the stele is nicely rounded and frame surrounds the stele in the same fashion that Aramean and Assyrian stelae around the area were made. It depicts in shallow relief, a schematic human figure of a warrior with a bull's head wearing a dagger. Four enigmatic small circular projections are seen next to its chest. The figure is connected to the frame of the picture by a strip that extends between his legs. The face of the bull is depicted in a straightforward view, in a nice minimal, but still discernible and identifiable relief. Two large crescent horns adorn his head, which reflect the crescent of the moon. The arms and legs of the figure are curved in a semi-circular fashion in a manner that resembles embracing. No details are rendered of the figure or of the arms and legs.

Only a handful of stelae or figures similar to this have been found elsewhere, and therefore, while it is difficult to speculate upon the meaning of the symbol, efforts have been made to place it in the context of other ancient religious groups from Syria to Turkey. Most were discovered in southern Syria and would most likely indicate an indigenous religious concept, presumably a Geshurite practice. It is suggested here that perhaps the gesture depicts a concept of a celestial god, standing above and viewed as he embraces the earth from on high.[16]

It is also quite possible that the stele may have had a dual purpose and served as a boundary marker for the ninth-century kingdom of Ben Hadad I, and the bull symbolism may only be a secondary religious/political usage. About 885 B.C.E., Ben-Hadad I of Damascus invaded and reduced "all the land of Naphtali" (I Kings 15:18–20; II Chronicles 16:2–5) to a vassal state, which would include our area as well. If so, the stele would be a border-post marking similar to the ones posted along the modern borders.

Another interesting and suggestive aspect of the placement of the standing stone is presented by the existence of another one nearby which has no artistic rendering on it and is on the floor and not on steps. If we are correct, it is possible that these two standing stones may symbolically represent the entire system of ancient religion of Israel which functioned in this area. Since the Ancient Israelites did not apparently depict their God in images, this blank stele next to the carved one may demonstrate how the two religions co-existed in ancient times. This interpretation of a multi-religious syncreticism at ancient Iron Age Bethsaida is aided, in part, by other small finds from the site. If confirmed, this interpretation would be an important contribution to the study of the ancient religion of Israel. It also would tell us that ancient Bethsaida served as a clearinghouse for religious creativity in the Iron Age, and this role may have continued into the Hellenistic and Roman periods.

Near the same Iron Age gate excavations was revealed partial remains of a large and massive structure which we refer to as a "palace." Two column parts, probably belonging to this structure, were discovered near and inside the building. The "palace' is of the so-called *Bit Hilani* ("house of columns") type[17] and contains an entrance with a vestibule

---

16. A chapter on this stele will appear in *Bethsaida,* Vol. III by Othmar Keel.

17. A much larger report on this appears in Volume II of *Bethsaida: A City by the North Shore of the Sea of Galilee.*

and a main hall and is ringed by adjacent rooms. Figurines with influence from the Ammorites, Egyptians, Hittites and other neighboring powers are present. An impressive Pataikos was found in the main hall (featured on the cover of *Biblical Archaeology Review* in January/February 1995)—possibly the most beautiful found in Israel/Palestine until now.[18] What this means is that the city of Bethsaida was an impressive and extremely important site in the Iron Age (especially the classical biblical period from tenth-sixth century) and this may be the reason why it continued to be an important city again in the Hellenistic and Roman periods. The palace, which apparently dates from the ninth century, was used again in the late Iron Age and extends into a Hellenistic/Early Roman era-type temple/shrine believed to be the Roman Imperial Cult site of the Temple/Shrine to Julia-Livia (wife of Augustus Caesar).

The storage rooms in this structure, and particularly a northeastern room, yielded rich finds, among which were jars, jugs, cooking pots, imported vessels from Phoenicia, and basalt vessels. Particularly interesting were a stamped handle showing a kneeling figure with uplifted hands, and a bulla that sealed an official document. The bulla represents the importance of the site and its direct connections with Samaria, the capital of the Kingdom of Israel, most probably during the ninth or the beginning of the eighth century B.C.E.[19]

In short, the finds represent a multi-religious, multi-ethnic society in antiquity, located on the crossroads between Mesopotamia to the east and Egypt to the south. It contains the makings of a syncretistic, integrated multi-religious society which generally parallels the society which we live in today in the United States, and very unlike the rather exclusive, specialized, and monotheistic image of ancient Israelite religion which we have come to know through the writings of the prophets in the Hebrew Bible. Its location on the border of the historic Land of Israel is I think important to the development of such a concept, and although it was a part of the Ancient Kingdom of David, its location far from the

---

18. See the short report and photo appearing in January/February, 1995, cover story of *Biblical Archeology Review*.

19. It should be emphasized that the seal's production date should be considered as a *terminus post quem date*. The dating and analysis of this bulla was carried out by B. Brandl of the Antiquities Authority of Israel and his article entitled: "An Israelite Bulla in Phoenician Style from Bethsaida" in *Bethsaida: A City by the North Shore of the Sea of Galilee*, Vol. I, (Kirksville: Thomas Jefferson University Press, 1995), 141–164.

centers of Israel religion may have allowed it to exercise a more liberal form of syncretism than would have functioned in Jerusalem.

Some of the most significant finds which have contributed to the understanding of the site as a first-century C.E. Jewish city involve comparisons and analyses of some of the small finds and coins with similar finds at sites that have been more clearly identified as Jewish cities of the period, especially in Galilee and Golan. The small finds include: fishing gear, stamped handles (with and without inscriptions), bullae; but more specifically, Jewish Hasmonean and Herodian coins, glassware, fine ware, and the common pottery. Since 1992, much of this material has been assigned to S. Fortner, a doctoral student at the University of Munich. Ms. Fortner is, in fact, writing her doctoral dissertation on the Hellenistic and Roman small finds at the University of Munich, has assembled thousands of unique finds from the period, and has painstakingly investigated the parallels of the finds, especially (but not limited to) the fishing gear and fine ware. The Hellenistic and early Roman small finds run into the thousands and will be published together in forthcoming volumes of *Bethsaida: A City by the North Shore of the Sea of Galilee,* Volumes III and IV. The coin finds have been analyzed by A. Kindler, emeritus of Tel Aviv University, and appear in the first two volumes of *Bethsaida,* and his coin interpretation has added immeasurably to our understanding of the site. There are now several hundred coins from the Hellenistic and early Roman periods, with the last systematic coin finds coming from the second and third centuries. Two finds will be highlighted here.

The earliest Hellenistic finds are black Athenian pottery and oil lamps dating to the mid-fourth century B.C.E. The latest finds (including pottery and coins) are from the Roman period. One unique find involves a clay seal found in one of the first seasons. The seal measures just over 2 inches by 2 inches and may have been used for official communications. It appears to depict two figures standing on the so-called "hippos" boat casting a ring net. More importantly, it appears to be in shallow, reed-filled water rather than on the open sea, perhaps lending greater credence to the geological information about the area. This seal has been the log for the Bethsaida Excavations Project since its discovery and it is called by pilgrims who visit the site, "The Seal of the Fisherman." It is another example of how important a symbol can become. Since our seal resembles the early Roman fishing boat which was discovered in the mud on the shores of the Sea of Galilee and is today housed at the Bet

Alon Museum (dubbed the "Jesus Boat"), the clay seal now is in need of comparative study and interpretation.

Another find which has provided a certain measure of comparative study is a bronze incense shovel found on May 7, 1996, Bethsaida Excavations, in an extremely disturbed Hellenistic-early Roman layer of occupation in Area A square G54, locus 152.[20] The shovel was found under debris in close proximity to a large Iron Age Bit Hilani-style palace structure, and 9 meters away from a structure which measures 20 meters by 6 meters and apparently was a public Hellenistic-early Roman style "temple" or shrine. This find and the discovery in 1998 of another shovel's decorated handle near the same area demonstrate that the site was probably a Roman period cult site. If this Roman style Temple/ Shrine identification is ultimately confirmed through further investigations, the hypothesis is that this is the site of a Julia cult established by Philip Herod when he raised up Bethsaida to a *polis* and renamed it Bethsaida-Julias in 30 C.E.

The dating of this shrine is important to our understanding of the earliest understanding of Christian origins at the site. If this site had an Imperial Cult shrine on top of its acropolis of Bethsaida as it now appears, the Apostles who resided there in this period (and Jesus's appearances there in this period) in particular would have been impacted by its presence. In short, what this has now made us reinterpret is the meaning of the religious polemic of early Christianity in light of the existence of a strong Imperial Cult presence precisely in the place where the Apostles were meeting and coalescing their mission.

The presence of what I call "The Jewish Imperial Cult of Rome in Palestine" means that again, Bethsaida served as a clearinghouse for a new form of religious syncretism in this period as well. The presence of the imperial cult at Bethsaida also affects our understanding of the message of Jesus as it is mediated in the New Testament. This would be only one of the few sites which have been discovered in Israel which is clearly dedicated to the imperial cult and especially to Julia, the Magna Mater, the Mother of God, Tiberius Caesar, and patron to the eastern cults of religion in the Roman Empire. The same area has also yielded a number

---

20. In the same locus above, below and around the find was found in the preceding days, May 2–6, 1996: Hellenistic cooking pots, casserole bowls, juglets, jars, decorated ware, so-called Galilean bowls, Roman glass, a bow-spouted Herodian lamps, and Eastern Terra Sigillata pottery shards among hundreds of other small finds.

of figurines, mostly from the Iron Age but with a few from the Hellenistic and early Roman periods according to their style. The small figurine of a woman was found (approximately 2 inches by 4 inches) near the Temple of Julia. It was made on a mold, and it depicts a woman which a curled headdress covered with a veil similar to the known statues of Julia Livia found in Rome.

Two other sites, Sebaste and Caesarea Maritima, have been or are presently being excavated and also provide insights into the Imperial Cult in this period. Incense shovels similar to the one discovered at Bethsaida has been found at locations in Israel, Asia Minor and Syria.[21] The meaning and purpose of these shovels has been a subject of debate because the incense shovel is prominently found in synagogue iconography of the third to the sixth centuries.[22] It is possible that the incense shovel was a part of religious syncretism either through the introduction of the Imperial Cult throughout Israel or even through the dedication of Roman religious vessels of this sort into the Temple in Jerusalem by Augustus Caesar in the early first century C.E. Since incense was such an important part of the Temple service, such items may have served a functional as well as religious purpose in religious services there. The last major discovery of incense shovels in a clear archaeological context in Israel was made by Yigael Yadin in the 1960's. He found three incense shovels together in a basket in one locus in the so-called "Bar Kokhba Cave of Letters." The close resemblance between the first century C.E. Bethsaida incense shovel and those found in the Cave of Letters has led me to conclude that perhaps the Cave of Letters was a repository for items from the Temple in Jerusalem.[23] If I am correct, it will be just

---

21. Y. Yadin, *The Finds from the Bar Kokhba Period in the Caves of Letters*, (Jerusalem: Israel Exploration Society, 1975), 55–57, lists nine incense shovels in Palestine, one in Gaul, three from Pompeii and Herculaneum, four from Lebanon and Syria (indicating that others are to be found in the National Museum in Damascus), but this is not a fully systematic study of the number of shovels. In the forthcoming volume, *Bethsaida: A City by the North Shore of the Sea of Galilee*, Vol. II (Kirksville, MO: Thomas Jefferson University Press, 1997) a full-length monograph includes a much more detailed study of the entire question.

22. M. Narkiss and M. Avi-Yonah, for example, concluded that the incense shovel was a Jewish symbol. M. Narkiss, "The Snuff Shovel as a Jewish Symbol," *Journal of the Palestine Oriental Society*, (1935), 14–28, and M. Avi-Yonah, "The Meaning and Use of Incense Shovels," *Journal of the Palestine Oriental Society* (1940), 87–97.

23. See my article: R. A. Freund, "A New Interpretation of the Incense Shovels in the 'Cave of Letters' in *The Dead Sea Scrolls: Fifty Years after Their Discovery*," edited by L. H. Schiffman, E. Tov and J. C. Vanderkam (Jerusalem: Israel Exploration Society, 2000), 644–600.

another way that Bethsaida has clarified more about the religion of ancient Judaism.

In an area to the north of the Temple of Julia, a large house with a courtyard dating from the Late Hellenistic-Early Roman period was discovered. The house was found in a destroyed state and contained a large number of examples of Late Hellenistic-Early Roman pottery, among which there was a significant amount of fine ware. The rooms ringing the central courtyard contained a large number of fishing implements such as net lead weights in two types, a flat bar with loops at the two long edges and the type known as a "musket type," and a long and crooked needle. Due to these finds it is reasonable to assume that the owner of the house was a fisherman.

Just to the north of the Fisherman's House, a private home with a large kitchen area has been uncovered. In this area a private wine cellar from the first century C.E. and a shard from the first century with a mysterious etched cruciform motif have attracted a significant amount of attention. In May 1994, during the summer excavations at the House of Winemaker (directly adjacent to the large courtyard of the Fisherman's House) in the same area, some unusual finds were made. It was here that the private wine cellar was found (with the wine jars still in the cellar) and nearby where the famous "Shard of the Cross" (gracing the cover of Vol. I of our book, *Bethsaida: A City by the North Shore of the Sea of Galilee*) was found.

This house, directly adjacent to the Fisherman's House, let to a street which passed from the present entrance to the top of the mound. An opening in the eastern wall leads to the rather large kitchen of the house. Some paved remnants at the southeast corner of the kitchen indicate that the entire floor might have been paved. Near the entrance there was an oven, and along the southern wall there was a large collection of kitchenware. Two basalt threshing boards together with a basalt stone flour mill were found near the pavement. In addition to it, three bronze pruning hooks, and a gold earring were among the finds of this house. Other notable finds were three bent iron nails that were found near the opening and perhaps belonging to the door hinges, and the iron key similar to known Hellenistic and Roman period keys found in places such as the Cave of Letters. This is the key which we presented to the Pope.

The overall numismatic evidence of Bethsaida is impressive. Between 1987–2000, over 400 coins have been discovered at the site. The numismatic record of Bethsaida begins with a fifth-century Phoenician (Tyre) coin and continues almost unbroken through the Roman period. There are four coins among the Bethsaida finds from the rulers who reigned over Galilee and the Golan during the first century CE. Three coins of Philip, the son of Herod the Great, who ruled over the Gaulinitis and the bordering territories from 4 BCE to 37 CE, have been found. On one Philip coin, the year 33 (of Philip's rule) can be read(29/30 CE).[24] Since the image of Philip appears on the Philip coins another insight into the type of people at Bethsaida immediately arises. Neither Antipas nor Archaelaeus, Philip's brothers, nor even the quixotic Herod the Great himself, ever had the audacity to put his own image on his coinage. He apparently knew that his constituency would never allow such egoism. That fact that Philip Herod was able to place his own image on his coinage tells us much about the constituency of Bethsaida: that they were highly Romanized Jews who would most probably have accepted such an innovation as a positive element. Since no systematic Byzantine structures or remains have been discovered at the site, the coinage of the early Roman period appears to be the last vestige of some type of sustained occupation.

It was during this final period that the Rabbis seem to have established themselves in this area. It was during the second century, following the ill-fated Bar Kokhba Rebellion, that the Rabbis established themselves in many cities in Galilee and Golan to preserve the Judaic tradition. It is perhaps a telling example of the tradition and how special it was that similar to the New Testament, rabbinic tradition has miracle stories associated with Bethsaida. Rabbi Simeon ben Yohai, an important second century CE teacher (later associated with much esoteric and mystical literature and knowledge), who was a student of Rabbi Akiva, has a miracle tradition associated with Bethsaida. In the *Song of Songs Rabbah,* Vol. I ed. J. Neusner, (Atlanta: Scholars Press, 1987), 89ff, one finds the following:[25]

There we have learned on Tannaitic authority: If one has married a woman and lived with her for 10 years and not produced offspring, he has not got the right to stop trying. Said R. Idi, it happened at Bethsaida—that

24. *Op. Cit.,* Strickert, "Coins of Philip," *Bethsaida: A City by the North Shore of the Sea of Galilee,* Vol. I, 164–192.

25. The *Pesikta De Rav Kahana,* Vol. I, B. Mandelbaum, editor (New York: JTSA, 1962), 327, cites this event as well.

someone who had married a woman and stayed with her 10 years, did not produce offspring. They came before R. Shimon ben Yohai (at Bethsaida?) and wanted to be parted from one another. He said to them, "By your lives! Just as you were joined to one another with eating and drinking, so you will be separated from one another only with eating and drinking." They followed his counsel and made a festival and made a great banquet and drank too much. When husband's mind was at ease, he said to her, "My daughter, see anything good that I have in the house! Take it, and go to your father's house." What did she do? After he fell asleep, she made gestures to her servants and serving women and said to them, "Take him in the bed and pick him up and bring him to my father's house." Around midnight he woke up from his sleep. When the wine wore off, he said to her, "My daughter, where am I now?" She said to him, "In my father's house." He said to her, "What am I doing in your father's house?—But I have nothing in the world as good as you!" They went to R Shimon ben Yohai and he stood and prayed for them and they were answered (and given offspring). This serves to teach you that just as the Holy One Blessed He answers the prayers of barren women, so righteous persons have the power to answer the prayers of barren women.

This tradition about this childless couple from Bethsaida and the miraculous intervention of Rabbi Shimon Ben Yohai is interesting because of the New Testament miracle stories associated with the site. Rabbinic miracle tales of this type are generally reserved for direct Divine intervention (or Angels) rather than for Rabbis, so it is extremely unique. Other miracles stories associated with Bethsaida could be cited,[26] but the important aspect of the Bethsaida connection here is that it was marked (even in the last part of its existence) as a "special" place. It is also perhaps quite telling about the final disposition of the city, that the name of Bethsaida was nearly forgotten as Rabbinic scribes changed the name in Rabbinic texts from the well-known second-century site called (Beth) Saidan to the similar-sounding (and written) and the better-known (but faraway) city of Sidon. I spent three years recovering the original name (Beth) Saidan from various manuscript readings and research.[27]

---

26. BT Hullin 49b (Tosefta Terumot 7.12).

27. See my article entitled: "The Search for Bethsaida in Rabbinic Literature" in *Bethsaida: A City by the North Shore of the Sea of Galilee,* Vol. I, pp. 267ff.

Small non-systematic finds continue through the modern-period,[28] which demonstrate that it still was within distance of the major trade routes until the modern period.

One small telltale sign of the importance still accorded to the site by indigenous peoples in the modern period is reflected in the Bedouin cemetery which rings the outside of the site. An oral history (video-taped) and documentation sub-project of the main Bedouin tribe, the Talawiyeh, was undertaken by the Bethsaida Excavations Project in 1993–95 and continues to the present. One of the main results of this history and documentation sub-project is that the local tribe considered the site to be "holy" (and therefore had chosen it for a burial site approximately 200 years ago) and preserved traditions about biblical and Roman settlements there! Unfortunately, much of the mound was seriously damaged during Syrian occupation of the mound from 1949–1967, when the site was used as a military staging ground. Syrian trenches and military gun positions crisscross the site to this day and create difficulty for systematic mapping of the site.

The obvious conclusion is that much more needs to be done in the varying strata to complete the final determinations of what happened to Bethsaida and when. The second volume of *Bethsaida: A City by the North Shore of the Sea of Galilee* was published in 2000 based upon papers prepared by our different directors and supervisory staff, with subsequent volumes to follow in 2002 and 2003. Thanks to the thousands of volunteers and students who have participated in the excavation since 1987, approximately three acres of the 20-acre site have been uncovered. The on-going commitment to the extensive care and restoration of the finds has been undertaken by the 20 universities of the Bethsaida Excavations Project Consortium, the Jewish National Fund, the Israel Tourist corporation, the Ministry of Tourism, the University of Hartford, and, of course, the project's headquarters at the University of Nebraska at Omaha.

As the world celebrates the Millennium, the prospects of Bethsaida playing a key role are promising. Although the present location of Bethsaida, just east of the Jordan River, raises questions about whether the site will be located in Syria or Israel after final peace negotiations are

---

28. R. Arav, "A Mamluk Drum from Bethsaida," *Israel Exploration Journal*, (IEJ) Volume 43, Number 4 (1993), pp. 241–245.

completed, the Consortium is hoping that the site will be an international Peace Park, which will be an appropriate symbol for a new era in the relations between Israel and its neighbors in this new Millennium— a very appropriate symbol since Bethsaida was, for nearly 2000 years (until its disappearance), a commercial crossroads between the superpowers of antiquity, Egypt and Mesopotamia, and one of the original points of contact for the beginnings of early Christianity and rabbinic Judaism. One can only hope that the site will serve a venerable purpose in this coming Millennium as well. It is in this Millennium/Jubilee year a fitting topicof this year of celebration and this lecture honoring Cardinal Bernardin.

An Ancient and Venerable People

Robert Louis Wilken
March 18, 2001

The sixth Jerusalem Lecture was delivered in Chicago on March 18, 2001, by Dr. Robert Wilken, the William R. Kenan, Jr. Professor of the History of Christianity at the University of Virginia. Dr. Wilken earned his doctorate from the University of Chicago, did post-doctoral research on the New Testament at the University of Heidelberg, and studied Modern Hebrew and the Talmud at Spertus College of Judaica. Dr. Wilken is thoroughly versed in early and medieval Christianity history and thought; Byzantine Christianity; history of biblical interpretation: early Christian ethics; Eastern Christianity; and Christianity and Islam. He is an Elected Fellow of the American Academy of Arts and Sciences and the former president of the American Academy of Religions and the North American Patristic Society.

IN a sermon preached in ancient Antioch, the home of the large Jewish community, John Chrysostom, the famous Christian preacher said:

> You Christians should be ashamed and embarrassed at the Jews who observe the Sabbath with such devotion. They refrain from all commerce beginning with the evening of the Sabbath. When they see the sun hurrying to set in the west on Friday they call a halt to their business affairs and interrupt their selling. If a customer haggles with them over a purchase in the late afternoon and offers a price after evening has come, the Jews refuse the offer because they are unwilling to accept any money [on the Sabbath].[1]

---

1. John Chrysostom, *Homilies on Romans* 12:20.3 (*Patrologia Graeca* (PG), 51:176). For further documentation of the attraction of Judaism to Christians in the Roman Empire see Robert L. Wilken, *John Chrysostom and the Jews: Rhetoric and Reality in the Late Fourth Century* (Berkley: University of California Press, 1983).

Chrysostom's views of the Jews, echoed by other Christian writers of the time, are a good place to begin a consideration of the relations between Christians and Jews during the early centuries of the Common Era. Jewish life, its customs and practices and rituals, made a deep impression on Christians, and one might add the society at large. John called the Jews "an ancient and venerable people."

The Jewish way of life was not simply admired, it was also alluring and it attracted some Christians to the point that they actually joined with Jews in celebrating Jewish festivals and adopting Jewish customs. In the early fall (prior to Yom Kippur and Rosh Hashannah) and again in spring (prior to Pesach), when Jews bought the special foods in the markets, decorated their homes and synagogues, constructed booths for Sukkoth, closed their shops at unexpected times, and danced in the public squares of the city (for Simkhat Torah), Chrysostom reports that some Christians (his word is "many" but his sermons are given to hyperbole) forsook the churches to go to the synagogue to hear the blowing of the trumpet or to celebrate with the Jews in their homes.

Hence when Jewish festivals approached, Christian leaders often took to the pulpit, Chrysostom preached a series of sermons against "Judaizing" Christians in Antioch in Roman Syria in the fall of 387. Before he began these sermons he had been preaching on the Arians, an early Christian heretical group. But he halted his sermons against them and began a new series on the Judaizers, because at this time of the year (late September and early October) the Jewish festivals come "continuously and one after another."

In the cities of the Roman Empire where Christianity first took root, the Jews belonged to self-confident communities whose history reached into the distant past, and whose way of life was respected and admired by fellow citizens. Christianity was a newcomer, a religion that had sprung up only recently. Its books were neither old nor hallowed, and its history was short and undistinguished (no kings, no great wars, no memorable tales).

It was known in the society at large that Christians had taken over the books of the Jews, the Tanakh, what Christians called the Old Testament, and the original copies—that is manuscripts written in Hebrew—could only be found among the Jews. Christians were able to read the Bible only in translation, the Greek of the Septuagint, a translation made by Jews before the beginning of Christianity.

In an illuminating exchange between a Christian and a Roman critic, the Roman said that Christians had claimed the coming of Christ was anticipated by the Jewish prophets. But, said the Roman, "You have forged these books for yourselves, you have seen what came to pass, and have written these things in whatever books you pleased, as if their coming had been predicted." The only response Christians could give was to send the critic to the synagogue where the original copies could be found. "Let the book of Isaiah be produced by the Jews," wrote Augustine to answer the critic. Christians were dependent on the Jews to present their message to others and could not make their way in the Roman world without appealing to the Jewish Scriptures, Jewish traditions, and Jewish history.

What is more, the books of the Jews, that is the Septuagint, the Greek version of the Tanakh, circulated independently of the Christian books that made up the New Testament. Porphyry, a leading neo-Platonic philosopher in the third century, neither a Christian nor a Jew, had read the Jewish Bible. The Christian Bible (that is, a book in which the Jewish Bible and the Christian writings, the New Testament, are bound in a single book, the one found in the drawers of chests in hotel rooms) did not exist at this time. Educated pagans could read what was written there without a Christian interpretation (or a Jewish one for that matter). And one thing that Romans discovered in the Septuagint was that it was a book of laws and only the Jews observed the Laws of Moses, for example, Sabbath, food laws, circumcision, Pesach, Yom Kippur. Christians did not keep the Law and ignored the legal passages of the Bible, interpreting them in such a way as to eliminate the plain sense of the text. Though they claimed to be faithful to the Jewish tradition and had created a Christian past by identifying with Jewish history, indeed making that history their own past, on examination it appeared that they had, contrary to their own claims, begun something quite new.

Accordingly, the most articulate pagan critics of Christianity before Constantine in the early fourth century—Celsus in the second century and Porphyry in the third century—charged that Christianity was an apostasy from Judaism. But it was the emperor Julian later in the fourth century, known in Christian memory as Julian the Apostate, who grasped the power of this argument and backed it up with texts from the Bible.

Julian had been raised a Christian and knew the Scriptures well. But he had given up his Christian faith and adopted the traditional religious practices of the cities of the Roman Empire. He speaks neither as a Christian nor as a Jew but as a representative of the traditions of Roman society, a cultured and educated pagan. Yet his critique of Christianity was devastating.

Julian realized that Jews continued to observe their ancestral traditions as documented in the Scriptures, and Christians who used the same Bible did not keep a Law of Moses. Hence in a writing against Christianity, contemptuously entitled *Against the Galileans,* he asked: "Did God give contrary laws, one to Moses and another . . . to this man from Nazareth?" Where in the Scriptures does Moses teach that a new Law will be established at a later time? Nowhere does God "announce to the Hebrews a second law besides that which was established." Where is there even talk of a revision of the established law? He cites Deuteronomy: "You shall not add to the word which I command you, nor take from it; keep the commandments of the Lord your God which I command you this day." And he asks the Christians: "Why do you not practice circumcision?"

What terrified Christians, however, was not so much Julian's words, but his bold attempt to rebuild the Jewish Temple in Jerusalem. Speaking of the Temple, Jesus had predicted that "there will not be left here one stone upon another that will not be thrown down." After the fall of the Temple in 70 C.E., Christians understood this to mean that the Temple would never be rebuilt. When Constantine became emperor a huge church was built in Jerusalem at the site of Jesus's death and resurrection, what we know of today as the Church of the Holy Sepulcher, and this building became the center of the new Christian city. The Temple Mount to the east was left vacant and over time became a dung heap. Jewish Jerusalem, symbolized by the site of the Temple, was now a thing of the past and the huge new "temple" (the term was sometimes used) dominated Christian Jerusalem.

Julian's plan was startling. By rebuilding the Temple he would prove Jesus a false prophet (and hence not divine) and Jews could resume animal sacrifices, thereby putting the lie to the Christian claim that the ancient form of worship (symbolizing by sacrifices) had given way to the new spiritual worship of the Christians symbolized by the Eucharist. Julian was able to enlist the support of the Jews, through his project was hardly a magnanimous gesture. His aim was to put the axe to the root of Christian belief. In the words of the Jewish proverb, what was done "not for the love of Mordecai but for the hate of Haman."

The project began in spring 363, but it was abruptly cut short by an earthquake or some other disaster. The pagan historian Ammianus Marcellinus said that balls of fire burst from underneath the foundation, and Christian historians said that fire came down from heaven to burn the site and the workers. As fate would have it, in June Julian was cut down in the midst of a battle with the Persians on the Eastern frontier. He was thirty years old. With his death the project was abandoned, though for generations afterward Christians were fearful another emperor would revive the idea. For Julian sensed, and Christians understood, that the Achilles heel of Christianity was its relation to Judaism. If Judaism was still a living religion, legitimated by the rebuilding of the Temple, Christians could not claim to be the rightful inheritors of the patrimony of Israel or that Jesus was the Messiah.

To understand, then, the relation of Christians and Jews in the Roman world, that is in the age of the Church Fathers, it is not enough to speak about Jews and Christians. There is a third player, that of the Romans, who knew both Christians and Jews and whose critique of Christianity drew on a knowledge of Jewish life and traditions. The society in which Christianity first sought to work out a relation to the Jewish people was not a Christian society, and it does not promote understanding to impose an image of medieval Christian Europe on the Roman Empire. Christians were a minority, as were of course the Jews, and for the first two centuries the Christian minority was smaller than that of the Jews. In the city of Sardis in western Asia Minor in the second century, for example, Christians formed a small conventicle meeting in homes, and the Jews gathered in a huge synagogue almost three hundred feet in length located adjacent to the central public square of the city.

Because Christianity was an offshoot from the Jews it could not present itself to outsiders without reference to the Jews. The continuing existence of observant Jewish communities in the cities alongside the Christian communities gave critics their most potent argument against Christianity. It is perhaps an exaggeration to say that Christianity lived in the shadow of the Jews, but that it not far from the truth. John Chrysostom said: "I know that many have high regard for the Jews and think that their present way of life is holy."

A single incident can illustrate the point. In one of his sermons Chrysostom says: "Three days ago, I saw a noble and free woman, who is modest and faithful, being forced into a synagogue by a coarse and senseless person who appeared to be a Christian. . . . He forced her into the synagogue to make an oath about certain business matters that were in litigation. . . . She kept calling out for help, hoping someone would stop this lawless show of force. Enraged and burning with anger I roused myself and rescued her from this unjust abduction. . . ."[2]

Note that it was not a Jew who forced the woman into the synagogue but a Christian. Why? John goes on to say: "I asked him why he had walked by the church and dragged this woman to the synagogue of the Hebrews. He replied that many had told him that oaths taken there [presumably before the Torah scroll] were more binding." Hence in the next paragraph of the sermon Chrysostom makes an *argument* as to why the churches "are truly places of awe and filled with religious fervor." No argument was needed to demonstrate that the synagogue was a place of awe.

So much then for the social world inhabited by Christians and Jews in the cities of the Roman Empire. What are we to make of it? If we look closely at the statements of Christians from this period, we discover that what troubled them was not the Jews as a people, but Jewish religion—that is, observance *(sh'mirath ha mitzvoth),* Jewish practices based on the Law. To Christians the Jews were a *dath* not an *am,* to use the Hebrew expression, a religion. By observing the Sabbath, circumcision, food laws, and festivals, Jews put into question the claims of Christians. Christianity ignored the Jewish Law, yet the Jewish Bible, the Septuagint, which Christians claimed as Holy Scripture, contained the laws that Jews observed and Christians ignored. Observant Judaism was a spiritual challenge to Christianity. Practice conferred legitimacy.

Judaism left deep marks on Christianity but Christianity made little impression on the Jews. From the middle of the second century through the fifth century there was a steady stream of writings by Christians dealing directly with the relation of Christianity to Judaism. These works are at once a defense of Christianity to the Jews and an explanation of how Christians can claim to be "Jewish," that is faithful to Jewish

---

2. *Against the Judaizers* 1.3 (PG 48:847).

tradition, the new Israel, in light of the embarrassing social fact that the "old" Israel was still very much alive and well.

There is nothing comparable on the Jewish side. Christians are seldom mentioned in Jewish writings and Jews could get along perfectly well without having to deal with Christianity, thank you, but Christians had no such luxury. Christianity was unintelligible without reference to the Jews. Hence it was spiritually and theologically necessary that Christians explain how the Church came to be, how they understood the book that the Jews continued to use, why they had given up the Law, why they believed prophecies about the Messiah had been fulfilled in a person who had died an ignominious death.

Origen, the seminal Christian thinker who lived in Alexandria in the third century, said that Jews put great pressure on us to explain how the words of the prophets can be fulfilled in the events surrounding Jesus of Nazareth. The prophet Isaiah said that when the Messiah comes he will "proclaim release to the captives," and he will rebuild the city of Jerusalem, and the wolf will "feed with the lamb and the leopard lie down with the kid and . . . a little child will lead them." But these things had not happened, the Jews argued. Hence Christians are deceived in thinking that Jesus of Nazareth was the promised Messiah.

This reproach put Christians on the defensive, especially the rank and file who lived alongside Jews in the cities of the Roman world and had no answers to offer Jewish neighbors. In response Christian thinkers mounted an elaborate defense that took the form of an alternate interpretation of the prophets and of Jewish history. The argument was simple in its outlines, but elaborate in the details. The words of the prophets are not to be understood literally—that is historically or politically, i.e., about establishing a Jewish kingdom in Jerusalem—but spiritually, an inward experience. They are speaking about the soul, about the inner life, about deliverance from sin and the building of a new kind of city, the community of the Church. Biblical texts that mention the City of God, Jerusalem, or Zion, were understood to be references to the Church.

There was more here than exegesis of the Bible. One can also discern the beginning of a new view of Jewish history, and here the matter becomes graver. For the events that took place in the first and second centuries, in particular the war with the Romans, the destruction of Jerusalem and the Temple, and the failure of the Bar Kochba revolt, gave

Christian thinkers a convenient weapon in their arguments against Jews (and to the Romans). The destruction of Jerusalem, the cessation of worship in the Temple and the demise of the priesthood, the displacement of the Jews from Jerusalem, called out for explanation. When the fall of Jerusalem was linked to the upheaval in Jewish life in the first and second centuries it appeared to others that the Jews would eventually cease to exist as a distinct people.

As this audience knows, Jewish thinking, particularly in biblical times, was formed by historical events. If God is the God of history and not simply of nature, historical events require interpretation, especially those that concern the elect people of God. The most notable event in the Bible was of course the deliverance of the Jewish people from Egypt. "Horse and rider he has thrown into the sea." But there were others: the fall of Jerusalem to the Assyrians in the eighth century and then to the Babylonians in the sixth century and the exile in the sixth century to Babylon. In the writings of the prophets one can see how these things could have happened and what they meant for the Jewish people.

In the same way, the fall of Jerusalem in the first century cried out for explanation, and Jewish writings from that time attempt to explain why God had allowed his city to be destroyed and handed over to the infidel.

It is understandable, then, that the first Christians who were Jews, and the generations that followed, instructed by the Jewish Bible, sought to make sense out of the destruction of Jerusalem. Christians, however, were not conventional Jews; they stepped to other rhythms and had begun to rewrite Jewish history in light of the coming of Christ. As Christians looked back then, it was not the fall of Jerusalem in 70 C.E. that needed explaining, but also the proximity of the death of Christ and the fall of the city.

Jesus died in 30 and the city fell in 70 of the Common Era. In the lifetime of a human being forty years is a long time, but a hundred years later the two events do not seem as distant, and by the time two hundred years have passed they appear to have happened at roughly the same time. In other words, as time passed Christians began to wonder whether there was a relation between the death of Jesus and the fall of the city. For Christian thinking, it was also significant that the catastrophe of the first century was not reversed in the second century. After the failure of the Bar Kochba revolt, the Romans had plowed over the Jewish city and built a new Roman colony, Aelia Capitolina, in the place where Jewish Jerusalem once stood. Jewish Jerusalem seemed a thing of the past.

Origen writes: "I challenge anyone to prove my statement untrue if I say that the entire Jewish nation was destroyed less than one whole generation later on account of these sufferings which they inflicted upon Jesus. For it was, I believe, forty-two years from the time when they crucified Jesus to the destruction of Jerusalem. Indeed, ever since the Jews existed, it has not been recorded in history that they were ejected for so long a time from their sacred ritual and worship, after they had been conquered by some more powerful people. . . . We will go so far as to say that they will not be restored again. [Origen has in mind Jesus's prophecy that "no stone will be left standing upon another."] The Jewish nation had to be overthrown, and God's invitation to blessedness transferred to others, I mean the Christians, to whom came the teaching about the simple and pure worship of God. And they received new laws which fit in with the others established everywhere. Those laws which had previously been given were intended for a single nation ruled by men of the same nationality and customs, so that it would be impossible for everyone to keep them now."[3]

This is a disturbing passage, and I am grateful that it was Origen (who was never made a saint) who wrote these words rather than Saint Augustine. Yet Origen does not express a private opinion; his was a view shared by most Christian writers from the early Church.

As unpalatable as his words may be, they must be placed in context, and the context, as we have seen, was the effort of Christians to defend the new religion in the face of formidable opponents, Roman as well as Jewish. Further, Origen's is a very Jewish argument, the kind that can be found in the Jewish Bible with respect to the Canaanites, the Egyptians, or the Babylonians. Victory was a sign of divine favor and defeat proof of celestial displeasure. However, what is "Jewish" in the Bible and among Jews comes out sounding much different when it is spoken by a Christian who is a member of what had become a rival religious tradition, and in time will become the dominant religion of the society.

What Origen says here is not all he has to say about the Jews. In another writing, a defense of Christianity to the Romans, Origen comes

---

3. Origen of Alexandria, *Against Celsus, Vol. 4*, (Whitefish, MT: Kessinger, 2004), 4.22.

to the defense of the Jews against his opponent, the philosopher Celsus. Celsus, who knew the Christians traced their origins to the Jews, embellishes his censure of Christians with an attack on the Jews. "The Jews," he writes, "were runaway slaves who escaped from Egypt; they never did anything important, nor have they ever been of any significance or prominence whatsoever." In response Origen says that what set the Jews apart is that God had given them the Law. They were the only people "who manifested a shadow of the heavenly life upon earth." They did not worship idols and venerated only the "supreme God." They constituted a virtuous society and their judges were "righteous men who had given proof of their good life over a long period." They took education seriously and to give people time to study the "divine laws" they observed the Sabbath and celebrated feast days. Jewish society, he says to Celsus, was unlike any other society. If Celsus would compare the Jews to other nations, "he would admire none more, since as far as is humanly possible they removed everything not of advantage to mankind, and accepted only what is good."[4]

Origen believed, of course, that there came a time when the Jewish way of life, which was confined to one people and one place, Jerusalem and the land of Israel, had to give way to a way of life that was suitable to other peoples and other lands. Yet even as he draws a contrast between the Jews and the Christians, he steadfastly maintains that the Jews are not to be placed in the same category as the pagans, that is idolaters. In defending worship of the one God, Christians considered the Jews allies. This is a point of no little importance, for it suggests that even after the coming of Jesus, on the matter of central importance, worship of the one God, Jews and Christians stand together.

Celsus also said that the Jews set themselves apart from others, arrogantly claiming that they had some "deeper wisdom." Origen agrees that this is the case, but takes it as a compliment. The Jews are unique for they are, he writes, God's "portion," his "elect" people, and chosen race.

Unfortunately within Christian tradition (until very recently), it was not this inheritance from the Church Fathers that was remembered. It was rather that the fall of Jerusalem and the destruction of the Temple seemed to signify an ending, the penultimate drama in a history that

---

4. Ibid., 4.31.

extended back to the days of Abraham and Moses and David and the prophets.

Yet Origen's comments on the uniqueness of the Jewish people, that they are the elect people of God, should not be dismissed. For they remind us that Christian attitudes to the Jews are complex and often very nuanced, not univocal, and that there are resources within Christian tradition to see things differently than earlier generations perceived them. Even as Christians mounted a religious critique of the Jews, they saw the Jews as the elect people of God, the people with whom God made an eternal covenant. This belief, this doctrine, is as foundational for Christian as it is for Jewish belief. It is part of the biblical revelation that we share, for example in the words of Psalm 89: "I will not violate my covenant, or alter the word that went forth from my lips." When Christians pray this psalm we are reminded that the covenant of God with the Jewish people is eternal, a teaching that is echoed in the New Testament by St. Paul. To the Israelites, he writes, "belong the sonship, the glory, the covenants [puzzling why he uses the plural], the giving of the law, the worship, and the promises; to them belong the patriarchs. . . ."

In the early Church, Christians said many harsh and harmful things about the Jews that were to have unforeseen, and deplorable, consequences in medieval Europe. There is nothing to be gained by hiding from the melancholy history of Christian treatment of the Jews. Yet Christianity's relation to the Jewish people cannot be reduced to abuse or hatred. Christians are capable of understanding the Jews as the Jews understand themselves. This is the lesson we need to carry with us—if we wish to move forward, if we seek to discover a usable past. Not only is Christianity inescapably bound to the Jewish Bible and to Jewish history, Christians are able to love the Jew as Jew, not only to hate. That may seem like small comfort, but it cannot be said of any other religion except Christianity.

Let me conclude with a personal story. Some years back when I visited Jerusalem, it was my privilege to go to the synagogue with a friend, Rabbi Pinchas Peli, may he rest in peace. One semester Peli came to teach at the University of Notre Dame where I was on the faculty and he said that he wanted to visit my church. So one Sunday morning, when his wife, Penina, was in South Bend visiting him, they joined our family for the Eucharist. It was a beautiful May morning and as we took our places in the pew, with warm spring sunlight streaming in the windows,

I was delighted to have Pinchas and Penina sitting next to us, and eager to have them share in our worship.

It happened to be the fifth Sunday of Easter and the first lesson was from the Acts of the Apostles, chapter 13. That morning the reader was a talented young woman, an actress, who was a skilled and effective reader. The text was the account of the visit of Paul and Barnabas to the synagogue in Antioch in Pisidia in Asia Minor and she reads the passage with power and enthusiasm. The text says that on the Sabbath almost the whole city gathered to hear the word of God, "but when the Jews saw the multitudes, they were filled with jealousy, and contradicted what was spoken by Paul, and reviled him." When the lector reached the final sentences of the passage, she raised her voice to highlight the dramatic ending: "And Paul and Barnabas spoke out boldly, saying, 'It was necessary that the word of God should be spoken first to you. Since you thrust it from you, and judge yourselves unworthy of eternal life, behold, we turn to the Gentiles.'" To which she responded: "This is the Word of God." And the congregation in return replied: "Thanks be to God."

It was as though Pinchas and Penina had been hit over the head by a sledgehammer. Penina began to cry and Pinchas was visibly agitated. But they stayed in their places and endured the rest of the service. After the service the Pelis were invited to our home for brunch and of course the chief topic of conversation was the reading from Acts. Penina was outraged and kept saying, "How can you continue to read such a passage after the Holocaust?" Pinchas, with what seemed to me a keener spiritual insight and religious sensibility, had something quite different to say. "It is a hard saying. But it is part of the Bible, and one cannot, after all, take the scissors to the pages of the Scriptures. The only way to deal with such a text is through interpretation."

Interpretation is an ongoing task, the work of purifying memory, as John Paul II put it. Like Jews and Christians who lived centuries ago, we too are historical beings. And how we view each other is shaped not only by what happened long ago, but by what has happened in our own times.

For two generations Christian theology has been engaged in a fundamental rethinking of Christianity's relation to Judaism and to the Jewish people. This work has been carried out by biblical scholars, by historians of Christian thought, by theologians, by Christian educators, and by bishops and other leaders of the various Christian communions. It has dealt with technical points of biblical exegesis, profound questions of theology, and, not least, with how words and images and ideas influence the attitudes of Christians.[5] Whether one thinks of the passages on the Jews in the decree *Nostra Aetate* of the Second Vatican Council and other Catholic statements over last two decades,[6] the various declarations of the World Council of Churches and Protestant denominations,[7] the historic meeting of Orthodox Christians and Jews in Athens in 1993,[8] the depth and seriousness of Christian engagement with the Jews is unprecedented. Something very new and extraordinary has taken place in our lifetimes.

We cannot, however, forget that this new movement of the Spirit was born out of Jewish suffering and of the struggles of the Jewish people. The occasion for the Church's reconsideration of her relation to the Jews was the Holocaust.[9] The first books and articles that laid the foundation for what followed were written in the late 1940s. To be sure, there were some earlier voices, Christian thinkers who had begun to write about Christianity's relation to the Jewish people in the decade before the war, notably Fr. John Oesterreicher, Erik Peterson, Jacques Maritain and Henri de Lubac.[10] But the great outpouring of Christian reflection did not begin until after the destruction of six million Jews.

---

5. See Eugene J. Fisher, *Faith Without Prejudice. Rebuilding Christian Attitudes Toward Judaism* (New York: Crossroad, 1993). For discussion of the theological issues see Bruce D. Marshall, "The Jewish People and Christian Theology," in. *The Cambridge Companion to Christian Doctrine,* ed. Colin Gunton (Cambridge: Cambridge University Press 1971).

6. "Declaration on the Relationship of the Church to Non-Christian Religions (*Nostra Aetate*)" in Walter M. Abbot, sj, editor. *The Documents of Vatican II,* ed. Walter m. Abbot, sj (New York: Herder & Herder, 1966).

7. *The Theology of the Churches and the Jewish People* (Geneva: World Council of Churches, 1988).

8. See *Orthodox Christians and Jews on Continuity and Renewal,* Third Academic Meeting between Orthodoxy and Judaism, ed. Malcolm Lowe (Jerusalem: Ecumenical Theological Research Fraternity in Israel: 1994).

9. A point that was recognized by Cardinal Bea in the introduction to his commentary on the decree *Nostra Aetate.* See *Church and the Jewish People: A Commentary on the Second Vatican Council's Declaration on the Relation of the Church to Non-Christian Religions* (New York: Harper & Row, 1966), 7.

10. Oesterreicher's periodical, "*Die Erfuellung,*" was begin in the early 1930's and had as its purpose to break down the walls of ignorance and discord by communicating a vision of Jewish existence to Christians. In 1939 he began to broadcast radio addresses in German from Paris to oppose with all his strength "Hitler's lies and hate." See Johannes Oesterrreicher, *Wider die Tyrannei des Rassenwahns: Rundfunkansprachen aus dem ersten Jahr an Hitlers Krieg* (Salzburg: 1986); Erik Peterson, *Die Kirche aus Juden und Heiden* (Salzburg: 1933); for Maritain, see Robert Royal, editor. *Jacques Maritain and the Jews* (South Bend, IN: University of Notre Dame Press, 1994); for de Lubac, see his *Christian Resistance to Anti-Semitism: Memories from 1940-1944* (San Francisco: Ignatius, 1990).

The other factor that awakened Christian thinking was of course the establishment of the State of Israel. For the first time since antiquity the Jews were able to reestablish Jewish life and institutions under Jewish rule in the Land of Israel. Jews, as it were, returned to history, and Christians began to look at the Jewish people, as well as the Bible and Christian theology, with fresh eyes. Jacques Maritain thought it providential that the Second Vatican Council was convened so shortly after the return of the Jews to the Land of Israel. "It seems to me very significant that these two events of such great bearing—on the Jewish side the return of a portion of a people to the Promised Land, on the Christian side the Second Vatican Council—took place at almost the same time, the first in 1948, the second in 1962–1965. They mark, each in its own way, a reorientation of history."[11]

What we have to say will be formed by the events of our century as well as by books written centuries ago. I am thinking not only of the work of historians or theologians, but the education of the affections, the sadness and shame that have come over Christian thinkers as they have come to know better the history of Christian relations to the Jewish people, and of the need for repentance. I am thinking also of actions, symbolic gestures, for example, the visit of John Paul II to Auschwitz in 1979, his visit to the Jewish synagogue of Rome in 1986, and his words to the Jews of Germany in 1980, in which he said that the covenant with the people of God of the "old covenant" is "never revoked by God," and of course his visit to Israel in the Spring of 2000 and his words of sorrow tucked into the stone of the Western Wall.[12]

Early Christian thinkers knew that what set the Jews apart from others was that they worshiped God by observing the Law of Moses. Even though they claimed that there was something better than the Law. Christians recognized that the Law was a gift of God (Rom. 9:1), and that the new way revealed in Christ was irrevocably bound to what had been revealed earlier. What St. John called "worship in spirit and in truth" was not simply a new spiritual worship; it was, in Origen's phrase, a "spiritual worship *of the Law*." Christians did not destroy the books of the Law, they preserved them and interpreted them anew.

---

11. Jacques Maritain, *On the Church of Christ,* translation by Joseph W. Evans (South Bend, IN: University of Notre Dame Press, 1973), 174.

12. For statements of Pope John Paul II see John Paul II, *Spiritual Pilgrimage: Texts on Jews and Judaism 1979–1995.* ed. Eugene J. Fisher and Leon Klenicki (New York: Crossroad, 1996).

Christianity cannot be indifferent to the people of God who continue to observe the Law, even though their existence is an abiding spiritual challenge to Christianity. For if there is no worship according to the Law, if there is no Jewish community that observes the Law as an act of covenantal obedience to the one God, what does it mean to say that there is a "spiritual worship of the Law"? In the most profound sense, this question was at issue in Paul's words in Romans cited in the decree *Nostra Aetate* of Vatican II: "If some of the branches were broken off, and you, a wild olive shoot, were grafted in their place to share the richness of the olive tree, do not boast over the branches. If you do boast, remember it is not you that support the root, but the root that supports you."

When Paul wrote these words he used the present tense, the "root that *supports* you." At the Second Vatican Council [1962–1965], it would have been easy to transpose the word "support" into the past tense, "supported." Hence it is of some theological significance that when *Nostra Aetate* paraphrases Paul's words in Romans, it retains the present tense. The Church "cannot forget that she *draws* sustenance from the root of that good olive tree onto which have been engrafted the wild olive branches of the Gentiles."[13] One might have expected, two thousand years later, to read, "*drew* sustenance" from the Jewish people. But what the decree says is, "draws sustenance from the root of the good olive tree." This mystery is at the heart of a Christian understanding of the Jews.

---

13. *Documents of Vatican II,* 664.

Medieval Christians and Jews: Divergences and Convergences

Robert Chazen
March 14, 2002

The seventh Jerusalem Lecture was delivered in Chicago on March 14, 2002, by Dr. Robert Chazen. Dr. Chazen is the S. H. and Helen R. Scheuer Professor of Hebrew and Judaic Studies in the Skirball Department of Hebrew and Judaic Studies at New York University.

Dr. Chazen has published widely in medieval Jewish history. He has been chair of the Graduate Fellowship Committee of the Wexner Foundation since inception of the program in 1987, and is currently chair of the Academic Advisory Council of the Center for Jewish History.

CHRISTIAN-JEWISH relations have come under enhanced scrutiny over the past few decades, largely as a result of the continued impact of the Holocaust on the Western world in general and on the Christian and Jewish worlds in particular. The French historian and Holocaust survivor Jules Isaac was the first major post-World War II thinker to highlight the deleterious impact of centuries of Christian anti-Jewish teachings upon Western perceptions of the Jews. Isaac focused on key elements in the Christian supersessionist view of Judaism. This supersessionist view posited the Jews as the initial bearers of the divine-human covenant and then claimed that the Jews—long subject to backsliding in their fulfillment of this covenant–had committed a sin so heinous that "normal" divine punishment could no longer suffice. Rather, in this view, God had no choice but to abrogate his relationship with the Jewish people and to transfer his covenant to another human community. This view—profoundly negative to Judaism and the Jews—developed fairly quickly in early Christian circles and became a cornerstone of Christian thinking over the ages. As Christian-Jewish relations have been persistently studied and analyzed over the past few decades, this early and fundamental Christian view has remained at the center of scholarly and popular attention.[1]

An American medievalist, Gavin I. Langmuir first aroused post-Holocaust sensitivity to the importance of the Middle Ages for the history of Christian-Jewish relations. Langmuir began with the simple assumption that Christian-Jewish relations could by no means have remained static over the course of two millennia. Over this lengthy time span, change had to take place and in fact did. Langmuir concluded that, during the Middle Ages, the Christian view of the Jews underwent considerable alteration, indeed considerable deterioration. Langmuir and those who have followed him have tended to concentrate on the turbulent twelfth century, a period of enormous intellectual and spiritual ferment in medieval western Christendom. This ferment resulted in major advances in Christian thinking and creativity; it also resulted in significant decline in the imagery of a number of out-groups living within Christian society, including the Jews.[2]

Intensifying twelfth-century Christian concern with Jews and Judaism was in part the result of internal dynamics in western Christendom. Too little attention has been accorded to a second factor that played an important role as well. During the twelfth century, the center of gravity in world Jewish population began to shift from the realm of Islam to western Christendom. Up to that point, the vast majority of the world's Jews had lived in Muslim lands, ranging from Mesopotamia across the eastern and southern shores of the Mediterranean Sea over onto the Iberian Peninsula. Prior to the twelfth century, Jews did not impinge in a serious way on the everyday consciousness of the Christian population of western Christendom. With the movement westward and northward

---

1. For a convenient English-language presentation of Isaac's views, see Jules Isaac, *The Teaching of Contempt: Christian Roots of Anti-Semitism,* trans. Helen Weaver (New York: Holt, Rinehart and Winston, 1964). Along these same lines, see the important works of Rosemary Radford Ruether, *Faith and Fratricide: The Theological Roots of Anti-Semitism* (New York: Seabury Press, 1974), and James Carroll, *Constantine's Sword: The Church and the Jews* (Boston: Houghton Mifflin, 2001).

2. See the essays collected in Gavin I. Langmuir, *Toward a Definition of Anti-Semitism* (Berkeley: University of California Press, 1990), and his synthetic study, *History, Religion, and Anti-Semitism* (Berkeley: University of California Press, 1990). For further studies of the twelfth-century decline in imagery of the Jews, see Anna Sapir Abulafia, *Christians and Jews in the Twelfth-Century Renaissance* (London: Routledge, 1995), and Robert Chazan, *Medieval Stereotypes and Modern Anti-Semitism* (Berkeley: University of California Press, 1997). For an influential study of the enhanced twelfth-century rejection of numerous out-groups in western Christendom, see R. I. Moore, *The Formation of a Persecuting Society* (Oxford: Basil Blackwell, 1987).

of Jews, Judaism was no longer simply a theoretical issue; Jews were an enhanced everyday reality, constituting in fact the only significant non-Christian presence in western Christendom.[3]

While the medieval alterations in Christian views of Judaism played a significant role in the broad evolution of Christian perceptions of the Jews, medieval western Christendom and its Jews have independent claims on our attention. The Middle Ages were more than simply a link in the chain of evolving Christian anti-Jewish thinking. During the Middle Ages, Christian men and women lived side-by-side with Jewish men and women, often in enmity and conflict but sometimes in amity and cooperation. It is my intention to explore a number of aspects of Christian-Jewish interaction in medieval western Christendom. I shall by no means obscure the negative elements in these interactions; I shall at the same time attempt to balance our sense of the negative with some of the positives as well.

To be sure, medieval Christians and medieval Jews saw themselves as locked in an intense religious and ideological struggle with one another. Indeed, medieval Christians and Jews often defined themselves in contradistinction to one another. The tensions between these two communities regularly escalated into hatred and violence. At the same time, the two communities challenged each other in useful ways, each invigorating the other through the challenges it posed. Moreover, medieval Christians and Jews often cooperated quietly but meaningfully with one another, with both sides enriched as a result. This lecture will explore the full range of medieval Christian-Jewish interactions, both negative and positive.

◆ ◆ ◆ ◆ ◆

The written legacy of medieval Christians and Jews tends to highlight the oppositional. The core of this opposition lay in conflicting claims to religious truth. As Christians looked out over the known world in its entirety, of which they became increasingly cognizant during the twelfth and thirteenth centuries, the Jews occupied a curious and ambiguous position. They were, from one perspective, the very best of non-Christian humanity, since they had been the first to recognize and acknowledge

---

3. For a broad overview of the movement of Jews into medieval western Christendom, see Robert Chazan, "Then and Now: Jewish Life at the End of the First and Second Christian Millennium," in Solomon Goldman, Dean Philip Bell, Hal. M. Lewis, editors. *The Solomon Goldman Lectures,* vol. 8. (Chicago: Spertus College of Judaica, 2003).

the one true God. At the same time, the Christian view that the first humans to recognize the one true God and to enjoy the responsibility and glory of his covenant had ultimately erred in their understanding of the divine and had failed in their fulfillment of the covenant made the Jews the very worst of humanity.

This ambiguous view of Judaism and the Jews was complicated by a sense that the Jews posed unique dangers to Christianity and Christians. Because of the evolution of Christianity out of first-century Palestinian Jewry, there was a great deal shared between the two groups. They venerated as sacred the same literature—for the Jews the unique repository of divine revelation, for Christians a literature—whose truths were fully realized with the coming of Jesus as Messiah. As the result of their common Scripture, Christian and Jews also shared a rich set of powerful symbols—for example: the patriarchal foundations of monotheistic faith, the prophetic challenge to religious thinking and practice, the religious meaning of the Land of Israel, the unique sanctity of Jerusalem. This sharing meant that the Jews and their perspective on the Hebrew Bible and its symbols posed special dangers to the Christian community—the dangers flowing from proximity. Unwary Christians always ran the risk of ensnarement by the views of their Jewish neighbors; the leadership of the Church bore heavy responsibility for obviating such dangers.

Given the religious threat that medieval Christians saw in the Jews, the ecclesiastical leadership of medieval western Christendom felt a responsibility to establish policies that would minimize the harm Jews might inflict. As the medieval Church became increasingly concerned with the well-being of its adherents in the face of a variety of challenges and as Jews became more numerous throughout medieval western Christendom, protective anti-Jewish policies proliferated. From antiquity the medieval Church inherited a set of stipulations that prohibited Jews from occupying any position that would entail power over Christians. Examples of such positions of power included Jewish ownership of Christian slaves, Jewish enjoyment of political office, and Jewish marriage with Christians which might lead to spousal control.[4] During the twelfth and thirteenth centuries, ecclesiastical legislation intended to curb potentially harmful Jewish impact upon Christians intensified

---

4. For a collection of Roman imperial decrees—with English translation—that includes many of these stipulations, see Amnon Linder (ed. and trans.), *The Jews in Roman Imperial Legislation* (Detroit: Wayne State University Press, 1987).

markedly. The drive to minimize the religious dangers that Jews might pose led to far-reaching efforts to segregate them altogether. New rules prohibited Jewish settlement in rural villages, where regular social interaction was inevitable, and established separate neighborhoods for Jews in urban enclaves. The most radical of these measures decreed identifying badges or clothing for all Jews. In this way, Christians could readily identify their Jewish neighbors and be fully prepared for the threats they might ostensibly pose.[5] Needless to say, these segregating devices did more than simply protect Christians; in the process they sharply diminished the position of Jews in Christian society.

Legislative steps did protect the Christian majority to an extent, in the process exerting considerable impact on Jewish life. Segregation of Jews, however, involved merely physical isolation. Since the dangers Jews posed were ultimately perceived as spiritual, it was far more important to forewarn Christians through teaching. This was achieved in two ways. The first—and more benign—involved engagement with specific Jewish teachings and rebuttal of those teachings. Since so much of the Christian-Jewish argument revolved around interpretation of verses from the Hebrew Bible, ecclesiastical thinkers poured considerable effort into presenting their followers with evidence for the rectitude of Christian interpretation and the error of Jewish interpretation. Likewise, as twelfth-century Christendom increasingly absorbed the scientific and philosophic legacy of Greece and Rome, Church thinkers made the case for the rationality of Christian belief and the corresponding irrationality of Jewish belief.[6]

Beyond engaging Jewish views on the intellectual plane, there remained yet another option—sullying the image of the Jews. As is true in all such intense spiritual and intellectual debates, it is tempting— almost inescapably so—to carry on argument by besmirching the image of the other side. The underlying notion here is that people of debased intellect and moral fiber could hardly be capable of having a genuine grasp on truth.

---

5. These materials for the late twelfth and early thirteenth centuries—again with English translation—are available in Solomon Grayzel and Kenneth R. Stow (eds. and trans.), *The Church and the Jews in the Thirteenth Century*, 2 vols. (Philadelphia and New York, 1933–89).

6. For a sense of this Christian *Adversus Judaeos* literature, see Bernhard Blumenkranz, *Les auteurs chretiens-latins du Moyen Age sure les Juifs and le Judaisme* (Paris: Mouton, 1963); Heinz Schreckenberg, *Die christliche Adversus-Judaeos-Texte und ihr literarisches und historisches Umfeld* (11.-13. Jh.) (3rd ed.; Bern: Peter Lang, 1997).

As noted, there were deep roots to this approach in early and ongoing Christian thinking. From earliest days, Christian leaders had argued that Jewish sinfulness and willfulness had led God to abrogate his covenant with the Jewish people. This image of the sinning Jew was embodied most graphically in the allegation of Jewish deicide, that is, of Jewish culpability for the death of Jesus. In this view, Jews, who should have acknowledged Jesus as the Messiah promised by the biblical prophets, instead insisted on Roman execution of the messianic figure they should have welcomed. For traditional Christian thinking, this was the unforgivable sin for which God sundered his covenant with the Jewish people. This purported evidence of Jewish sinfulness served as effective proof that no genuine truth might reside in the claims of such a flawed people. While Jewish claims had to be continually addressed, their potential for truth was severely vitiated by Jewish shortcoming. Such a depraved people could hardly know and teach truth.

All through the Middle Ages, the imagery of Jews as deicides remained potent. During the twelfth century, this negative imagery took an ominous turn. A number of Christian thinkers, perhaps most importantly the famed abbot of Cluny, Peter the Venerable, insisted that the Jews of these later times continued to manifest the same blind hatred toward Christianity and Christians that their ancestors more than a millennium earlier had exhibited toward Jesus. This notion of ongoing Jewish sinfulness very much exacerbated the negativity of traditional Christian views of Jews. Once again, such a negative sense of twelfth-century Jews served to buttress the conviction that no truth could reside with such a people and that reasonable Christians should in no way be subverted by the teachings of such a group. Beyond that objective, however, the new imagery transformed the Jews into more than simply an errant people, posing a spiritual danger; they became a hostile people, posing physical danger as well—constantly threatening the *sancta* of Christianity and their Christian neighbors.[7]

For Peter the Venerable—a major spiritual and intellectual leader—alleged Jewish malevolence expressed itself essentially in blaspheming the *sancta* of Christianity. The popular imagination went far beyond Peter the Venerable. The twelfth and thirteenth centuries saw the emergence

---

7. For full analysis of this turn in Christian thinking, see Chazan, *Medieval Stereotypes and Modern Anti-Semitism.*

of a number of popular slanders that portrayed the Jews as viciously malevolent and harmful. The earliest of these slanders seems to have involved the notion that Jewish hatred for Christianity expressed itself in a compulsion to murder Christians, whenever opportunity might present itself.[8] This initial perception of homicidal Jewish rage was embellished fairly quickly into the slander of ritual murder. In attempting to make his case for the sanctity of the young murder victim William of Norwich, the Christian chronicler Tomas of Monmouth accused the Jews of the English town of doing the pure young lad to death via crucifixion, in conscious imitation of the sin of their ancestors.[9] These imaginative embellishments proliferated through the rest of the twelfth century and on into the thirteenth; the embellishments included the notion of Jewish sacrificial slaughtering of Christians, of Jewish utilization of Christian blood for ritual purposes, of Jewish abuse of the host, and of Jewish well poisoning. Again, discrediting the Jews as spiritual and intellectual rivals proceeded well beyond that limited goal and transformed the Jews into an omnipresent physical threat to Christian society.

Both the early and the evolving Christian imagery of Jews inevitably evoked powerful animosity toward the Jewish minority of medieval western Christendom. The early imagery of the Jews as decides was widely celebrated in Christian liturgy and art, arousing the masses to deep antipathy toward those who had allegedly been responsible for the death of Jesus. This animosity expressed itself decisively during the course of the First Crusade. While the Church leadership that set the crusade in motion clearly promulgated no suggestion of assault on Europe's Jews, and while the organized armies that responded to the papal call did not absorb any such notion, the popular bands that coalesced in the wake of the dramatic papal message did connect the call to arms with traditional Church teaching of Jewish deicide. German crusading bands assaulted a number of major Jewish communities in the Rhineland. Their slogan is reported in Christian and Jewish sources alike. Following is a version of this battle cry, bequeathed to us in the earliest of the Jewish chronicles of the First Crusade attacks. The crusaders are portrayed as crying out: "Behold, we travel to a distant land to do battle with the kings of that land. We take our lives in our hands in

8. For the emergence of this slander, see ibid.

9. See the classic study of Gavin I. Langmuir, "Thomas of Monmouth: Detector of Ritual Murder," *Speculum* 59 (1984): 86–127.

order to kill and to subjugate all those kingdoms that do not believe in the Crucified. How much more so [should we kill and subjugate] the Jews, who killed and crucified him."[10] The call to battle against the Muslim infidels, that is, those who do not believe in Jesus, is here turned into a rationalization for killing Jews, who are alleged to be so much worse, by virtue of their purported role in the death of Jesus. To be sure, there is no hint of such rationalization of anti-Jewish violence among the spiritual or military leaders of the First Crusade. During subsequent crusades, ecclesiastical leaders spent considerable energy defining the objectives of crusading, insisting relentlessly that anti-Jewish violence had no place in the enterprise.[11] Nonetheless, the potential of traditional Church teachings for evoking intense anti-Jewish feelings is obvious.

The more extreme slanders that began to proliferate during the twelfth and following centuries bore even greater potential for arousing hatred and violence. Conditioned to fear Jewish neighbors as mortal enemies poised at every moment to inflict harm, twelfth- and thirteenth-century Christians could be easily moved by one or another crisis to see the grounds of their problem in the Jews. When devastating plagues broke out in mid-fourteenth-century Europe, those towns that still harbored Jews attributed their suffering to Jewish well-poisoning, resulting in wide-ranging attacks on scores of Jewish communities. Thus, views that originated in an early rationale for Christian supplanting of the Jews on the religious plane evolved into notions of Jewish malevolence in the here-and-now, which in turn sparked profound hatred and considerable violence.

The object of everyday fear and occasional violence, the Jews were ultimately utilized as a touchstone for degrading comparisons. Jews came to be seen as the antithesis of Christian virtues. They were philosophically irrational, in contradistinction to Christian rationality; in the all-important reading of Scripture, they were obtuse, in contradistinction to Christian sophistication; on the religious and moral plane, they were steeped in the body, in contradistinction to Christian spirituality. Christian superiority was made manifest through tendentious contrast with the Jews.[12]

---

10. For this passage, see Robert Chazan, *European Jewry and the First Crusade* (Berkeley: University of California Press, 1987), 225.

11. See ibid., chapter 6.

12. See again, Sapir Abulafia, *Christians and Jews in the Twelfth-Century Renaissance.*

◆ ◆ ◆ ◆ ◆

For the Jews of medieval western Christendom, the Christian majority was, in turn, deeply threatening. The threat was of course somewhat different from that which Christians perceived as emanating from the Jews. Jewish sacred literature did not project significant concern with Christianity, and Jews did not feel threatened by a sense of common origin. For medieval Jews, Christianity represented simply an aberrant reading of the books they held sacred. On the other hand, medieval Jews were fully aware of the power and achievements of the Christian world and of Christian claims to the biblical legacy. To live as a small minority in flourishing Christian societies was in and of itself threatening. We recall that in fact Jews were attracted—from the twelfth century on—to medieval western Christendom by virtue of its vitality and strength. Jews had to ask themselves whether that vitality and strength translated into religious rectitude. Was Christian achievement reflective of religious truth? Christians were very much convinced that this was the case; Jews had to defend themselves against such conclusions.[13]

In fact, the inherent religious appeal of Christian power was doubly intensified for the Jews of medieval western Christendom. In the first place, the legislative regime of limitation noted earlier, the resultant difficulties endured by the Jews, and the occasional violence stimulated by anti-Jewish imagery intensified the feeling of Christian might and Jewish weakness. Jews were regularly faced with specific and everyday evidence of their powerlessness vis-a-vis their potent Christian neighbors. Moreover, by the middle of the thirteenth century, portions of medieval western Christendom had committed themselves to aggressive missionary efforts; by the end of that century, this proselytizing impulse had spread throughout the length and breadth of medieval western Christendom.[14] The new missionary zeal was in significant measure related to the crusading ardor noted earlier. For many, the aggression of crusading was meant to be supplemented by a spiritual engagement with the non-Christian world; indeed, for some, military aggression was to

---

13. I have studied late twelfth- and thirteenth-century Jewish perceptions of this Christian spiritual pressure and lines of response in *Fashioning Jewish Identity in Medieval Western Christendom* (Cambridge: Cambridge University Press, 2009).

14. For the onset of this missionary effort, see Robert Chazan, *Daggers of Faith: Thirteenth-Century Christian Missionizing and the Jewish Response* (Berkeley: University of California Press, 1989).

be replaced by spiritual confrontation.[15] In any case, the Jews of medieval western Christendom were regularly faced with aggressive proselytizing. Forced sermons, forced disputations, and new lines of argumentation all developed during the thirteenth century, much exacerbating the inherent religious threat to the small but growing Jewish minority of medieval western Christendom.

Jews, as a relatively powerless community, could not impose counter-legislation that would affect the Christian majority. Within their own communities, however, Jews did establish many of the same barriers instituted by the Christian majority. Measures to minimize social contact between Christians and Jews were regularly decreed by the rabbinic leadership. The hope, once again, was to insulate—in this case to insulate susceptible Jews against Christian harm.[16]

For Jews—like their Christian counterparts—it was yet more important to erect intellectual and spiritual defenses. While the pre-twelfth-century legacy of Jewish anti-Christian polemics was sparse indeed and included nothing written in western Christendom, from the 1160s to the 1260s these leaders were clustered across southern France and northern Spain, the area in which Christian aggressiveness first manifested itself.[17] By the end of the thirteenth century, Jewish anti-Christian polemics began to emerge elsewhere as well—in Italy, Germany and northern France.

The most traditional Christian thrust that had to be identified and blunted involved recourse to the Hebrew Bible. From its inception, Christianity had insisted that the Hebrew Bible foretold in detail the coming of Jesus as Messiah. This line of argumentation was enhanced and embellished all through late antiquity and the Middle Ages. The European Jewish polemicists engaged this line of Christian argumentation fully, presenting Christian claims and offering detailed rebuttal. Much of the advance in biblical exegesis of the Middle Ages—for example, a more scientific approach to language and heightened emphasis on

---

15. On this relationship, see Benjamin Z. Kedar, *Crusade and Mission: European Approaches toward the Muslims* (Princeton: Princeton University Press, 1984).

16. See Jacob Katz, *Exclusiveness and Tolerance: Jewish-Gentile Relations in Medieval and Modern Times* (Oxford: Oxford University Press, 1981), chapter 4.

17. I have studied this first wave of Jewish polemical writings in *Fashioning Jewish Identity in Medieval Western Christendom*.

contextual reading—makes its way into both the Christian exegesis and the Jewish counter-exegesis.[18]

In many ways, the line of Christian argumentation most threatening to Jews involved the appeal to current realities—the rapidly expanding power and achievement of western Christendom and the dolorous circumstances of its Jews. Jewish polemicists portray their Christian opponents as regularly citing this contrast and drawing from it the traditional Christian conclusion of divine rejection of the Jews, meaning of course the utter hopelessness of the Jewish circumstances. Considerable Jewish effort and ingenuity were invested in combating this potent line of Christian argumentation. Jewish authors appealed regularly to biblical assurances of redemption, which they argued could only be understood as referring to the Jewish people. At the same time, these Jewish polemicists lashed out at Christianity, asserting that the biblical assurances of redemption—which Christians saw as references to themselves—were in fact not fulfilled by Jesus in his lifetime or by the faith he founded over the ages.[19]

During the twelfth century, Christian intellectuals were much involved in the examination of Christian doctrine in the light of the new science and philosophy that were making their way into western Christendom. In this arena, the Jewish polemicists did very little defending, but in fact proceeded to attack Christian doctrine as profoundly irrational. The Christian teaching the Jews attacked most regularly was the Incarnation, which they saw as intellectually indefensible and in fact demeaning to the deity. Jewish assault on the doctrine of Incarnation—and to a lesser extent on the doctrine of the Trinity—was intended to show that the entire Christian religious challenge was fatally flawed by the majority faith's essential irrationality.[20]

Jewish polemicists further introduced into the intellectual and spiritual fray the element of moral achievement. They argued that a religion must be judged in terms of both the rationality of its teachings and the moral achievement of its adherents. This led to a contrastive portrait of alleged Christian failings in the realm of morality and purported Jewish

---

18. See ibid., chapters 6–7.

19. See ibid., chapters 8–10.

20. See Daniel J. Lasker, *Jewish Philosophical Polemics against Christianity in the Middle Ages* (New York: Ktav Publishing, 1977), and Chazan, *Fashioning Jewish Identity in Medieval Western Christendom*, chapters 11–12.

successes. Items singled out for this contrast included the bellicosity of medieval Christian society (this was, after all, the period of crusading and of intense internal warfare all across Europe) as contrasted with the peacefulness of the Jewish community, and alleged sexual lapses throughout Christian society (including prominent charges of such lapses among the Christian clergy) is contrasted with the purportedly high level of sexual restraint and purity within the Jewish world.[21]

Beyond the specifics of all this argumentation, the Jewish polemicists were in fact creating a larger contrast, between a powerful but irrational and immoral Christian majority and a weak but rational and moral Jewish minority. The Jewish authors hoped to persuade their followers that the choice between these two alternatives was quite obvious. Jews had of course to choose to remain within their weak but intellectually sensible and morally elevated minority community. Scripture throughout had portrayed great powers—Egypt, Assyria, Babylonia, Persia, for example—that were flawed and essentially meaningless from a divine perspective. For the Jewish polemicists attempting to inoculate their co-religionists against the blandishments of a powerful medieval Christian society, that society was simply one more in the sequence of theologically meaningless foes that God had created over the ages. In the same way as Christian thinkers defined Christianity and its superiority through a contrast with Judaism and the Jews, Jewish thinkers defined Judaism through a tendentious contrast with Christianity and Christian society.[22]

◆ ◆ ◆ ◆ ◆

All of the foregoing makes it clear that the Middle Ages did in fact constitute a point of genuine deterioration in Christian-Jewish relations, with each side intensifying negative imagery of the other. Especially when viewed from the perspective of the long and important history of Christian views of Judaism and the Jews, the Middle Ages deepened negative imagery and laid the groundwork for much modern anti-Jewish thinking. Yet, as I urged at the outset, Christians and Jews living during the Middle Ages were caught up in everyday concerns and were unlikely

---

21. Ibid., chapter 14.

22. Ibid., chapter 16. Note that the Christian critique of Jewish society, as delineated by Sapir Abulafia, and the Jewish critique of Christian society just now noted, adopt the same criteria for religious achievement, while coming to diametrically opposed conclusions as to who in fact achieved these virtues.

to focus on the long history of Christian anti-Jewish views and their intensification. In this regard, the most important fact to note is that despite the evidence of profound anti-Jewish thinking and its carry-over into steady antipathy and occasional violence, Jews—who had chosen to make their way in increasing numbers into medieval western Christendom from the twelfth century on—did not by and large choose to leave the Christian sphere. To be sure, the Jews of medieval western Christendom suffered a series of expulsions—most notably from England in 1290, from France in 1306 and periodically during the four-teenth century, and from Spain in 1492. Yet overall those Jews expelled from their homelands elected to remain within the orbit of western Christendom, generally tending to move into lagging areas where eco-nomic opportunities still beckoned and where governments were still inclined to offer protection.[23] The evidence of Jewish desire to remain within the Christian sphere and the corresponding reality that Jewish population within medieval western Christendom continued to grow as a percentage of world Jewish population all through the Middle Ages, together suggest that the realities of Jewish living were far more complex that accelerating deterioration of imagery, enhanced popular antipathy, and occasional outbreaks of violence might at first blush suggest.

While much of the opposition described from both the Christian and Jewish sides was deeply harmful to Christian imagery of Judaism and Jewish imagery of Christianity, opposition is not entirely a negative element in human experience; opposition often provides a useful stimu-lus to creativity. It has often been suggested that Jewish criticism of Christianity played a constructive role in the development of medieval Christian thinking. To cite a prominent example, one of the milestones in the twelfth-century maturation of Christian thinking was the lifetime effort of Anselm of Canterbury to clarify and rationalize Christian doc-trine. Anselm was one of the giants of medieval Christian thought, and his masterpiece—*Cur Deus Homo (Why God Became Man)*—was a land-mark achievement. In this work, a student named Boso brings insistently before his distinguished teacher Anselm the objections of non-believers to the central Christian belief in Incarnation. The great English student of Anselm's life and thought, R. W. Southern, has argued that one of the

---

23. See again Chazan, "Then and Now: Jewish Life at the End of the First and Second Christian Millennium."

two major goads to Anselm's creative endeavor in the *Cur Deus Homo* was the challenge mounted by the Jews in twelfth-century Europe. The student Boso was in fact paraphrasing key Jewish objections to the doctrine of the Incarnation.[24] While medieval Christians may not have welcomed such Jewish criticisms, indeed may have resented them deeply, as moderns we have the right to note that Jewish criticisms in fact stimulated Christian creativity.

Much the same conclusion can be offered with regard to the impact of the Christian challenge on medieval Jewish thinking. The Christian challenge was—as we have seen—wide-ranging and intense. It was surely feared and resented by the Jews. Yet this Christian pressure fostered much creative Jewish thinking. Jewish biblical exegesis was improved, as it strained to rebut Christian claims; the philosophic foundations of Jewish faith were clarified in the face of Christian pressures; overall assessment of the nature of the religious enterprise was enhanced by the competition of Christian thinking and living. Again, both Christians and Jews by no means welcomed the pressures applied by the rival faith, but we can suggest that these pressures often had a positive outcome.

In numerous instances, there was more than simply the stimulus of challenge; there was active cooperation as well. The pioneering work of Beryl Smalley has laid bare the extent to which advances in medieval Christian biblical exegesis were rooted in cooperation between Christian scholars and their Jewish neighbors. This cooperation was sometimes carried out through Christian reading of Jewish writings; more often, it was actual face-to-face cooperation, as Christian scholars tapped the Hebrew knowledge of their Jewish peers. Smalley has shown that medieval Christian exegetes such as Andrew of Saint Victor and Herbert of Bosham were profoundly stimulated by their contacts with medieval Jewish exegetes and exegesis; she attributes much of the advance in medieval Christian biblical exegesis to these creative contacts.[25]

The same kind of cooperation is occasionally manifest on the Jewish side as well. Reference has been made to the emergence of Jewish anti-Christian polemical literature from the middle years of the twelfth century on. One of the very earliest Jewish polemical works is a well-organized

---

24. R. W. Southern, *Saint Anselm: A Portrait in a Landscape* (Cambridge: Cambridge University Press, 1990), 198–202.

25. Beryl Smalley, *The Study of the Bible in the Middle Ages* (3rd. ed.; Oxford: Basil Blackwell, 1983), chapter 4.

manual entitled *Milhamot ha-Shem (The Wars of the Lord)*, composed by an otherwise unknown Jew named Jacob ben Reuben. In his introduction, Jacob lays out the unusual circumstances that gave rise to his opus. He describes his circumstances in the following terms: "I shall explain in the light of what happened to me while I was in exile in Huesca. It was my fate to dwell there among gentiles. There, where I lived, a certain Christian took a liking to me. [He was] one of the leading citizens of the town and one of the learned of the generation. He was a priest expert in logic and sophisticated in esoteric wisdom."[26] Jacob proceeds to indicate that his priestly mentor eventually challenged him religiously, arguing that the contrasting status of Christians and Jews should surely serve as grounds for Jacob's rethinking his religious commitments. Beyond the stimulus afforded by the Christian challenge, there is in *Milhamot ha-Shem* evidence of an erudite Christian and an eager Jew learning together in amity, with the latter's creative understanding much enhanced by the contact.

Indeed, here and there the extant sources preserve unmistakable evidence of Christians and Jews forming close personal ties, negative imageries from both sides notwithstanding. Let us begin with Christian testimonies. Joseph Shatzmiller has examined in great detail a fascinating court case from early fourteenth-century Marseilles.[27] A Marseilles Jewish moneylender, Bondavid of Draguignan, was accused by a Christian burgher of Marseilles, Laurentius Girardi, of twice seeking restitution of a loan of sixty shillings. The court records still extant show an impressive set of Christian burghers testifying to the good character of Bondavid. These character references include many specific tales of Bondavid's decencies to Christian borrowers and are freely provided by Christian townspeople, ranging from the top to bottom of the social scale. These specific statements are capped by a number of broad character assessments. A clergyman, Guillelmus Gasqueti, testified that Bondavid was considered the most righteous Jew in Marseilles. Beyond that, he attested to the following: "Actually [Bondavid is] more righteous than anyone he ever met in his life. He [Guillelmus] does not believe that there is [one] more righteous than he [Bondavid] in the whole world.

---

26. Jacob ben Reuben, *Milhamot ha-Shem*, ed. Judah Rosenthal (Jerusalem: Mossad ha-Rav Kook, 1963), 4–5.

27. Joseph Shatzmiller, *Shylock Reconsidered: Jews, Money Lending, and Medieval Society* (Berkeley: University of California Press, 1990).

For, if one may say so, he [Guillelmus] never met or saw a Christian more righteous than he [Bondavid].[28] Reflected here are two levels of amity. In the first place, Bondavid the Jew is repeatedly portrayed as extending his benevolence to Christian neighbors. Secondly, these Christian neighbors are lavish in their recognition of the Jew's largesse. While the official literatures of the two faith communities rarely provide insight into such everyday human connections and feelings, they nonetheless obviously existed.

There is occasional reflection of such amity in Jewish sources as well. Here let me cite a few examples, beginning with a curious episode that took place in tenth-century LeMans in western France. The episode revolves around a scurrilous former Jew, determined to bring harm upon his one-time co-religionists. Locked in some kind of business competition with a LeMans Jew, the rogue hired assassins from nearby Blois to kill the Jew, and they did. Our Jewish source portrays the Christian townsmen of LeMans rushing to the aid of the stricken Jew. Despite the evidence—throughout this brief Jewish source—of anti-Jewish sentiment exploited and manipulated by the villain, the everyday folk treated the murdered Jew with kindness and concern.[29]

As noted already, the call to the crusade aroused some of the popular bands to expand the message of crusading in unanticipated directions. We have cited the slogan that justified—indeed demanded—preliminary violence against the Jews prior to departing for the assault upon the Muslims. Jews in such Rhineland communities as Speyer, Worms, Mainz and Cologne were taken unawares by the crusading violence. They essayed a number of uncertain steps to save themselves and their families. The most common was to seek refuge with the powerful authorities of their towns—the bishops and their fortified palaces. At the same time, others placed their trust in friendly Christian neighbors. In Worms, for example, the Jewish community seems to have divided itself up, with half retreating to the bishop's palace and half to the homes of Christian burghers. Eventually, both groups were attacked and murdered, with those who had elected to flee to burgher homes the more readily vulnerable. On the other hand, when the Jews of Cologne fled incipient violence by turning to Christian neighbors, the ploy was successful.

---

28. Ibid., 118.
29. See Robert Chazam, *Church, State, and Jew in the Middle Ages*, 295–300.

The Christians themselves who befriended their Jewish neighbors courted serious danger in these violent circumstances. The earliest of the Hebrew narratives preserves a striking story of the entrance of a crusading band into the town of Mainz, led by a woman and her allegedly wonder-working goose. Inspired by the woman and the goose, "the crusaders and burghers gathered against us, saying to us: 'Where is your source of trust? How will you be saved? Behold the wonders that the Crucified does for us!' Then all of them came with swords and spears to destroy us. Some of the burghers came and would not allow them to do so."[30] Note that, on the one hand, the aroused crusaders were joined by Mainz burghers who were ready to participate in the anti-Jewish violence. At the same time, it was other Mainz burghers who stepped in to protect the endangered Jews.

A particularly striking incident—also involving the Jews of Mainz—is recorded by a later Hebrew narrative. On May 27, 1096, the crusading force of Emicho of Flonheim entered the town of Mainz and quickly assaulted the Jewish community that had been sequestered in the palace of the archbishop. The destruction of this enclave and its Jews was nearly total. Only a small group of Jewish warriors, under the leadership of Kalonymous ben Meshullam, survived the destruction. This warrior group had hidden out in the basement of the palace. After nightfall, an emissary of the archbishop, who had himself fled across the river to the village of Rudesheim, approached Kalonymous with an offer to save him and his followers. The surviving Jews were ferried across the Rhine River. "The archbishop was exceedingly happy that R. Kalonymous was still alive, and intended to save him and the men who were with him."[31] In the event, the archbishop did not succeed in saving these Jews. Nonetheless, the Jewish chronicler—filled with hatred for the crusaders and the religion in whose name the crusaders had set forth—indicates nonetheless the genuine affection between the archbishop of Mainz and a leading Jew of his town.

While evidence of Christian-Jewish cooperation and Christian-Jewish amity is impressive, perhaps the most striking index of genuine Christian-Jewish interaction is the extent to which the two competing faiths often mirrored one another in important ways. We have just now

---

30. Chazan, *European Jewry and the First Crusade*, 233.
31. Ibid., 269.

cited the fierce mutual opposition engendered by crusading enthusiasm. Over-zealous crusaders redefined their enterprise as beginning with anti-Jewish violence. The Jews of the affected Rhineland town suffered deeply at the hands of over-zealous crusaders. Beyond suffering, these Jews developed for themselves a counter-crusade ideology every bit as intense as that of the crusaders. The exhilaration manifest in crusading ranks was mirrored among the Jews as well, with ferocious religious fervor moving these Jews to extreme acts of self-sacrifice. Parallel intensity and parallel symbolism are manifest.[32]

To cite but one example, the centrality of Jerusalem to the crusading enterprise is well known. Far less well known is the extent to which the Jews of 1096 were motivated in parallel fashion by imagery of Jerusalem. The Jews of the Rhineland saw themselves and were portrayed by their chroniclers as recreating the Jerusalem Temple through their acts of self-sacrifice. In effect, these Jews argued that the march of crusader armies eastward to Jerusalem was of merely temporal significance; the truly impressive pilgrimage to Jerusalem was made by religious giants who actually stayed in place, that is to say by the Jews of the Rhineland ready and willing to take their own lives and the lives of their wives and families out of devotion to their faith and their God. The genuine religious heroes of the First Crusade—in this Jewish view—were the Jewish victims of crusader aggression, building as it were a spiritual Jerusalem along the banks of the Rhine River. There is in this remarkable congruity between Christian and Jewish views of religious commitment and heroism.

We have earlier noted the ways in which Christians and Jews defined themselves through contrast with one another. For Christians, Jews were irrational in their understanding of God, unreasonable in their grasp of Scripture, and mired in the bodily; for Jews, Christians were irrational in their understanding of God, unreasonable in their grasp of Scripture, and mired in the bodily. While the conclusions are diametrically opposed, the two communities are in remarkable agreement as to what constitutes exemplary religious faith and behavior. The criteria were congruent; the conclusions diverged.[33]

---

32. For analysis of some of these parallels, see ibid., chapter 5.

33. Recall the Sapir Abulafia, *Christians and Jews in the Twelfth-Century Renaissance,* and Chazan, *Fashioning Jewish Identity in Medieval Western Christendom.*

◆ ◆ ◆ ◆ ◆

The transplanting of Jews from their earlier Muslim milieu to the lands of western Christendom had fateful consequences. Jewish history became bound up with a Christian environment; Christian history was henceforth marked with the complex issue of the Jewish minority. To a significant extent, the story of subsequent Christian-Jewish relations is tragic, marred by animosity and violence. The hope has only been partially realized that the new order of modernity, with its removal of religion from its heretofore decisive place in societal organization, would minimize the significance of Christian-Jewish tensions and create a more cooperative environment. The tale, however, is far more complex than simply tragedy. Along with tensions, animosities, and violence have come creative challenge, cooperative endeavor, amity, and a genuine level of congruence in religious thinking. This complex story is read and will continue to be read from a variety of perspectives, some more negative and some more positive. It is a tale that requires ongoing re-telling and re-evaluation, in an effort to minimize for the future the negative legacy and augment for the future the positive.

9 How Jewish and Christian Mystics Read the Bible

Bernard McGinn
March 3, 2003

The Eighth Jerusalem Lecture was delivered in Chicago on March 3, 2003, by Dr. Bernard McGinn, the Naomi Shenstone Donnelley Professor of Historical Theology and of the History of Christianity at the University of Chicago Divinity School.

Dr. McGinn has written extensively in the areas of the history of apocalyptic thought and most recently, in the areas of spirituality and mysticism. His current long-range project is a five-volume history of Christian mysticism in the West under the general title The Presence of God, three volumes of which have appeared: The Origins of Mysticism; The Growth of Mysticism; and The Flowering of Mysticism.

THE great Jewish thinker, Alexander Altmann, whom I am honored to count among my teachers, once wrote the following:

> For the philosopher, God is; for the mystic, God lives. Even where, for the philosopher, the notion of God stands at the center of his thinking, God is merely an object of thought; he is not the actively felt, suffered, encountering experience of man. Only mysticism is ultimately and radically serious about positing God as actual. Only mysticism, therefore, is radically serious about the word of God. The world of the Bible lies clear and finished and concise before the gaze of the mystic. But all that is finished and dead. Hence the finished state of the Bible, which is the living word of God, must reveal itself to be mere appearance. The important thing is to eavesdrop on the living grounds of the unmoving surface and to penetrate to the

secret life of revelation. This is the achievement of mystic contemplation, the demand for which arises naturally out of the idea of revelation itself.[1]

The remarks that follow may be considered a gloss on Altmann's observation.

I wish to consider two themes. The first, briefly touched upon is the nature of mysticism, which I see as the ongoing search for an experience, consciousness, or awareness of the presence of the living God—the God who makes a difference not only in what we think, but also in how we struggle to live.[2] The second, treated in more detail, is the fact that for Jews and Christians this search for the living God is inherently biblical. It is biblical not insofar as the seeker uses the Bible as a document of the past or as a proof text for some belief or practice, though the Bible certainly tells us the history of salvation and teaches the fundamentals of belief and action. But the mystical use of the Bible is more than that. It is a form of what Moshe Idel has called "strong reading,"[3] an attempt not just to live according to the biblical message, but rather to re-write the Bible in the heart, to find in the depths of the text a direct encounter with God's presence.[4]

Mysticism is often seen as a phenomenon belonging to the arena of the paranormal, an affair of autobiographical accounts of visions of God, raptures, experiences of union, and the like. There are, to be sure, many such accounts, more in the Christian tradition than in the Jewish. But the "book of experience," as Bernard of Clairvaux and other Christian mystics called it, was secondary to the book of God's word, which served not only as the measure or norm for determining the validity of mystical claims, but more importantly as the inexhaustible living source from which the book of experience drew its sustenance. Down to the end of the twelfth century, Christian mysticism was largely exegetical in a direct way—that is—it found expression in the work of reading, commenting on, and preaching the biblical text. During the past eight centuries the

---

1. Alexander Altmann, "Jewish Mysticism," *The Meaning of Jewish Existence, Theological Essays 1930-1939,* ed. Alfred L. Ivry (Hanover: Brandeis University Press, 1991), 72.

2. For more on the notion of mysticism employed here, see Bernard McGinn, *The Foundations of Mysticism: Origen to the Fifth Century* (New York: Crossroad, 1991), xiii-xx.

3. Moshe Idel, *Absorbing Perfections, Kabbalah and Interpretation* (New Haven: Yale University Press, 2002), 17–19.

4. The need to write the biblical covenant on the heart, of course, is already found in the Bible itself, notably Jer 31:33–34.

relationship between the scriptural book and the book of experience in Christianity has been more complex and varied. At times the book of experience has seemed almost to overwhelm the biblical book, especially among some women mystics. Nevertheless, the guiding principle for most Christian mystics has remained the same: personal experience is not the norm; it is what is made the norm by scripture.

In Jewish mysticism, at least since the rise of Kabbalah in the twelfth and thirteenth centuries, the bond between text and mystical practice and states of consciousness is even stronger. Numerous studies by scholars like Gershom Scholem, Moshe Idel, Michael Fishbane, Elliot Wolfson, and others have investigated the exegetical character of Jewish mysticism.[5] Borrowing terminology from Idel, we can say that Christian and Jewish mysticism are both bibliocentric, but that Jewish mysticism is more linguocentric and textcentric in the sense that the Hebrew text and written form of the Torah itself is conceived of as divine.[6] "The Torah is no other than the Holy One, blessed be He," as the *Zohar* puts it.[7] For the Christian mystic the biblical text remains an instrument for attaining God, while in any types of Jewish mysticism Torah, as the Body of Christ, is the very goal itself. In both traditions, however, we should remember that it is the contextualized Bible, by which I mean the Bible as it is read and used in the community, that serves not only to confirm the validity of mystical consciousness, but also to generate and mediate it.

When we begin to think about how Jewish and Christian mystics found transformation in the act of interpreting the inner message of the

---

5. Gershom Scholem, "The Meaning of the Torah in Jewish Mysticism," in *On Kabbalah and Its Symbolism* (New York: Schocken, 1996), 32–86; Moshe Idel, *Absorbing Perfections*; Michael Fishbane, "The Book of Zohar and Exegetical Spirituality," in *Mysticism and Sacred Scripture*, ed. Steven A. Katz (New York: Oxford University Press, 2000), 87–117; Elliot Wolfson, "Beautiful Maiden Without Eyes: *Peshat* and *Sod* in Zohariric Hermeneutics," *The Midrashic Imagination in Jewish Exegesis, Thought, and History*, ed. Michael Fishbane (Albany: SUNY, 1993), 155–203. For a general introduction to medieval Jewish exegesis, see Frank Talmadge, "Apples of Gold: The Inner Meaning of Sacred Texts in Medieval Judaism," *Jewish Spirituality from the Bible through the Middle Ages*, ed. Arthur Gerrn (New York: Crossroad, 1986), 313–55. An overview of scholarship on the history of Jewish exegesis during the past century can be found in Michael Fishbane, "Bible Interpretation," *The Oxford Handbook of Jewish Studies*, ed. Martin Goodman et al. (New York: Oxford University Press, 2002), 680-704.

6. Idel, *Absorbing Perfections*, 416–22.

7. *Zohar* 2:60a, as cited in Idel, 426. Seeing the Torah as itself divine, the body of God, is intimately tied to the Rabbinic description of the Torah as written with letters of black fire on white fire (i.e., the Divine Body); see the midrash '*Aseret ha-Dibberot*. For a treatment of the rabbinic texts and the subsequent history of the theme, see Idel, chap. 2.

Bible, we are immediately confronted with a serious problem that is also, perhaps, an opportunity. The problem is that Jews and Christians read the Bible in fundamentally opposed ways, at least on the level of doctrine, or when they are staking out their respective positions. As Luke Timothy Johnson has recently reminded us, Christians read what they call the Old Testament in the light of the New Testament and their belief in the resurrected Jesus as Messiah, while Jews read Tanakh in the conviction that the Messiah is still to come. For Jews, Jesus is a failed Messiah because he did not "make things better for the Jews."[8] Christian interpretation is founded on a special form of realized messianism according to the pattern that Oscar Cullmann referred to as "already but not yet," that is, that the messianic age has already begun with Christ's resurrection, but that it will not reach its fulfillment until the Second Coming.[9] While hope for the coming messiah has remained an important element in the Judaism of the past two millennia, not least among Jewish mystics,[10] Jewish reading of Tanakh centers more on using the text for the present, that is, for sustaining and enriching the life of the community and its common observances and practices.

From the doctrinal perspective, the orthodox understanding of Christianity has usually been taken to imply supercessionism, that is, the belief that after the coming of Jesus, Judaism is no longer a valid form of worship of God. Paul of Tarsus has been most often seen as the foremost spokesman of supercessionism, though recent Pauline research has begun to question this view.[11] From the second century C.E. onward, Christians also created a doctrine that might be called exegetical, or hermeneutical, supercessionism designed to denigrate Jewish reading of Tanakh as something hopelessly old-fashioned because of its rejection of Jesus and its alleged literalism. Origen, the great third-century biblical interpreter, in a famous passage in his handbook of exegesis in book four of *On First Principles,* lists three groups of incorrect readers, beginning with "the Jews . . . because they suppose that the prophecies that

---

8. Luke Timothy Johnson, "Christians and Jews: Starting Over. Why Real Dialogue Has Just Begun," *Commonweal* CXXX.2 (January 31, 2003), 15–19.

9. Oscar Cullmann, *Christ and Time. The Primitive Christian Conception of Time and History* (London: SCM, 1962), 14–48.

10. See Moshe Idel, *Messianic Mystics* (New Haven: Yale University Press, 1998).

11. See e.g., John G. Gager, *Reinventing Paul* (New York: Oxford University Press, 2000).

relate to Christ must be understood literally."[12] What followed was centuries of accusations of "judaizing" directed not only against Jews, but also against Christians whose forms of exegesis were considered suspect for a variety of reasons.

Now anyone who has read much Jewish exegesis, be it rabbinic or mystical, will know that it is far from literal in many particulars. This is especially true of the use of the Bible by Jewish mystics from the thirteenth century on. It is only when we allow Christianity to define Judaism that Jewish exegesis appears to be literal. But this is what doctrine does—it stakes out a position and in doing so not only defines itself, but is often tempted to define the other in light of the self. The purpose of my reflection is not to deny the role of belief and doctrine in establishing religious identity; rather, it is to remind us that defining the other in the light of the self often results in misconstrual and misunderstanding.

This is where the study of mystical exegesis provides us with an opportunity. Granted that Jewish and Christian mystics employed the study of the Bible to deepen and fortify their doctrinal identity within their respective traditions, the ways in which they did so through uncovering the hidden presence of God in the text show remarkable similarities, analogies, and perhaps even some examples of conscious borrowings. These analogies in the interpretive process challenge the standard Christian misconstrual of Jewish exegesis as literal and therefore can help us to remove some of the misunderstandings that have plagued Christian views of Judaism.

From my own perspective as a scholar of the history of Christianity, I find the exercise of comparative mystical exegesis one useful tool in the ongoing task of overcoming the supercessionism of much of the Christian past. Such a move, I believe, is also in line with the position expressed in the document "The Jewish People and Their Sacred Scriptures in the Christian Bible" issued by the Pontifical Biblical Commission in 2001, which states:

> Christians can and ought to admit that the Jewish reading of the Bible is a possible one, in continuity with the Jewish Sacred Scriptures from the

---

12. Origen, *De Principiis* 4.2.1. For a translation of Book Four, see *Origen: On First Principles*, translated and annotated by G. W. Butterworth (New York: Harper Torchbooks, 1968). It is interesting to note that some medieval Jewish mystical interpreters accused Christians of excessive literalism. See Elliot Wolfson, "Beautiful Maiden without Eyes," 169.

Second Temple period, a reading analogous to the Christian reading which developed in parallel fashion. Both readings are bound up with the vision of their respective faiths, of which the readings are a result and expression. Consequently, both are irreducible."[13]

This is irreducible, certainly; but perhaps also comparable and mutually illuminating.

In a brief essay I can do no more than to provide a few comparative examples of the ways in which Jewish and Christian mystics read the Bible. I will start with Origen, the teacher who set the main lines for so much Christian hermeneutics, including its mystical goal. Though Origen is a clear example of hermeneutical supercessionism, paradoxically, no early Church writer learned more from the Jews about reading the Bible.[14] If Christ is the key for understanding the Bible according to Origen (*De Prin.* 4.1.1), the goal of this reading is, as he put it, "to portray the meaning of the sacred writing in a threefold way upon one's own soul" (4.2.4). For Origen, the human person consists of three aspects: flesh, soul (i.e., the principle of life), and spirit, that aspect in us that is open to God. Since scripture is given for our salvation, it too must have three aspects or levels. We read the letters to make out the grammatical sense of the words and to determine the narrative, whether actual history or not. We then ask what the words mean, that is, what they teach us in terms of belief and virtuous action. But the goal is not just to believe and to be virtuous; the aim of interpretation is to begin to live the mysteries about the nature of God and the return of fallen humanity to God revealed by the Logos, the Word of God within the text. The isomorphism, or formal equivalence, between the text of the Bible and the text of the human person is a dynamic one: the harmonization of the three components of humanity and their anagogy, or movement up to God, takes place through the act of discerning the mystical message hidden within the letter. The believer has to come to live within the text to find these depths. The goal of interpretation is ascension to God, a process Origen described as wishing "to gallop through the vast spaces of mystic and spiritual understanding" (*Commentary on Romans* 7.11).

---

13. Quoted in Donald Senior, "Rome Has Spoken. A New Catholic Approach to Judaism," *Commonweal* CXXX, 21.

14. See Nicholas de Lange, *Origen and the Jews* (Cambridge: Cambridge University Press, 1976).

The highest level of this process is the kind of knowledge, or science, the Origen called "epoptics" in the prologue to his *Commentary on the Song of Songs*.[15] This is the "inspective discipline" which "instills love and desire of celestial things under the image of the Bride and Groom [of the Song of Songs], teaching how we come to fellowship with God through paths of love and charity." Such knowledge of "dogmatic and mystical matters" allows the soul "to arise to the contemplation of divinity with pure spiritual love." It is the insight that belonged to Jacob who became Israel (i.e., "he who sees God"); a unitive knowing that in one place Origen calls a *ta mystika,* that is, "mystics" (*Commentary on Lamentations* frg. 14).

In speaking of the inner meaning of the Bible as mystical, Origen was not original. For several generations before him, Christians had been using the Greek adjective *mystikos,* or hidden, to describe the dynamic inner source of Christian living. The word was most often used in reference to the hidden meanings of the Bible, but it was also employed in referring to the inner dimension, or mystical aspects, of rituals such as baptism, or of the stages leading to the vision of God *(theoria theou).*[16] Origen himself spoke of "mystical and ineffable contemplation" (*Commentary on John* 13:24). It was not until two and a half centuries after Origen that the mysterious writer who called himself Dionysius coined the term *theologia mystike* to describe this form of knowing and loving, but the reality was already there in the Alexandrian teacher.

One of the essential characteristics of Origen's form of mystical exegesis is the way it sees the biblical narrative as revealing the itinerary of the soul, and even of the classes of souls, in the descent from the ascent back to God. Toward the end of the book four of *First Principles,* he lays down the general rule that whenever the prophets speak about Judaea or Jerusalem they are using "mystical narratives" *(mysticis quibusdam narrationibus)* that refer to Israel according to the Spirit, that is, "the race of those who are Jews inwardly, the soul having acquired this nobility of race in virtue of certain unspeakable words" (*De prin.* 4.3.7–8). This form of "mystical anagogy" (4.3.6) undergirds the Alexandrian's

---

15. For a translation, see *Origen, The Song of Songs. Commentary and Homilies,* translated and annotated by R. P. Lawson (Westminster, MD: Newman Press, 1957), 21–57.

16. E.g., Clement of Alexandria, *Stromateis* 7.10.57, For a survey of early Christian use of *mystikos,* see Louis Bouyer, "Mysticism/ An Essay on the History of the Word," *Understanding Mysticism,* ed. Richard Woods, OP, (Garden City: Image Books, 1980), 42–55.

reading of Numbers 33, where he interprets the forty-two stations of the departure of the children of Israel from Egypt as both the forty-two generations of the ancestors of Christ and the forty-two stages by which the Christian ascends to God, by virtuous practice in this life and by continued stages of ascent to heaven after death. "Let us begin to ascend through the stages by which Christ descended," he announces. The interpretation is complex, even cumbersome at times, but the goal is clear. The final stage, Moab by the Jordan (Num. 33:48), signifies that our goal is to arrive at the river of God, "so that we may be made neighbors of the flowing Wisdom and may be watered by the waves of divine knowledge, so that purified by them all we may be made worthy to enter the Promised Land."[17]

This understanding of the biblical text as expressing an itinerary of the soul, a succession of states on a journey, had far-reaching repercussions in Christian mystical exegesis. As already noted, Origen spoke of three progressively deeper understandings of the text—literal, moral/psychic, and spiritual—though his exegesis in practice was never so artificial. By about 400 C.E. this threefold progression had increased by one and been enshrined in the famous doctrine of the four senses of scripture, as we find it classically expressed by the monk, John Cassian. In his fourteenth *Conference*, Cassian divides contemplative science, which is nothing else than the study of the Bible, into two main parts: historical interpretation and spiritual insight. Spiritual insight involves three aspects: tropology (i.e., moral practice); allegory (i.e., doctrine); and anagogy (i.e., the spiritual mysteries that lead to heaven). He gives the following example:

> And if we wish to see it, these four modes of representation flow into a unity so that the one Jerusalem can be understood in four different ways, in the historical sense as the city of the Jews, in allegory as the Church of Christ, in anagogy as the heavenly city of God "which is the mother of all" (Gal 4:26), in the tropologial sense as the human soul.[18]

---

17. *Homily XXVII on Numbers* as translated in *Origen. An Exhortation to Martyrdom, etc.* translated by Rowan A. Greer (New York: Paulist Press, 1979), 245–69 (quotation at 268). Michael Fishbane informs me that in some Hasidic texts these forty-two letters of the Divine Name indicate a process of spiritual purification after the slavery of Egypt—a fascinating parallel to Origen.

18. John Cassian, *Conferences* 14.8 as translated in *John Cassian. Conferences,* translated and preface by Colin Luibheid (New York: Paulist Press, 1985), 160. On the role of Jerusalem as a symbol in Kabbalistic exegeis, see Idel, *Absorbing Perfections,* 284–87.

Note that these four senses pertain to one and the same image. In mystical exegesis they are meant to work together as part of a dynamic process of appropriation, though in practice the ways in which this is realized are quite varied.

In his tenth *Conference,* one devoted to prayer, Cassian discusses how the monk should make the psalms his own through a process of inner re-writing. "Instructed by our own experience," we do not learn what the Psalmist is saying by hearsay. "They are not like things confided to our capacity for remembrance but, rather, we bring them to birth in the depths of our hearts as if they were naturally there and part of our being." This practice of praying the psalms culminates in a mystical form of prayer. "This prayer centers on no contemplation of some image or other. It is masked by no attendant sounds or words. It is a fiery outbreak, an indescribable exaltation, and insatiable thrust of the soul."[19] Thus, for Cassian, praying the text of the Bible is meant to lead on to praying in the same Holy Spirit who inspires the Bible.

It is revealing to compare this Christian view of interior reading, or recreating the Bible from within, with a text from an Hasidic mystic writing more than a millennium later. Rabbi Barukh of Medzibezh, the Besht's grandson, proposes the example of the Israelites at Sinai as the model for Torah study. He explains this as follows:

> The principle is that everyone has to first hear it in his heart . . . and afterwards to study what the heart is saying . . . God said "*anokhiy,* and it is incumbent on man to hear in his heart and afterwards in the Torah. They [i.e., the Israelites] have seen what has been heard, namely, they have seen in the Torah what they heard in their heart . . ."[20]

Both the book of the heart, what Bernard of Clairvaux called the book of experience, and the book that is the Bible, are correlative texts for Cassian and Rabbi Barukh.

The implied or expressed itinerary suggested by the stages of mystical interpretation, whether of three or of four senses, was fundamental to many Christian mystics. Let me give just one later example. Bernard of Clairvaux's *Eighty-six Sermons on the Song of Songs* are not structured according to any overarching plan, but follow the meandering of the

---

19. *Conference* 10.11, as in *John Cassian,* 138.
20. R. Barukh of Medzibezh as cited in Idel, *Absorbing Perfections,* 425–26.

conversations of love between the Divine Bridegroom and the ardent Soul-Bride expressed in the Song. Nevertheless, an itinerary of stages of love is always implicitly present, and sometimes breaks through to reveal how progress in deepening understanding of the text is also movement into the inner place where God and human become united in love. In Sermon Twenty-three Bernard uses Song 1:3 ("The King has brought me into his cellars") to lay out a roadmap of three stations of the Bride's interior spiritual progress through the action of the internal senses brought to life through the three levels of reading the Bible.

The cellars of Song 1:3 remind the Cistercian of two other places in the journey of love mentioned in the Song—the garden of Song 5:1 and the bed chamber of Song 3:4. Each of these locations (note that Bernard freely reorganizes the sequence) represents a level of reading that must be made one's own through the book of experience. "Let the garden be the plain and simple historical sense, the cellar the moral sense, the bridal chamber the mystery of visionary contemplation" *(theorica contemplatio)* (SC 23.3)."[21] The details cannot be followed here, but the sermon invites the reader to consider first the garden embracing the literal meaning, that is, the history of salvation set forth in the whole Bible; then to move on to the riches of the Bridegroom's cellars where the Bible teaches about the fundamental monastic virtues of discipline, fraternity and active charity (SC 23, 4–8). Finally, Bernard says that the bed chamber indicates three forms of contemplation of which he does not claim exhaustive knowledge, though he admits, "If I knew nothing, I would say nothing" (SC 23.9).

The notion of an itinerary, both a description of the steps in reading the Bible and a matching journey of the soul, does not appear to have emerged in Jewish mysticism until the last third of the thirteenth century, when we find it in Spain with such mystics as Moses de Leon, Joseph Gikatilla, Isaac bin Latif, and Bahya ben Asher, some of the most important figures in Spanish Kabballah. These mystics created the acronym PaRDeS (i.e., Paradise) to signify a fourfold reading of the Bible. This is how Moses de Leon, one of the main figures connected with the production of the *Zohar,* describes it in his *Book of the Rational Soul,* written about 1290:

---

21. For a translation of the sermon, see Bernard of Clairvaux, *On the Song of Songs II,* translated by Kilian Walsh, OCSO (Kalamazoo: Cistercian Publications, 1976), 25–41.

> Under the title *Pardes* I have written a book about the mystery of the four ways, which the title in itself denotes, insofar as it refers to the four who entered the *pardes*, which is nothing other than *peshat, remez, derashah,* and *sod.* In this book I have commented at length on these matters in con-nection with the mystery of the stories and facts related in the Torah, in order to show that they all refer in a mystical sense to eternal life and that there is nothing in the Torah that is not contained in the mystery of His Name.[22]

According to this paradigm, *peshat* stands for the plain, or literal, meaning; *remez* (literally "hint") refers to allegorical explanation; *derash* is the level of homiletic exposition; and finally sod, or mystery, is the secret symbolic interpretation that is the goal of Kabbalistic exegesis.

Two centuries later the Renaissance sage and Christian Cabalist Giovanni Pico della Mirandola noted the similarity between this schema and the traditional Christian four senses,[23] and much ink has been spilled over whether or not the schema may have been adopted from Christian sources. We will probably never know for sure. What is impor-tant is to note that the use of the PaRDeS paradigm has both a somewhat different content than the Christian four senses, and as Moshe Idel has emphasized a different function from its Christian counterpart.[24] The Kabbalists used the theory of four senses both to express the integration of their new form of mystical literature into the broader Jewish tradition and to stress its superiority, at least for the esoteric circles that were able to grasp it. The various senses indicate the different bodies of literature formative of the Jewish community. The plain sense had already been richly explored by traditional Jewish exegesis such as Rashi. Despite negative comments made by some Kabbalists about the literal sense, on the whole they presuppose it and even employ it in their mystical com-mentaries on the Bible. The same is true for the practical teaching found in the sermonic material of *derash,* long a staple of medieval Jews.

---

22. Cited in Scholem, "The Meaning of Torah in Jewish Mysticism," 59.

23. Giovanni Pico della Mirandola, *Apologia,* cited in Scholem, 62 n. 1.

24. Idel, *Absorbing Perfections,* Appendix I, "The Fourfold Method of Interpretation" (429–37); see also Scholem, "The Meaning of Torah in Jewish Mysticism," 56–63; and A. Van der Heide, "PARDES: Methodological Reflections on the Theory of the Four Senses," *Journal of Jewish Studies* 24 (1983), 147–58. On the difference in content, see Talmage, "Apples of Gold," 319–21. For a contemporary appropriation, see Michael Fishbane, "The Teacher and the Hermeneutical Task: A Reinterpretation of Medieval Exegesis," *The Garments of Torah. Essays in Biblical Hermeneutics* (Bloomington: Indiana University Press, 992), 112–20.

Allegorical interpretation *(remez)* can be identified with the use of allegory in Jewish philosophical readings of the Bible found in the twelfth and thirteenth centuries, such as that of Maimonides. The *sod,* or mystery, is the highest form of reading, the goal toward which the others are directed. Therefore, the fourfold paradigm was used by groups of Kabbalists both conservatively, to affirm their connection with the broad tradition of Judaism, and innovatively, to emphasize their claims to a higher viewpoint. Although they did not feel called upon to engage in all the forms of exegesis themselves, R. Bahya ben Asher's *Commentary on the Pentateuch* shows that they could integrate all four readings in one work.

Moshe Idel characterizes the dominant form of Kabbalistic exegesis, such as we find in the *Zohar,* as "symbolic narrative," which he describes as a "narrative symbolic interpretation . . . where the biblical story was decoded as pointing to another supernal story," that is, an account about the activities and interplay of the *sephirot,* or divine powers, in the heavenly world, one that is meant to be appropriated into the life of the Kabbalist himself.[25] As Michael Fishbane puts it: ". . . the dynamics of the Bible's surface sequence were used to ascend to spiritual wisdom."[26] While this form of symbolic narrative reading has its own rules and a distinctive richness, it is analogous to forms of Christian mystical interpretation based upon itinerary narratives closely linked to the letter of the Bible, similar to those briefly mentioned above.

A good example of Jewish mystical itinerary based on the fourfold reading of PaRDeS can be found in the noted parable of the "Old Man and the Beautiful Maiden" found in the *Zohar.*[27] The account is both a mystical tale describing the activities of the circles of second-century rabbis who are the purported authors of the *Zohar* and a reconstruction and reinterpretation of the Song of Song. The tale opens with Rabbi Yose

---

25. *Absorbing Perfections,* 435, and note 26 on 604. For a more detailed study, see Chapter 10, "The Symbolic Mode in Theosophical-Theurgical Kabbalah" (272–313, especially 296–97).

26. Fishbane, "The Book of Zohar and Exegetical Spirituality," 108.

27. *Zohar* 2:99ab. There is a translation in Daniel Chanan Matt, *Zohar. The Book of Enlightenment* (New York: Paulist Press, 1983), 121–26, with helpful notes on 249–54. Many discussions of the passage exist. See especially Elliot Wolfson, "Beautiful Maiden Without Eyes." It would be interesting to compare this parable with another well-known text from the *Zohar,* Rabbi Simeon's description of the Garments of Torah in 3:152a. For studies, see Talmage, "Apples of Gold," 324–25; and especially Fishbane, "The Garments of Torah—Or, To What May Scripture Be Compared?" *The Garments of Torah,* 33–46.

telling Rabbi Hiyya about an Old Man, a donkey driver, who had pestered him on his trip with riddles, such as: "What is a beautiful maiden who has no eyes and a body concealed and revealed? She comes out in the morning and is hidden all day. She adorns herself with adornments that are not." The two rabbis call in the Old Man to question him, whereupon he is revealed as a sage in disguise. His teaching is richly symbolic and imbued with transcendental erotics based on mystical readings of the Song of Songs.[28] The Blind Maiden is Torah, who conceals and reveals herself in various meanings. The puzzle of her being without eyes may point to the Zoharic emphasis on the role of the exegete as one "full of eyes," that is, a strong reader ready to draw out multiple readings from the divine text that has no eyes because its eyes, or meanings, are infinite and can only be opened by the skilled reader.[29] The hidden lover is the mystic, the Kabbalistic seer enthralled with the revealing-concealing text in an exegetical game of love based on the Song of Songs. This gradual enticement offered by the Blind Maiden is nothing other than an ever-deepening experience of God achieved in and through the biblical text.

Torah takes the initiative "when she reveals herself to a human and beckons him with a hint," a stage which corresponds to the literal sense of the Bible. But the letter, like the teasing maid, wants to lead the seer deeper, inviting him to more profound and more satisfying experiences of her divine self, the *Shekhina*. She beckons him with a hint ("Come on up to my place, honey"), and if he doesn't take the hint, she criticizes his manhood, calling him a fool. These attractions advance the Kabbalistic program by moving the enticed lover to come to converse with Torah from "behind the curtain," that is, *dersaha,* or homiletic interpretation, and then to encounter her "through the veil, words riddled with allegory." (The account here conflates the middle two registers of PaRDes, i.e., homiletics and philosophical allegory, into one.)

Once the devout reader has become more accustomed to Torah, the ever-enticing female, he is ready for the main event. She tells him all her hidden secrets. The text continues: "Now he is a perfect human being, husband of Torah, master of the house. All her secrets she has revealed

---

28. On the use of the Song of Songs in Jewish mysticism, see the introduction by Arthur Green, "The Song of Songs in Early Jewish Mysticism," *Orim* 2 (1987): 48–62.

29. For this suggestion, see Wolfson, "Beautiful Maiden without Eyes," 185–86. Michael Fishbane notes that the norm *"ayin* as eye can also mean color or hue, so that the Maiden without Eyes might point to a pure and unmediated vision of God.

to him, withholding nothing, concealing nothing. At this stage of consummating mystical-erotic knowing, a true *hieros gamos,* or sacred marriage, there is an emphatic insistence on the continuing authority of the taken away. Now the *peshat* of the verse, just as it is! Not even a single letter should be added or deleted." Finally, when the Old Man completes his teaching, the implied subtext of the whole story, the Song of Songs, is explicitly cited, as Rabbi Hiyya quotes a verse from the end of the Song: "Set me as a seal upon your heart, as a seal upon your arm" (Song 8:6), to emphasize the meaning of the entire parable.

This type of mystical exegesis, and other forms of symbolic reading closely bound to the biblical text and its narratives, while not the same as Christian mystical readings of the Song, or of the history of the patriarchs of Genesis, or the life of Moses or Job, are at least broadly comparable. There are other forms of Jewish mystical reading of the Bible, however, that appear more alien to the Christian mystical exegete.

Jewish mystical exegesis, as pointed out above, centers on the sacred character of the text itself—each word in Hebrew, even the very letters that composed the word, have divine meaning. The linguocentric and textcentric character of Jewish mysticism is based upon a belief in an immediate link between the Hebrew language and the divine world. One of the additions to the *Zohar,* the *Zohar Chadash,* expresses it this way: "Those who are engaged in Torah with intention and deliberation . . . do not contemplate the word alone, but rather the supernal place upon which the word depends; for there is not a scriptural word that is not dependent upon another supernal mystery."[30]

To be sure, Christian exegetes used the etymology of Hebrew names, numerology, and sometimes even *gematria* (i.e., calculating the numerical value of words)—procedures all richly developed in Jewish mystical exegesis. But for Christian mystics, with the exception of a few Christian Cabalists, other mystical techniques widely used by Jewish mystics, such as the transposition of letters for theurgical purposes, were so closely tied to intimate knowledge of the Hebrew text and to Jewish traditions that they were a closed book. Hence, Jewish mysticism features bolder forms of decoding the biblical text—not only the narrative elements, but

---

30. *Zohar Chadash* 105c, as translated by Fishbane, "The Book of the Zohar and Exegetical Spirituality," 115, n. 35. On this text, see also Elliot R. Wolfson, *Through a Speculum that Shines. Vision and Imagination in Medieval Jewish Mysticism* (Princeton: Princeton University Press, 1994), 390–91.

even the very words and letters of the text—in order to create new units, both semantic and non-semantic, that are seen as containing transcendent meaning and power to effect mystical transformation.

Such forms of mystical interpretation are found across a broad continuum in Jewish mysticism. They are important in theosophical Kabbalistic texts like the *Zohar*, but are even more significant for mystics like Abraham Abulafia, the thirteenth-century Spanish exponent of Ecstatic Kabbalah. Moshe Idel speaks of Abulafia's mystical reading of the Bible as "text-destroying."[31] In Abulafia's atomizing exegesis, each letter of the text represents a world, so that, in his own words:

> It is incumbent to revolve the entire Torah, which consists in the names of the Holy One, blessed by He, and it is incumbent to innovate new wonders on each and every letter and on each and every word, from time to time. And it is incumbent to inquire into one word and connect it to another, and then to leave the second and look for a third to connect it with the first, and then another, sometimes at their middle, sometimes at their beginning, sometimes at their end, sometimes by their numbers, sometimes by their permutations, until he will exit from all his initial thoughts and will innovate others, better than then, always one after another.[32]

How this innovating reconfiguring of the biblical text worked in practice, and how it became the central mystical exercise for attaining states of ecstatic contact with God, cannot be detailed here. Abulafia is worth mentioning, however, not only because his freedom in deconstructing the biblical text is among the most extreme in Jewish mysticism, but also because he appears to have held that the supernal message contained in the letters of the Bible need not be necessarily tied to the Hebrew language alone, but, due to the presence of the Agent Intellect in all humans, may also be accessible in other languages.[33] The practice of a few Christian mystics provides some corroboration for this.

While the radical deconstruction and reconstruction of the words and letters of the Bible are distinctive to Jewish mysticism, there are a few

---

31Moshe Idel, *Kabbalah. New Perspectives* (New Haven: Yale University Press, 1988), 208.

32. Abraham Abulafia, *Sefer Gan Na'ul*, as translated in Idel, *Absorbing Perfections*, 341. For more on Abulafia's exegesis, see Moshe Idel, *Language, Torah, and Hermeneutics in Abraham Abulafia* (Albany, SUNY, 1989).

33. This, at least, is the suggestion made by Idel on the basis of a text translated and discussed in *Absorbing Perfections*, 343–44.

Christian mystical exegetes who went beyond the standard symbolic readings that generally used the narrative structure of the text to create mystical itineraries. One of the most interesting cases is that of the German Dominican Meister Eckhart, a contemporary of the Castilian Kabbalists who wrote the *Zohar*, as well as of Abulafia. Most of Eckhart's surviving work is in the form of biblical commentary, both the long Latin interpretations he composed on the books of the Old and New Testaments to provide material for preachers and his more than a hundred vernacular sermons on biblical texts based on the readings for the Christian liturgical year. In several places in his Latin works, as well as in at least one vernacular sermon, Eckhart reflects on his interpretive procedure.

Eckhart stands much traditional Christian exegetical theory and practice on its head, and it is interesting to note that he does so partly in dependence on Maimonides, whose notion of parabolic (i.e., allegorical) exegesis for philosophical purposes he cites approvingly.[34] For Eckhart, philosophy, theology, and mystical transformation are all one and the same, and the goal of these seemingly different disciplines is achieved through a form of "excessive" exegesis that he insists conforms to the excess of meaning given in the divine language of the Bible itself. Commenting on John 21:25 (The entire world could not contain the books that would describe everything that Jesus did), he says:

> Such a mode of speaking, that is, excessively, properly belongs to the divine scripture. Everything divine, as such, is immense and not subject to measure. . . The excellence of divine things does not allow them to be offered to us uncovered, but they are hidden beneath sensible figures.[35]

Unlike many Christian mystics, Eckhart avoids laying out a mystical itinerary; for him, mysticism is a new awareness of the identity of God and human in the *grunt,* the deepest inner reality of the soul. This new consciousness is something that can be attained even in an instant. Hence it is not enough merely to break through the shell of the letter of scripture in order to find an inner meaning that can be used to structure some kind of mystical journey. Rather, as he puts it in Sermon 51, "all likeness must be broken through," that is, all images, even divine images,

---

34. For an account of Eckhart's hermeneutics and the relevant secondary literature, see Bernard McGinn, *The Mystical Theology of Meister Eckhart. The Man from Whom God Hid Nothing* (New York: Crossroad-Herder, 2001), 24–29.

35. Meister Eckhart, *Expositio sancti Evangelii secundum Iohannem,* n. 745.

must be destroyed as the exegete pursues his task of annihilating the particularity of created nature. He says:

> I have said before the shell must be broken through and what is inside must come out, for if you want to get at the kernel you must break the shell. And also, if you want to find nature unveiled, all likeness must be broken through, and the further you penetrate, the nearer you will get to the essence. When the soul finds the One, where all is one, there she will remain in the Single One.[36]

When one breaks through all images and likenesses to attain the One beyond images, then the biblical text, in kaleidoscopic fashion, can be reconfigured by the exegete into a variety of patterns that Eckhart paradoxically describes as new literal meanings. In the prologue to his *Book of the Parables of Genesis,* he says: "Since the literal sense is that which the author of a writing intends, and God is the author of holy scripture, . . . then every truth comes from the Truth itself. . . ."[37] The import of this remarkable statement is that the traditional spiritual meaning of the Bible, when viewed from the perspective of the exegete who speaks out of realized identity with the divine ground, has become a new form of infinitely malleable matter. The outer and the inner have traded places, or even merged. The exegete has become the text in the sense that it is he or she who provides the meaning that is adjudged divine. This claim might seem like excessive hubris, but in actuality it is not, because there really is no exegete any more in Eckhart's view. There is only Divine Truth proclaiming its infinite meanings through the vanished individuality of the mystical preacher.

Time precludes giving examples of just how Eckhart puts his form of "text-destroying" hermeneutic into practice, especially in his sermons. I cite him here only to show that Christian mysticism has analogues to the more radical forms of Jewish mystical exegesis.

At the conclusion of this essay I want to return to the title rephrased as a question: "How did Jewish and Christian mystics read the Bible?" "Very strangely," I suppose is the response that most of you would be

---

36. Meister Eckhart, German Sermon (Pr.) 51.

37. *Liber Parablorum Genesis,* prol. n. 2.

inclined to give by now. From the perspective of modern historical-critical study of the Bible, this is certainly the case.[38] But the mystical exegetes were not writing for modern academics. They were writing for communities whose faith was founded on the conviction that God was the author of the Bible and that the message contained in sacred writ is meant for present application, especially for personal transformation. A sacred text *qua* sacred is a text that is intended to be applied, and the antiquity of Tanakh and its fixation in a closed canon meant that exegetical ingenuity would always be necessary to apply the text to radically different historical situations.[39] The mystical exegetes were more ingenious, or "stronger," readers than others precisely because for them the desire to appropriate the text was more total and more profound. Even if we have lost the key to the creation of such forms of exegesis, we can at least learn to appreciate what these mystical exegetes were trying to do. We may also, after some effort, come to admire their ingenuity and boldness. On a practical level, the study of comparative mystical hermeneutics reveals that, in some respects at least, Christian and Jewish readers were far more alike than the misunderstandings of the past have led us to believe.

---

38. It is important to note that modern historical-critical reading is also "allegorical," in the etymological sense of "saying other," that is, using an interpretive framework *outside* the bare letter (in this case, modern historical investigation) to give the letter contemporary meaning for an historically conscious audience.

39. On the reciprocity of canonicity and ingenuity leading to "exegetical totalization," see Jonathan Z. Smith, "Sacred Persistence: Toward a Redescription of the Canon," *Imagining Religion: From Babylon to Jonestown* (Chicago: University of Chicago, 1982), 36–52.

10

Christian-Jewish Relations in the Enlightenment Period

Arthur Hertzberg
May 10, 2004

The ninth Jerusalem Lecture was delivered in Chicago on May 10, 2004 by Rabbi Dr. Arthur Hertzberg, Bronfman Visiting Professor of Humanities at New York University and Professor Emeritus of Religion at Dartmouth College.

Rabbi Hertzberg has held major posts in Jewish organizational life and has been active in Catholic-Jewish dialogue since the papacy of Pope John XXIII. He is the author of numerous books, including The French Enlightenment and the Jews: The Origins of Modern Anti-Semitism.

MY early connections with Cardinal Bernardin began many years ago, when he was the secretary general of the Catholic Bishops' Conference and I worked with him on Catholic-Jewish relationships. Let me be absolutely candid: what stood in the way those early days were the letter, and what seemed to be the spirit of classic Catholic theology. The young prelate Bernardin was one of the people in the Church who was trying to transcend that past. I attributed his new spirit then in part to his being an American who had grown up not only with a Catholic education but also with the separation of church and state that had been written into the American Constitution as the first article of the Bill of Rights. For Bernardin, I then thought this was a signpost toward a society in which the various religious communities were set to live as equals with traditions that had a stake, in the American view, in each other's survival. But then I got to know the man, and I understood that what moved him was what was moving a great man and a great miracle in the Church in those days, Pope John XXIII. It was love of humanity, the sense that we were all God's children, and He could not have put us on earth without leaving something to His children, to all of them, of His love and His grace. It was no accident that at Cardinal Bernardin's funeral, the cathedral was crowded with almost as many leaders of the Jewish community as Catholic dignitaries, and that Chicago stopped that day to take part in the last rites for the man who was universally recognized as the pastor and conscience of the entire city. I cannot begin to thank his successor, Cardinal George, and the leaders of the Jewish community for the honor of inviting me to give this memorial lecture. Cardinal Bernardin's last major lecture was at the Hebrew University in his search for common ground between the two religious groups. This lecture is the ninth in an annual series in memory of this occasion. As you shall see before the end of what I shall be saying, I am following in the path that he marked out in Jerusalem.

Now to the subject: I must confess that I am not surprised that the particular subject tonight: "Religion in the Age of the Enlightenment" has been assigned to me, and not merely because I once wrote my doctoral dissertation under the title *The French Enlightenment and the Jews,* to establish the revolutionary and scandalously difficult point that the Enlightenment itself, and some of its leaders, represented a secular counter-religion which persecuted and even excommunicated those who did not join their "church." But Judaism and Christianity did part company in the modern era when the Enlightenment led the European intellectuals toward enmity to religion. In widely varying degrees, the bulk of the Jewish community and the bulk of the Catholic community reacted quite differently. For many Jews, the Enlightenment was a religious plague, but it ushered in an age of social benefit. Jews were now given civic equality, often at the price of their semi-abandoning their inherited faith, but after many, many centuries of persecution, this price seemed worthwhile to many. For the Roman Catholic Church, the Enlightenment was an undercutting of the faith, which had to be fought at all costs. For the next century, and beyond, the religious histories of Jews and Catholics were radically different.

I know that the next sentence is a difficult one to utter and that it will not add to my popularity, but it needs to be said. In its battle with the Enlightenment, the Church lost. With its encounter with the Enlightenment, the synagogue had to redefine itself in many ways, but the Jews, who had long been a persecuted and embattled people, won. Therefore, two hundred years later, we have to re-estimate what this historic turning means now for both of our faiths. It has had radically different results in the nineteenth century and in the first decades of the twentieth, leaving a legacy for the future which is different for each of our faiths and communities. It would be self-delusion to obscure this radical difference. We cannot and should not try to talk it out of its existence, because that would leave us with an account of its history which is muddled. It is our obligation here, standing in the shadow of a great and holy man, Cardinal Bernardin, to face the truth—and, at the end of our journey through history, to be able to find the key with which he transcended it and made it possible for his successors in the Archdiocese of Chicago and in the multicultural and multireligious civic community of Chicago to live together and to revere his memory.

Let me begin with the Jewish story, and not primarily because I happen to be a rabbi and thus supposedly more familiar with the history of my own community. By the eighteenth century, as the Enlightenment seemed to be becoming ever more the dominant faith of the European intelligentsia, many Jews—and, indeed, the bulk of Jewish opinion—were ready to embrace it. Jews had been languishing for many centuries under the attack of the anti-Semites. They had long been defined by the accepted Christian doctrine as "the synagogue of Satan," and they were thus judged to be capable of the most unforgivable conduct. The Black Plague of the fourteenth century, the medical calamity which wiped out a quarter of Europe's population, was attributed to Jewish hatred of Christians. Unspeakable crimes were attributed to the Jews through the centuries, such as the recurrent attack that they required the use of the blood of Christians as an ingredient in the unleavened bread which they baked for Passover. By the eighteenth century, Jews had tired of these recurrent assaults and of the persecutions which they engendered. In their view, better that religion should be removed from its central and dominant role in human society. Better that religion should be made to accept the much more modest definition of itself as the faith of individuals, but not as the dominant outlook and even law of the state. Therefore, the promise of the Enlightenment to move religion from its centrality in society, at least in the West, seemed to be a good and welcome change.

Of course, even at the height of the fervor for the secularization of the state, there were Jews who joined Christians in deploring this change. In France during the Revolution, synagogues were closed, and their sacred vessels and objects were confiscated, along with those of the churches. Indeed, in various parts of the empire which the armies of the French Republic, and later of Napoleon, conquered, there were elements in the Jewish community which resisted accepting civic equality in return for the abandonment of the dominant role of religion in the internal life of their people. This happened in Holland in the 1790s where a vehement debate was evoked by such an offer. As late as 1812, when Napoleon's army seemed to be on the verge of conquering European Russia, the believing Jewish community was divided between those who wanted to welcome Napoleon as the herald of freedom for the Jews, and those who insisted that he might be good for the body of the Jews but would represent a disaster for their souls. The two dominant leaders of the new religious movement, Hasidim (which emphasized the need to improve the inner and outer destiny of the Jewish believer) were on opposite sides: "the seer of Lublin" insisted that the Jews needed personal freedom. The heads of the more philosophical element who were devotees of the Rebbe of Lubavitch said with uncompromising clarity that the tsar of Russia might continue to persecute the bodies of the Jews, but Napoleon would infect their souls with dangerous new doctrines about the meaning of life. And yet, the most active and Western-educated Jews of Europe followed after the Enlightenment with great enthusiasm. Many knew, or most knew, that the new doctrines would require radical changes in their spiritual thought and in their religious lifestyle, but better to cope with these changes than to continue to live in the misery of persecution. On balance, Jews were partisans of the New Age.

Christianity, and especially its Roman Catholic component, was on the other side. When the French Revolution took place, the Church in France was overwhelmingly in opposition. To be sure, a few clerics did take the oath of allegiance to the new Republican regime, but the large majority of Christian clergy remained in Royalist opposition. The Church as a whole was either underground or in exile; it continued to denounce the makers of the Revolution as the enemies of God and to excommunicate those who collaborated with the Revolution or with any further expressions of the Enlightenment elsewhere in Europe. At no point in these struggles in the nineteenth century for political equality for the Jews, not anywhere in Europe, were such demands supported by the dominant local Church—not in Eastern and Central Europe where the Church was usually Roman Catholic or Orthodox, and not in Great

Britain where the dominant church was Anglican, or in Prussia where the most powerful church was Lutheran. After a century of living with the power of the Enlightenment in Europe, the ablest of midnineteenth-century popes, Pius IX, called a Vatican Council in the 1860s. There he asserted, without compromise, the powers of the Church and the papacy in society, and he denounced, one by one, the prime doctrines of the Enlightenment: the separation of Church and state, the rule of democracy, and the freedom of individual conscience.

Thus the legacies that the encounter with the Enlightenment left for both Jews and Christians were contradictory. For Jews the Enlightenment had opened the door to the righting of the most ancient and painful wrongs. For Christians the Enlightenment announced the dethronement of religion from the center of the life of society.

In Europe throughout the nineteenth century and into the twentieth, Jews and Christians remained at war over the Enlightenment. The Roman Catholic Church was the prime force in insisting that Christian religion must remain as the central affirmation of society. Jews could pin their hopes for social advancement and personal freedom only on the success of those parts of society which had accepted the Enlightenment. Nevertheless, the lines between these two faiths were becoming ever less clear-cut. This was most true in the United States, where the Constitution of the United States, made a radical change in the relationship of religion to society. Religion was declared to be a private matter. Individuals might choose to believe or not to believe, to join a church or synagogue, or to avoid any such commitment, but none of this was a matter, at least in theory, of the concern of the state. On the contrary, in basic American law, all of the faiths were declared to be good for society, but only if they did not push any of the other faiths in the direction of their own particular beliefs. It may seem a bit bizarre to emphasize this point now in the early years of the twenty-first century, when so much is being made of the teachings of some of the religions about abortion and other issues which are involved in human reproductions, but my own research has discovered that the Catholic Encyclopedia as late as the 1970s repeatedly asserted the need of the Catholics to be left alone and untroubled in their faith so that they could teach their own people those rules about the profound issues to which others were opposed and which they refused to accept. The Church in those days found the separation of church and state to be a congenial doctrine because it kept the pressure of other communities off the back of the Roman Catholic establishment.

Nonetheless, America was different. It was from its very beginning a multi-religious society, and never mind what individual faiths were saying about each other, and especially, the claims that many were making to being the sole repository of God's true teaching. It was a fundamental part of American experience to accept the idea that each of the traditions represented and protected something of the Divine teaching. American society was the very frontier of the Christian culture and experience of the West. It was impossible for many Americans, perhaps even most of them, to imagine that those men and women who arose within that society to found new denominations, and thus to speak for God in unprecedented ways, were to be shrugged off as entirely false and fanciful messengers. In American society no religion dominated but all the religions were respected.

No formal theology was constructed in the nineteenth century, or for that matter the twentieth, to define this attitude, but it surely existed and it was, indeed, the dominant assertion about religion. It amounted to a robust belief that God was good and that He could not have created billions of His children through many centuries only to condemn them to unimaginable suffering in Hell, or perhaps purgatory, because they did not accept the correct theology. Never mind what some of the religious theories said, in austere and condemning tones. The basic optimism of the American spirit encouraged people to lay aside negative judgments on the faith and practices of the other, if only their intentions could be judged to be moving in the direction of love—the love of God and the love of the other.

It would be wrong to limit this description of the modern trend in religion only to American society. By the middle of the twentieth century, and especially on the site of ideological and religious hatred in Europe, there was a revulsion among many believers. The old religious distinctions seemed to be one of the breeding grounds of the hatred which had created the Second World War. When those battles ended, the victors asked the question: How can we stop such madness from ever happening again?

In most of the attempts to exile the "great hatred" from human society, men and women were persuaded that no faith, secular or religious, could be permitted to claim that it contained all of the truth about the human condition. Each of us was commanded to serve God and man faithfully, but such fidelity required that we walk before God in humility. So, right after the end of World War II, Jules Isaac, a French-Jewish intellectual, wrestled with the question of the source of that disaster. He explained anti-Semitism as the most poisonous "great hatred" of them all. His book was published in 1959 and it was soon read by the new Pope John XXIII. What Isaac had written remained on the Pope's table; it was a major influence in moving him to call the Second Vatican Council, to move the teachings of the Church away from any appearance of justifying religious war with the Jews—for that matter with any of the major religions of the world. At Vatican II the Roman Catholic Church did not change its doctrinal assertions that it was God's true messenger, but it accepted the principle that God was present in all the other religious traditions.

The religious teachings of the last decades of the twentieth century have increasingly been determined by the belief that God was present in all the great religions. That meant, and continues to mean, that the Divine presence is felt in all of the traditions. It simply could not be imagined that He absented Himself and allowed the bearers of the great faiths to make their own ways. The explanation for the horrors that had happened in the middle of the century could not be that God had gone on vacation or that He left the moral decisions to the choice of men and women, and whatever evil was done had been permitted by God through man's choice. No, men and women, and especially those who followed the major religious traditions, believed in the good and had clung to it even in the most difficult and dangerous times. Thus, goodness prevailed and it always reflected our commitment to God's teachings. No tradition had a total monopoly on the good. On the contrary, those who did not practice evil were, all of them, the faithful children of God.

This doctrine of universal love, and, therefore, the broadest kind of forgiveness, made it possible to look at the history of mankind during terrible years without passing final judgment on any tradition. Indeed, at this point, Jews and Roman Catholics did part company. In Roman Catholic faith, forgiveness is always a present option, after the sinner has confessed his crimes. This is much more difficult a matter in Judaism where forgiveness can come only from the persons injured and only after the sinner has gone a long, long way to make up for his crime. So, in the matter of the Holocaust, the Christians with whom I have debated some of these issues have remained constant. There is still a deep divide between Roman Catholic thinkers and moralists, who keep asking of Jews to find forgiveness in their hearts for the Nazis, and Jewish moralists who keep insisting that forgiveness will be possible only if the perpetrators of the crimes accept their guilt and make every physical effort that might be possible to atone for their sins. But, on both sides of these deep questions, we are far closer to resolution than we have ever been. We know, at the very least, that we are living in a generation that still remembers a terrible crime and that this memory can be erased only if we change our ways.

Here we have reached the essence of the possibility of reconciliation. Jews do not need, or want, the removal of any chance of reconciliation. Jews have no desire that the war between our faiths should continue. On the contrary, we are looking beyond the near past to a new day in which the principle of our living together will be a joint proclamation of our love for each other and for all humanity. It is here, at this very point, that religious leaders such as Pope John XXIII and Joseph Cardinal Bernardin are central and seminal figures. It is not accidental that John XXIII was widely mourned all over the world by men and women of all faiths and of no faith. When Joseph Cardinal Bernardin died, his funeral was attended by a very eminent and moved delegation of all the religious leaders of all the faiths in Chicago. When his cortege was being driven the nine miles from his cathedral to the Roman Catholic cemetery on the outskirts of the city, movement stopped and the streets were lined by all the faithful. The pastor of Chicago, the moral leader of all of God's children in the city, was on his way home.

What then was Cardinal Bernardin's ultimate legacy? He certainly remained an orthodox, believing Roman Catholic who continued to express and defend the Magisterium of the Church, but from the beginning to the end, Joseph Bernardin loved all of humanity. He could not imagine excluding any one of God's children from his grace and concern. Those with whom he worked in Chicago knew that he cared for them always and without fail. Jews have been for a long, long time birds in a mine shaft: if they cannot breathe, that proves that the air is contaminated. The Jews who knew this Cardinal breathed freely, for they knew that the atmosphere around him was not noxious and threatening. On the contrary, we are here tonight at the ninth memorial lecture because he inaugurated this series before his death by visiting Jerusalem and giving one of the superb explanations and expressions of what binds us together.

Nearly fifty years ago, even before the Second Vatican Council, in which the spirit of Pope John XXIII dominated, the Christian theologians and thinkers in America were deeply occupied with the question of what binds and unites the major religious traditions, and especially Judaism and Christianity. The eminent Protestant theologian Reinhold Niebuhr made as his own a doctrine that had been defined several decades earlier in pre-Nazi Germany. This is the theory of the "two covenants," that God had sent the Christians into the world to convert all of mankind to his biblical teachings and that He had charged the Jews with the responsibility of living the life that God had prescribed as proof that such a society was possible and attainable. I loved and revered Reinhold Niebuhr but I could not agree with him. I did not think that the "two covenant" thesis solved the problem of religious equality and mutual respect. What of Islam? More seriously still, what about the Oriental religions such as Buddhism, which did not belong to the biblical tradition? And yet, the question remained: How could we live together in the world of the future with mutual respect?

In an essay which Niebuhr never answered (he was already very ill), I suggested that a future of decent peace and respect among all the religions could be fashioned only if we made a distinction between our conduct in the here and now and of our hope for the future, for the end of days. In the here and now, we were commanded to act as if all the religions represented great values which were ultimately not in conflict. We could live—and indeed we had to live—with religious pluralism. We had to accept this estate for all the believers, not grudgingly, but with real zest for what we can and could discover in the teachings and practices of other faiths. Nonetheless, each of us was commanded to carry forward the specific teachings, the Divine revelations, which he had inherited through his own specific traditions. Until the end of days, I proposed that we had to live with religious pluralism, but when the end of days actually arrives, I expect we will find out which of the traditions is really God's herald in the world. I never discussed this essay with Joseph Bernardin but I suspect he had read it, and not only because he read everything. Some weeks after it was published, he greeted me a bit more effusively than usual and a bit more upbeat. I suspected, more from the atmosphere than from any specific exchange of letters, that I had sounded a note that the then young bishop regarded as suitable.

Now, some thirty years later, I am much more certain that he and I had moved closer in the ways that we thought about agreement among the major faiths. I have in evidence the lecture that he gave in Jerusalem in 1995, which I, of course, re-read in preparation for our discussion tonight. At the Hebrew University he spoke in the light of the experience of a church and synagogue in the last six decades, that is, in the years of both our adult lives. It was a mature statesman of religion and the mature believer who spoke that day with remarkable clarity, both in what he affirmed and in what he chose to leave out. Most characteristic of Cardinal Bernardin, the scholar within him did not allow him to avoid any of the difficult questions. The title of his talk was "Anti-Semitism: the Historical Legacy and the Continuing Challenge of Christians." Joseph Bernardin knew the early Christian history too well to lay aside, or to obscure, the amount of anti-Semitism that the Church Fathers and even the fourth gospel had imported into the earliest Christian religion, in large part from Hellenistic, pagan sources. He quotes St. John Chrysostom as linking the "now permanent exilic condition of the Jew with the killing of Christ." In the same generation, St. Augustine spoke of Jews several times in his classical work *The City of God* as having "their backs bent down always." Cardinal Bernardin, the Archbishop of Chicago, stood before a largely Jewish audience in Jerusalem and said:

> This legacy of anti-Semitism, with its profoundly negative social consequences for Jews as individuals and for the Jewish community as a whole, remained the dominant social pattern in Western Christian lands until the twentieth century.

Cardinal Bernardin had the courage to assert a few lines later that:

> At the dawn of the twentieth century the theology of perpetual divine judgment upon Jewish people did not vanish overnight. Rather, it continued to exercise a decisive role in shaping Catholicism's initial reactions, for example, to the proposal for restoring a Jewish national homeland in Palestine. It also was of central importance in shaping popular Christian attitudes toward the Nazis and their stated goal of eliminating all Jews from Europe and beyond through deliberate extermination.

But Cardinal Bernardin did not find even in the most anti-Jewish of the four Gospels, the story of the founding of Christianity according to John, and certainly not in the Church Fathers, the definitive teaching of the Church on Jews and Judaism. On the contrary, the true Christian doctrine did not teach that the Jews had been superseded and laid aside in the divine scheme of salvation. They remained indissolubly the children of God, as the Church had taught most recently in the Second Vatican Council:

> The Council clearly asserted that there never existed a valid basis either for the charge of collective guilt against the Jewish community for supposedly "murdering the Messiah" or for the consequent theology of permanent Jewish suffering and displacement.

Bernardin emphasized that this view had been stated and firmly defended, repeatedly, by Pope John Paul II. In 1985 the Vatican issued a document entitled "Notes on the Correct Way to Present the Jews and Judaism in Preaching and Catechesis in the Roman Catholic Church": "The permanence of Israel (while so many ancient peoples have disappeared without a trace) is a historic fact and a sign to be interpreted within God's design." John Paul II has been strongly supportive of the right of the Jews to return to live in their own ancient homeland. And the document of 1985 "rejects any idea that all Jews, then or now, can be charged with the responsibility of Jesus's death."

But the most difficult issue remains the Holocaust, the murder of six million Jews by the Nazis. Here Cardinal Bernardin was of two minds. He could not resist quoting the Jewish scholar Yosef Yerushalmi, to absolve the Church of being the basic source of Nazi Jew-hatred. On the contrary, near the very end of his lecture in Jerusalem, Cardinal Bernardin asserted that

> I must side with the perspective of those scholars such as Yosef Yerushalmi who have insisted that "the Holocaust was the work of a thoroughly modern, neopagan State," not merely a "transformed" medieval anti-Semitism rooted in Christian teachings. The *Shoah* cannot be seen as simply the final and most gruesome chapter in the long history of Christian anti-Semitism. Rather, it was a plan for the mass destruction of human lives, supposedly undertaken in the name of "healing" humanity, as the psychologist Robert J. Lifton has put it, rooted in modern theories of inherent biological and

racial inferiority coupled with the escalation of bureaucratic and technological capacities.

And yet, in the paragraph before, Cardinal Bernardin contradicts himself
on this very central issue. He insists that the roots of anti-Semitism in
Christian theory and practice is a moral responsibility to this day, and
beyond, of the Christian community.

> As I have already pointed out, relying on the research of Father Flannery
> and the late Professor Tal, there is little doubt that classical Christian pre-
> sentations of Jews and Judaism were a central factor in generating popular
> support for the Nazi endeavor, along with economic greed, religious and
> political nationalism, and ordinary fear. For many baptized Christians,
> traditional Christian beliefs about Jews and Judaism constituted the pri-
> mary motivation for their support, active or tacit, of the Nazi movement.
> Some even went so far as to define the Nazi struggle against the Jews in
> explicitly religious and theological terms. In the Church today, we must
> not minimize the extent of Christian collaboration with Hitler and his
> associates. It remains a profound moral challenge that we must continue
> to confront for our own integrity as a religious community.

It is clear from these two contrasting statements that a lesser man
than Joseph Bernardin would have found refuge for the Church in the
assertion that Hitler and his minions were neo-pagans, but this man of
God could not take such defensive refuge. He had to repeat, again, that
classic Christian presentations of Jews and Judaism were an essential
factor in generating popular support for the Nazi endeavor. Joseph
Bernardin could not let go of the issues of the Holocaust until he talks
of the number of courageous "Christian leaders, groups and individuals"
who stood against Nazi racism, and yet he insists that their stories
"should never be used against the need for a full scrutiny of Church
activities by reputable scholars." Education about the Holocaust, so
Bernardin insisted at the very end of this important lecture, should not
be left to Jews; it "should become a prominent feature in Catholic education and at every level." Bernardin concludes his talk by quoting the
bishops of Germany, who had issued a statement on the fiftieth anniversary of the liberation of Auschwitz. They acknowledged that "Christians
did not offer due resistance to racial anti-Semitism. Many times there
were failure and guilt among Catholics. . . . The practical sincerity of

our will of renewal is also linked to the confession of this guilt and the willingness painfully learned from this history of guilt."

Surely Cardinal Bernardin knew that this declaration by the German bishops was not universally popular in the Church. No doubt that is why he introduced it by saying that they made a point "with which I whole-heartedly concur."

I have quoted at great length from his historic lecture to demonstrate that Cardinal Bernardin knew, and insisted, that all Catholics must know, and remember, the complicated and painful history of their relationship to Jews and especially to anti-Semitism. Standing here in his Archdiocese of Chicago, and weeping within myself that he is no longer with us in the flesh, I permit myself to hope that I shall have the privilege someday of continuing these discussions with him in a better world. I am reminded of a teaching of the Talmud that the words of the wise are eternal: they must be studied and restudied, age after age; we must continue to find their hidden meanings. I thank those who have arranged for me to take part in this sacred discussion and to commune again with the soul of a holy man.

11

Catholics, Jews, and American Culture

Francis Cardinal George, OMI
February 21, 2005

The tenth Jerusalem Lecture was delivered in Chicago on February 21, 2005 by His Eminence, Francis Cardinal George, OMI, the Archbishop of Chicago.

Cardinal George, a member of the Missionary Congregation of the Oblates of Mary Immaculate, served as Vicar General in Rome from 1974–1986. Pope John Paul II appointed him Bishop of Yakima, Washington in 1990, and in 1996 appointed him Archbishop of Portland, Oregon. In 1997, Pope John Paul II appointed him Archbishop of Chicago and in 1998, elevated him to the Sacred College of Cardinals.

LET me begin by thanking Rabbi Michael Segal and Anshe Emet Synagogue, the American Jewish Committee, the Chicago Board of Rabbis, the Jewish Federation of Metropolitan Chicago, and the Spertus Institute of Jewish Studies for ten years of partnership with the Archdiocese of Chicago in sponsoring the Joseph Cardinal Bernardin Jerusalem Lectures. As we come to the tenth anniversary, it is important to recall that the address in the Senate Hall of the Hebrew University in 1995, when my predecessor made his now famous "Dialogue Visit" to Israel, the West Bank, and Gaza, was not so much a breakthrough as a culmination of then nearly twenty-five years of Catholic-Jewish relations in Chicago. Sister Joan McGuire mentioned that it represented the maturity of the relationship up to that point, while breaking new ground. But above all, it was a forward-looking event, a commencement. This is why when the question was asked a few weeks later here in Chicago, "What's next?" it was natural to conceive a project that would stretch out ten years into the future, to this very evening.

We who gather tonight have all been part in different ways of shaping that future, by looking back into history, ancient and recent, and by looking forward to the possibilities now available to us. As I stand before you tonight, I am very grateful not only to celebrate the last ten years but also to celebrate the greater maturity of the Catholic-Jewish relationship. One example of this maturity was evident in the last two years in the Archdiocese of Chicago and the Jewish Federation's joint Demonstration Project in the village of Fassouta in northern Galilee. Once it was unthinkable that a Catholic Cardinal would journey to the Middle East in the company of his Jewish friends. Even when that happened, it was equally unthinkable that Jews and Catholics here would raise $100,000 to create a computer literacy center in the north of Israel to respond together to the problem of Christian emigration from Israel. So, as we celebrate ten years of Jerusalem Lectures tonight, we should ask ourselves, "What is unthinkable tonight that perhaps in ten more years we or our successors will be celebrating?"

I am confident in stating the future in these terms because of our shared faith in the God of Abraham, Isaac, and Jacob. As one reads the biblical narrative, the doctrine of providence is clear in the text. God leads His people toward a future that God has planned for them. I believe that advances in Catholic-Jewish relations in the past fifty years have been guided by the providence of God.

This confidence I have in the providence of God leads me to introduce tonight's topic: "Catholics, Jews, and American Culture." As many of you know, one of my interests for many years has been the relationship between faith and culture, an interest born of my missionary visits to Catholic communities around the globe. Before I was appointed Bishop of Yakima in 1990, I directed an institute dedicated to reflecting on this relationship, and much of my intellectual work as a professor of philosophy also dealt with American culture. Since becoming a bishop, I have served in three different local churches or dioceses. While bishops do not have the leisure to read and write the way a professor might, we do have a certain perspective from our pastoral ministry which gives us lived insight into the relationship between faith and culture in the lives of the people we serve. The episcopate is a vantage point from which to assess the effects of culture on faith and the effects of faith on culture.

It's a relationship that is dynamic. Culture has a powerful influence on believers, and a lived faith creates culture. Both faith and culture are normative systems, telling us what to think and how to behave. But the relationship is not always benign, the intention not always friendly. Sometimes the mutual influences are quite negative, where culture erodes the practice of religion or when religion-inspired violence threatens the stability of a society or a culture. As believers in a revealed religion, there is a necessary critique of any culture by religious truth, since the Word of God is a purifying word and can never be co-opted.

Said another way, culture can get it wrong. A simple example from Chicago history will suffice to illustrate this point. In 1893, the Protestant majority in this country conceived the idea of holding a World Parliament of Religions as part of the Columbian Exposition here.[1] Part of the goal of the organizers was to mark the entrance into a new century, the Christian Century. The parliament was conceived as the first-ever conversation between the religions, but many of its organizers were certain that it would establish the superiority of Protestant Christianity as the most reasonable and excellent religion.

They made a mistake on a number of levels. The World Parliament of Religions was an historic event. It marked the inauguration of the interreligious movement more than a decade before the beginnings of the ecumenical movement among Christians, inspired largely by Protestants, early in the twentieth century. It marked the entrance of several Asian religions into North America. And it is remembered as the event at which Judaism and Catholicism were recognized as American religions. The United States ended the nineteenth century thinking of itself as it truly was, a Protestant nation, and entered the twentieth century with a broadened sense of itself as a nation of Protestants, Catholics, and Jews.[2]

For both Jews and Catholics during our early periods here, the public schools got it wrong. These schools promoted a state sanctioned, non-denominational Protestantism, complete with daily Bible reading and prayer.[3] Both of our communities reacted because we saw the schools as a challenge to our faiths. Our responses were different, however: Catholics organized a separate parochial school system and the Jewish

---

1. See Richard Hughes Seager, *The Dawn of Religious Pluralism: Voices from the World's Parliament of Religions, 1893.* (LaSalle, IL: Open Court, 1993).

2. See Will Herberg, *Protestant, Catholic and Jew: An Essay in American Religious Sociology* (Garden City, NJ: Anchor Books, 1960).

3. John T. McGreevy, *Catholicism and American Freedom* (New York: W.W. Norton, 2003), 7.

community promoted the public policy of making the schools neutral regarding religion, a neutrality that sometimes slides into hostility. Nevertheless, our two communities, shaped by previous dialogue between faith and many cultures over many centuries, have been in a faith and culture dialogue with America since our co-religionists first set foot on these shores. That is the dialogue I want to explore tonight. Before I begin this exploration, however, I would like to review the principal themes that were treated over the last ten years of these lectures.

Survey of the Catholic Jewish Dialogue in Chicago

Cardinal Bernardin's Dialogue Visit to Israel, the West Bank, and Gaza built upon many efforts in the Catholic and Jewish communities of Chicago before that event.[4] The formal or institutional commitment to a relationship between the two communities can be dated to 1958 and Albert Cardinal Meyer's establishment of the Office for Urban Affairs, which he placed in the hands of Monsignor Jack Egan. The first joint project of the two faith communities began during the civil rights movement, with the formation of the Chicago Conference on Religion and Race. The Chicago Board of Rabbis and the Archdiocese joined with the Episcopal Diocese of Chicago and the Church Federation of Greater Chicago to create an organization that would address the sin of racism in what has been called the most segregated city in America. At the same time, the Second Vatican Council was debating its declaration on the relationship of the Catholic Church to non-Christian religions and, as Sister Joan mentioned, *Nostra Aetate* was promulgated in 1965. That same year, John Cardinal Cody established the Commission on Human Relations and Ecumenism, headed by a young monsignor, Edward M. Egan, now the Cardinal Archbishop of New York.

Immediately after he came to Chicago, Archbishop Bernardin increased the Archdiocese's commitment to these relationships by establishing a fully staffed Office for Human Relations and Ecumenism to carry out the Archbishop's agenda for Christian ecumenism and for Catholic-Jewish relations. That same year, Sister Anna Marie Erst and

---

4. See Thomas A. Baima, editor. "Catholic-Jewish Relations in Chicago" in *A Blessing to Each Other: Cardinal Joseph Bernardin and Jewish-Catholic Dialogue* (Chicago: Liturgy Training Publications, 1996), 9–17.

the American Jewish Committee established the Institute for Catholic-Jewish Religious Education. In 1984, the Chicago Conference on Religion and Race was reorganized into the Council of Religious Leaders of Metropolitan Chicago, which still today is the principal roundtable for heads of religious communities to share concerns and plan joint action on the critical issues that face metropolitan Chicago. It is a forum where Christian churches and the Chicago Board of Rabbis have met regularly. It now includes others, especially the Muslims. One of the first major celebrations undertaken by the Archdiocese's Office of Human Relations and Ecumenism took place in 1985 to mark the twentieth anniversary of *Nostra Aetate*. Held at Mundelein College on the Loyola campus, this anniversary celebration had an animating effect on the relationship. Shortly after that, the parish-synagogue dialogues were begun, some of which have continued for these many years.

A unique project developed at Spertus College in the Joseph Cardinal Bernardin Center for the Study of Eastern European Jewry. Since Chicago is the largest Polish city after Warsaw, it was appropriate for Spertus and the Archdiocese to develop this project together. A high point for the Center was the visit to Chicago of a group of seminary professors from Poland, who spent seven weeks here studying Judaism and interreligious dialogue. All of this helped set the stage for Cardinal Bernardin's historic Dialogue Visit to the Holy Land.

Survey of the Jerusalem Lectures

The Dialogue Visit was therefore the culmination of 37 years of some form of Catholic-Jewish cooperation in Chicago. The centerpiece of the visit was Cardinal Bernardin's major address in the Senate Hall of the Hebrew University of Jerusalem. I know some of you were there and were responsible for creating the occasion for the address entitled *Anti-Semitism: The Historic Legacy and the Continuing Challenge for Christians*. This is how the Archdiocese and its Jewish partners later described that address:

> Cardinal Bernardin detailed the development of Christian thought on anti-Semitism, in particular pointing out how in recent years the Catholic Church has undertaken important efforts to acknowledge responsibility for that legacy. He repudiated any remaining vestiges of anti-Semitism in

the Church's contemporary teaching and practice as sinful. The Cardinal called upon Jews and Christians to recommit themselves to counter any resurgence of anti-Semitism, together with other forms of racial and ethnic violence. In responding to these realities, Cardinal Bernardin [suggested] several ways that Jews and Christians [could both] together and separately, build a better future of relations. He [called] for renewal of Catholic teaching material on anti-Semitism, expansion of awareness of Vatican II's rejection of anti-Jewish theology. The Cardinal [called] for Jewish educators also to rethink the Jewish community's understanding of its relationship with the Church. In these and other ways, Jews and Christians can, together, build a new relationship for the future.[5]

These Jerusalem Lectures were conceived as a way to "reflect on the themes introduced in Cardinal Bernardin's Hebrew University lecture."[6] The first lecturer was Professor Emil Fackenheim. His address attempted to engage the same subject as Cardinal Bernardin's lecture, but from a Jewish theological perspective. If any of you have not read the lecture, I would encourage you to read it or to reread it; but now I simply want to note something Professor Fackenheim said toward the end of his conference, when he shared some remarks he had heard at a Jewish-Christian conference in Germany.

> . . . Christians must begin again at the beginning, with the first two questions of the Bible: "Where are you, Man?" and "Where is your brother?" Christian anti-Judaism will never end until Christians relate positively to Jews, not despite their non-acceptance of [Jesus] Christ, but because of it.[7]

I'll come back to this idea toward the end of this talk, because I see in it something important for the next phase of our relationship. I'd like to continue now with a brief survey of the lectures.

Edward Cardinal Cassidy, in his role as president of the Pontifical Commission for Religious Relations with the Jews, delivered the second

---

5. Joseph Cardinal Bernardin, *Anti-Semitism: The Historical Legacy and the Continuing Challenge for Christians*. (Chicago: Archdiocese of Chicago, March 23, 1995).

6. Emil L. Fackenheim, *Jewish-Christian Relations after the Holocaust: Toward Post-Holocaust Theological Thought*. (Chicago: Archdiocese of Chicago, April 17, 1996).

7. Ibid., 21. (Professor Fackenheim cites these statements as follows: "The first two statements I heard at a Jewish-Christian conference, held in the Pabst Johannes Haus, Krefeld, Germany in 1983").

lecture. In his remarks, Cardinal Cassidy proposed a new agenda based on certain principles. He wrote:

> The first such principle is the fact that we are speaking in this context of joint action in favor of the moral values which as faith communities we share. We are not two humanitarian societies, far less are we two debating clubs. We are two faith communities and as such we are being called to respond to a common challenge.[8]

Continuing to flesh out this principle, Cardinal Cassidy brought up two more points. Recalling Pope John Paul II's visit to the Synagogue of Rome, he wrote: "His Holiness called for cooperation for the well-being of humankind and common reflection on how to help men and women today to achieve true justice and freedom in truth."[9] Further, Cardinal Cassidy reminded the audience of the unique relationship between Christians and Jews, not shared by any other religions. He said:

> It is important for us to keep this "unique" aspect of our relationship in mind, especially when we enter into a wider interfaith dialogue. [Jews and Christians] have an agenda based on what John Paul II has described elsewhere as being "linked together at the very level of their identity." With no other faith community, not even Islam, do Christians have such a relationship.[10]

As with Professor Fackenheim's comments, I would ask you to hold these ideas for a few moments while we continue this survey.

Rabbi Dr. David Hartman continued the theological exploration with his lecture on "The Theological Significance of Israel." In it he "explored the implications of this subject for the future of Judaism, and discussed the implications of the perspective he offered for relationships between Judaism, Christianity and other world religions."[11] In the opening section of his lecture, Dr. Hartman set the stage for one of his principal claims: the importance of particularity. By quoting the anti-Zionist German-Jewish philosopher, Herman Cohen, Dr. Hartman noted the

---

8. Edward Cardinal Cassidy, *Catholic-Jewish Relations: A New Agenda?* (Chicago: Archdiocese of Chicago, April 30, 1997), 6.

9. Ibid., 7.

10. Ibid. See *Attività della Santa Sede 1982*, pp. 184–185.

11. David Hartman, *The Theological Significance of Israel* (Chicago, Archdiocese of Chicago, March 17, 1998).

universalizing claims of the "German spirit" a century or more ago. This universalizing spirit, described here for the German nation, asked each particular group within the nation-state to hide its particularity in favor of the universalizing elements in national culture. German Jews were to imbibe the German-ness of the nation. Against this Dr. Hartman claims that "Israel, in the deepest sense, represents the choice of visibility, the choice not to hide."[12] In his conclusion, he wrote:

> Israel is not the embodiment of the universal. Israel is an expression of the dignity of particularity. In the eighteenth century, Jews felt that in order to speak ethically, you had to embody the universality of Kantian ethics. In order to be dignified, you had to embrace universality and reject particularity, which many of them did by giving up their particular traditions. Jews assimilated in droves because they believed mistakenly that you became universal by discarding the particular. The reborn State of Israel is an intensified expression of a people's particular identity. And it is this very particularity that can teach us the meaning of universalism as an outgrowth of a commitment to particularities.[13]

The next six lectures took a historical approach to the relationship between Jews and Christians.[14] This historical survey of each epoch over the last two thousand years was a very important contribution to our mutual understanding of one another. I want to acknowledge again, as others have, my appreciation for this scholarship and my hope that we might find a way for it to be more widely shared and disseminated. I'm not going to refer to these lectures in the detail that I did with the first four because, except for the last one, they do not directly address the topic that I want to raise with you now. The ninth lecture, delivered last year by Rabbi Dr. Arthur Hertzberg, does provide us with a transition to our topic today.

---

12. Ibid., 3.

13. Ibid., 25.

14. Anthony J. Saldarini, *Christian Anti-Judaism: The First Century Speaks to the Twenty-First Century* (Chicago: Archdiocese of Chicago, April 14, 1999); Richard A. Freund, *Bethsaida: Home of the Apostles and the Rabbis* (Chicago: Archdiocese of Chicago, April 10, 2000); Robert Louis Wilken, *An Ancient and Venerable People* (Chicago: Archdiocese of Chicago, March 18, 2001); Robert Chazan, *Medieval Christians and Jews: Divergences and Convergences* (Chicago: Archdiocese of Chicago, March 14, 2002); Bernard McGinn, *How Jewish and Christian Mystics Read the Bible* (Chicago, Archdiocese of Chicago, March 3,2003); Arthur Hertzberg, *Christian-Jewish Relations in the Enlightenment Period* (Chicago: Archdiocese of Chicago, May 10, 2004).

Dr. Hertzberg's lecture completed the historical survey of Christian-Jewish relations from the 1st century to the twentieth. In that lecture he mentioned his doctoral dissertation where he argued:

> . . . the revolutionary and scandalously difficult point that the Enlightenment itself, and some of its leaders, represented a secular counter-religion which persecuted and even excommunicated those who did not join their "church." But Judaism and Christianity did part company in the modern era when the Enlightenment led the European intellectuals toward enmity toward religion. In widely varying degrees, the bulk of the Jewish community and the bulk of the Catholic community reacted quite differently . . . in its battle with the Enlightenment, the Church lost. With its encounter with the Enlightenment, the synagogue had to redefine itself in many ways but the Jews, who [in Christendom] had long been a persecuted and embattled people, won. Therefore, two hundred years later, we have to re-estimate what this historic turning means now for both of our faiths.[15]

Rabbi Hertzberg went on to assert that the opinion of these Enlightenment Jews was that it would be "better that religion should be removed from its central and dominant role in human society," and that [religion] "accept a much more modest definition of itself as the faith of individuals . . ."[16] Dr. Hertzberg gives us a very good definition of the problem which confronts us as we enter this twenty-first century. The problem, simply stated, is that, with the advent of the Enlightenment, a new dialogue partner has entered our conversation: secularism. And with the entrance of secularism on the stage of public life, the Jewish-Catholic dialogue takes on the quality of a trialogue. We have not sufficiently recognized this fact, I believe, in our bilateral conversations, because we share it without too much conflict. Given that the form of secularism we have in the United States is different in significant respects from its counterpart in Europe or even Canada, our consideration of it must recognize that secularism, like religion, inculturates in particular ways in different societies.

It is for this reason that I titled my lecture *Catholics, Jews, **and** American Culture,* instead of *Catholics and Jews **in** American Culture.*

---

15. Arthur Hertzberg, *Christian-Jewish Relations in the Enlightenment Period* (Chicago: Archdiocese of Chicago, May 10, 2004), 2. See also, *The French Enlightenment and the Jews* (New York: Columbia University Press, 1968).

16. Ibid.

American Culture is an actor in our mutual relationship; it is a semantic system, which interacts with the semantic systems of our respective faiths as they dialogue with one another. Following Dr. Hertzberg, I would argue that it is a religious competitor with Judaism and Catholicism, sometimes helpful and sometimes malign.

I have presented this survey very quickly as a way for us to remember some of the key insights we gained through the last ten years of this lecture series and of our dialogue. With these as foundation for the topic I want to consider tonight, let me quickly summarize. We are two ancient faith communities entering the twenty-first century and called to respond to a common challenge—two premodern faiths in a postmodern culture.[17] That challenge includes, among other things, the universalist pretensions of nation-states and how their claims affect the particularity of peoples, and the presence of a secularism with all the qualities of a religion co-opting society for its own ends.

The Current Situation in Civil Society

Towards the end of last year, I spoke to the First Friday Club of Chicago. This was before the general election, and the topic they gave me was "Catholicism in American Public Life," hoping, I suspect, that I would say something about politics that would be controversial. In that talk, I noted that "public life is, of course, much broader than political life. Catholicism, [and tonight I could add Judaism] is a way of life, with its proper behaviors and convictions and ideas, based upon . . . [biblical] faith."[18] In America today, because secularism is becoming the state religion, faith is suspect, any faith, for at least two reasons:

> One reason stems from the suspicion that faith will limit freedom. Since freedom is our most precious value, both in public life and private life, any obstacle to human freedom, anything that is a threat to personal freedom, is suspect. Ever since American freedom was expanded after the Second

---

17. There is a sense in which Catholic faith, founded in Christ's resurrection from the dead two thousand years ago, nevertheless sees itself reaching back to creation itself. Without succumbing to supersessionism, theologians such as Yves Congar, O.P., can write about *Ecclesia ab Abel*, "the Church from Abel." See Yves Congar, O.P., "Ecclesia ab Abel," *Abhanglungen uber theologie und Kirche,* Heinrich Elfers and Fritz Hoffmann, eds., (Dusseldorf: 1952), 79–108.

18. Francis Cardinal George, O.M.I., "Catholicism in American Public Life", Unpublished lecture to the First Friday Club of Chicago, October 1, 2004.

World War to include sexual freedom of all sorts, religion, and particularly Catholicism, has come to be regarded as a threat.[19]

A second reason that faith is suspect stems from the conviction that religion is a cause of violence. This conviction ignores the historical fact that more people have been killed for the cause of national independence or to protect an already established state or even for values such as freedom than were ever killed in the name of Moses, Christ or Mohammed.

Whatever its ideological rationale, the secularization of society takes place:

> When the public realm is constructed without reference to a way of life based on faith, when public life doesn't admit that faith is compatible with its own nature as public. . . . Philosophically, a secularized society rests on the conviction that spirit does not have power. Matter has power. We harness the power of matter for our own purposes all the time. But spirit, which believers say is the most powerful reality of all, does not have power in a secularized worldview. At best, [therefore] religion is poetry that can console, but it doesn't give the truth about anything and it doesn't have any access to a power that is not material, because matter is all that there is.[20]

Believers can react to secularization by clarifying their sense of who God is, hoping that secularists, confronted with a God who is not a caricature, will rethink their opposition to religion. During a conference at the Library of Congress to mark advances in human knowledge at the end of the twentieth century, speaking about religion in the world today, I noted:

> Because God is not one being among others but rather the sheer energy of to-be itself, God does not make the world through manipulation, change or violence, as the gods of philosophy and mythology do. Since there is literally nothing outside of God, he makes the entirety of the finite realm *ex nihilo*, through an act of purest and gentlest generosity.[21] God's is a non-possessive love. And since God is the act of to-be, all creaturely things exist in and through God, "participating" in the power of his being and the graciousness of his love. And we can draw a final implication: because

---

19. Ibid.
20. Ibid.
21. Thomas Aquinas, *De potentia*, q. 3, art. 1.

all created things are participants in the divine generosity, they are all related to one another by bonds of ontological intimacy.[22]

What this means is that our way of conceiving social relationships must be in accord with the most fundamental relationship of God to the created order. Religious people and religious institutions have often failed to be true to the God we believe in, and non-believers base their anti-religious convictions as often in reaction to our behaviors as to our beliefs.

Where we can see the religious conflict with secularism most starkly is in the behavior of the institutions of the state. Now that secularism has assumed something akin to the role of an established religion, we see the state intervening to protect its citizens *from* religion rather than to promote the free exercise *of* religion. This creates a quandary for the Catholic American, and I suppose, for many other people of faith as well.

> The definition of life itself, of the nature of marriage, and of what is religious or not, are now in the hands of the government, through the courts. The United States no longer has the type of limited governmental institutions that preserved individual freedom. A state increasingly bureaucratized and courts that meddle in areas that [should be] outside of governmental jurisdiction in free society, have broken the social contract.[23]

This development is a logical consequence, I believe, of the Hobbes-Locke tradition "which profoundly shaped the minds of the founding fathers of this country . . . ."

> . . . in Hobbes and Locke, . . . rights are individualistic—my liberty and life over and against yours. These rights are somewhat correlated to moral ends outside of themselves by the greater or lesser religious sense of common destiny and purpose in the minds and beliefs of many of the Founders; but it is, tellingly, the pursuit of happiness–unguided, unanchored, unfocused by truth–that is guaranteed as a [personal] right. And government is instituted among men in order to protect these prerogatives and hence assure some level of peace and order in a still primarily antagonistic community. . . . This approach to religion, however, is still basically

---

22. Francis Cardinal George, OMI, "Catholic Christianity and the Millennium: Frontiers of the Mind in the 21st Century," Unpublished manuscript, June 16, 1999.

23. Francis Cardinal George, OMI, "The Quandary of Being a Catholic and a U.S. Citizen," in *Chicago Studies*: Vol. 43, No. 2, Summer 2004: 119–129.

Hobbesian, since it proceeds from the distinctively modern creation of a secular space, untouched by religious questions, concerns or finalities.[24]

As a result, I would respectfully and somewhat gingerly challenge (and one always challenges Dr. Hertzberg gingerly!) the optimism about the American situation which I read in Dr. Hertzberg's lecture. One can find similar tensions in the documents of the Second Vatican Council. At that historical moment, a general optimism about modernity seemed appropriate. Blessed Pope John XXIII, for example, saw the Church in a position of great internal strength, ready to engage boldly in a dialogue with a world weakened by divisions and conflict and wars but filled also with trust in God's love and goodness. The last forty years have seen a weakening of the Church's vital internal unity, as renewal has been confused with self-secularization. Secularism itself, the ethos of the world divorced from divine providence, has become assertive as it has gained control of the reins of state power. None of this means that the dialogue between faith and culture is now a stalled conversation between a sectarian faith and a hostile culture, a dialogue of the deaf. It means only that the conversation continues more cautiously, aware of inherent contradictions that were able to be forgotten in the enthusiasm of the 60s and 70s of the last century.

In the dialogue between biblical faith and American culture, the sociological counterpart of culture's co-opting faith ideologically is the assimilation of individual believers to cultural mores not rooted in faith. When both Catholics and Jews immigrated to the United States, we came to a culture which was shaped by Protestantism. This meant that both Jews and Catholics were assimilating into what was basically a biblical culture, with many points of contact. While never formally exploring the question in the contemporary faith-culture framework, the instinct of early American Catholic liberals, as exemplified in prominent Catholic prelates such as Cardinal Gibbons of Baltimore and Archbishop Ireland of St. Paul, was that the biblical faith we had in common with Protestants would allow for successful assimilation of Catholics into American society without loss of their Catholic faith. In the 1930s, with the cutoff of European immigration to this country after the First World War, Cardinal Mundelein of Chicago, a leader among the second generation of Americanizers in the Catholic hierarchy, held

---

24. George, "Catholic Christianity and the Millennium." Op. Cit.

similar convictions. In 1990, with these same convictions, I suggested in a book I wrote then that Catholics might look to Protestants for help in the religious dialogue with modernity, since Protestantism was born at the beginning of the modern age. . . ."[25] Fifteen years later, and from the vantage point of a diocesan bishop, I would be far more cautious. The very elements within American Protestant culture that would have allowed this linkage and help have been eroded by the same secularizing trend that affects Protestantism itself. What remains of that original Protestant ethos in contemporary American culture are some secularized echoes of Calvinism, especially notions of individuals determined by situations beyond their personal control, which makes everyone a victim not of a sovereign God but of inadequate parenting, societal prejudices and institutional injustice. As a result, we find ourselves in a situation where the biblical message of freedom rooted in truth is treated at best as just one more personal option and at worst as a reactionary opposition to progressive cultural trends liberating individuals from societal and institutional oppression of all sorts. The communitarian ethos of both Jews and Catholics gets cultural short shrift.

Speaking about these themes during one of his visits to Canada, Pope John Paul II said that secularized culture is really a "new culture," in the sense that it is a collection of values distinct from the biblical culture it is replacing.[26] He also named some concerns about where the "new culture" would move on ethical questions, and he questioned whether that culture had the capacity to be a foundation for understanding and fostering our common human identity. Fifteen years later, I believe the Pope's words prophetic. Our faith's problems with American culture today are etched most clearly in ethical questions and in various understandings of the anthropology of the human person.

These are central issues in the public debates shaping our shared future, yet the way we speak about church-state relations in this country makes it difficult to address them. The reduction of the faith-culture dialogue to the conversation between the institutions of church and state can't be overcome unless we recognize that community is not exhausted by political concerns or their institutionalization in state agencies. The

---

25. Francis E. George, OMI, *Inculturation and Ecclesial Communion: Culture and Church in the Teaching of Pope John Paul II*, (Rome: Urbaniana University Press, 1990), 107.

26. See John Paul II, "Address to Priests, assembled at the Oratory of Saint Joseph, Montreal, Canada, September 11, 1984," *AAS* 77 (1985): 389–397.

state is not, nor should it ever assume to be, the same as society. When society collapses into the state, totalitarianism is born. The state is its best when it sees itself as an institution at the service of society, and society is shaped by culture, which is broader than any state or political society because vital cultures, throughout human history, have always been created by religious faiths.

Part of the problem with the church-state conversation here is that it has proceeded along the route of what Avery Cardinal Dulles has called the "secular-dialogic" method.[27] Cardinal Dulles describes this method as secular "because it takes the world as a proper theological locus," and dialogic "because it seeks to operate on the frontier between the contemporary world and the Christian tradition, including the Bible, rather than simply apply the latter as the measure of the former."[28] While Cardinal Dulles notes a number of very positive elements in this method of dialogue, he also criticizes it because it fails to allow religion *to be itself* in the process of the dialogue. It would be my judgment that, while this method has occasionally been helpful for people of Jewish and Christian faith to live at home in this culture, it has now exhausted its potential. Because it presumes a benign secular state, it cannot deal with the development of secularism as a state religion. What we need, I would argue, is a new humanism, and Pope John Paul II has offered a foundation for it.

A New Humanism

One of the contributions which the present Pope [John Paul II] has made to theology is to take culture seriously as a *locus theologicus* (John Paul II). Let me quote George Weigel, who wrote:

> Beginning with his late teenage years under Nazi occupation, [Karol Wojtyla] gradually came to the conviction that the crisis of the modern world was first of all a crisis of ideas, a crisis of the very idea of the human person. History was driven by culture, and the ideas that formed culture.

---

27. Avery Cardinal Dulles, *Models of the Church*. (New York: Doubleday, 2002), 84.
28. Ibid.

Ideas had consequences. And, if the idea of the human person that dominated a culture was flawed, one of two things would happen. Either the
culture would give birth to destructive aspirations, or it would be inca-
pable of realizing its fondest hopes, even if it expressed them in the most
humanistic terms.[29]

First of all, it is important to understand that the Pope's critique of
modern culture is not born solely of philosophical speculation but, again,
from his experience, above all as a priest and bishop. His experience of
the Nazi occupation of Poland and then of atheistic communism and,
later, his experience of secularism and relativism in the West caused him
to think beyond our standard church-state framework for social questions and faith-science tensions for intellectual questions.

On June 13, 1984, Pope John Paul II said in Switzerland, discussing
"the purpose and the limits of scientific method," that the challenge now
is "to work toward a new synthesis of knowledge. Such a synthesis would
be 'wisdom', [and] it cannot be created without a philosophy, a meta-
physics. It can be accomplished, [furthermore], only if intellectuals can
work in freedom, guided by truth."[30] The Pope clearly defends freedom,
but always as a precondition for seeking for and arriving at truth. It is
beneath human dignity to live in falsehood, and all peoples and disciplines should be welcome to a public discussion about the truths and
falsehoods which underlie public policies. Unfortunately, in the present
day almost any religious truth claim brings public dialogue to a halt.

When I studied the Pope's teaching and his pastoral initiatives I
found recurring themes illustrating his own sense of the truths behind
public discourse:

1.   [a] broadly humanistic understanding of culture (that by which and
in which each person becomes ever more human);

2.   a deep conviction that every human person must both participate
fully in his or her own culture and, at the same time, live in solidarity
with all of humanity; and

---

29. George Weigel, *Witness to Hope: the Biography of Pope John Paul II*. (New York: Harper
Collins, 1999), 7.

30. George, *Inculturation and Ecclesial Communion*, op. cit., 120–121.

3.   a series of programmatic themes prompted by concern for creating a healthy culture: education, social and national vitality, human rights, family life and moral principles, communications, science and technology, humanistic research and the relation between culture and Christian faith.[31]

The Pope, in all of these discussions, never calls for "culture wars." "Every culture can be considered an apt 'substratum for [biblical religion]', though some cultures are more apt than others, depending on their pattern of cultural values and actions."[32] Consequently, what is needed from believers who wish to contribute to the transformation of their culture in the light of their faith is an analysis of its values, with special attention given:

> . . . to the concrete embodiment of cultural values in action. In acting, in its people's behavior, a culture expresses itself for what it is and takes responsibility for itself. If the analysis of values remains abstract, it can lend itself to ideological manipulation, [even] in the name of justice or freedom. Further, since the human person is both individual and [social or] related, cultural values must respect and express both the private and the social dimensions of personal subjectivity. A culture which reduces freedom to individual liberty or [reduces] justice to collective programs is as evangelically deficient as a culture which reduces truth to the search for technological means to attain arbitrary goals. Even more deficient, however, would be any cultural analysis which diminishes personal responsibility and looks only at abstract structures to explain patterns of action.[33]

If, as I would contend, religious communities are the primary carriers of any culture, then the dialogue between faith and culture will move us beyond the limits of the now sterile church-state debate to an analysis of values in action to discussion among believers and non-believers alike about the future of our society. Moreover, since, in a multi-religious society, the faith-culture dialogue must necessarily be an interreligious dialogue, the dynamics of such dialogue will shape every public conversation.

In the almost eight years that I have been Archbishop of Chicago, something I have most enjoyed is my involvement with interreligious

---

31. Ibid., 43.
32. Ibid., 44.
33. Ibid.

dialogue here. Tonight, I want to publicly thank Sister Joan McGuire and the staff of the Office for Ecumenical and Interreligious Affairs for all that they have done with so many of you to make Chicago one of the best venues in the world for interreligious engagement. I am very grateful.

In those same seven years, through all the addresses, talks, and remarks I have made at interreligious events, I don't think I have ever spoken directly to the subject of interreligious dialogue. Let me do that in conclusion here.

At the end of my Library of Congress address in 1999, I advanced the claim that:

> In the next millennium, as the modern nation state is relativized and national sovereignty is displaced into societal arrangements still to be invented, it will be increasingly evident that the major faiths remain carriers of culture and that it is more sectarian to be French, [Russian or] American than to be Christian or Muslim, [Jewish], Hindu or Buddhist. Interreligious dialogue is more basic to the future of faith, therefore, than is church-state dialogue, important though that remains.[34]

In 2005, I am more than ever convinced of this claim. And since my proposal tonight is that we commit ourselves to a new engagement in interreligious dialogue, I would like to share with you my convictions about the nature and rules of this dialogue. When I use the word "rule" in this context, I am referring to a tool of measurement, like a carpenter's level, which ensures that, as the work progresses, it will be stable and properly grounded. It is not directive as much as regulative.

Let me offer, then, four measures of the authenticity of dialogues, four "rules" for interreligious engagement.[35] Interreligious engagement is not an exercise in comparative religion. This necessarily secular academic discipline, which lays aside or brackets convictions of faith prior to engaging the other in dialogue, is the opposite of what dialogue is authentically about. In fact, laying aside our faith convictions is exactly what should never happen in interreligious dialogue. Partners in interreligious dialogue are first of all believers. The first rule is therefore a commitment to faith. Participants' faith commitments must guide and govern their lives and their speech even in dialogue. Only in this way

---

34. George, "Catholic Christianity and the Millennium," op. cit.

35. See George, *Inculturation and Ecclesial Communion*, op. cit., 216–218.

will they be authentic representatives of their own religious community to the dialogue partner, the other.

The second measure of dialogue is a commitment to the common. Again, I am not referring to finding the lowest common denominator between two traditions. Rather, I am calling for a personal religious commitment to what is at least analogously common between two traditions. *Nostra Aetate* states it this way:

> The Catholic Church rejects nothing that is true and holy in these religions. She looks with sincere respect upon those ways of conduct and of life, those rules and teachings which, although differing in may particulars from what she holds and sets forth, nevertheless often reflect a ray of that Truth which enlightens all. . . . She therefore has this exhortation for her sons: prudently and lovingly, through dialogue and collaboration with the followers of other religions, and in witness to Christian faith and life, acknowledge, preserve and promote the spiritual and moral goods found among these men and women, as well as the values in their society and culture.[36]

This is more than a mere description of what we have in common. In a sense it's a description of what we don't have in common, but what we respect together. As a Catholic, I must both respect the truth in Judaism and preserve and promote the spiritual and moral goods of Jewish faith and the values of Jewish culture and society.

Obviously, such a rule is demanding. It is personally demanding in the sense that it is a religious obligation for me. But it is also quite demanding on my relationship with you. For our relationship to be guided by this rule or measure, another rule is required to enable both of us to do this honestly. The third rule of interreligious dialogue is a commitment to the truth. Partners must "attempt to agree on criteria for judging what each would accept as true, even when it is to be found in a different belief system" and when that truth is not shared.[37] Without question, this third rule is the most demanding on the dialogue. But it is also the condition of the possibility of the rule of commitment to the common. It is also essential because it enables this commitment to flower into action.

---

36. *Nostra Aetate: The Declaration on the Relationship of the Church to Non-Christian Religions*, no. 2, in *The Documents of Vatican II*, Walter M. Abbot, S.J., ed. (New York: American Press, 1966), 662–663.

37. George, *Inculturation and Ecclesial Communion*, op. cit., 217.

The fourth rule of dialogue is the commitment to action. We are not in dialogue with disembodied ideas, but with persons. As we discover our respective commitments and personally commit ourselves to their promotion, we should find ourselves making common cause. These are the commitments that I think need to govern our dialogue: a commitment to faith, to the common, to the truth and to action in Chicago.

The Catholic-Jewish interreligious dialogue in Chicago has already begun to engage cultural issues, even if unintentionally. Cardinal Bernardin touched on one of the questions that will be as important for us in the future as it has been in the past ten years. He called on the Jewish community to rethink its understanding of its relationship to the Church. I would suggest that this is all the more important as we engage together in dialogue about faith and culture. In effect I am reframing, and in a sense reversing, what Professor Fackenheim asked of the Christian community ten years ago: that the Jewish community relate positively to Christians, not despite their acceptance of Christ, but because of it.

Cardinal Cassidy anticipated my call for this faith-culture dialogue when he reminded us that we are religious communities. And he named my fourth rule of dialogue which calls for committed action in favor of the moral and other values we find in our shared biblical faith.

With all that we have done, dear friends, over the past forty-seven years here in Chicago, we can, I believe, look forward to doing still more. As heirs to God's self-revelation witnessed to in Scripture and lived out in our faith communities and on the basis of the unique relationship that Judaism and Christianity have among the world religions, we carry a special responsibility to work for the transformation of the world and of American society, our own part of the world. While Dr. Hartman's provocative claim that "the very particularity of Israel can teach us the meaning of universalism as an outgrowth of a commitment to particularities" does not directly apply to the United States, his insights about the relation between particular and universal should, I believe, be discussed further by Catholics and Jews in America.[38] How can a religion be itself, with full particular authenticity, and at the same time contribute to the enrichment of all in American society? I have suggested several times that my way of being a Catholic is qualified by my experience

---

38. Hartman, op. cit.

of being a Catholic in America, which is distinct from being a Catholic in another cultural setting. If we fail to engage this question, what is left for us is to become cults or separated sects waiting out the collapse of our own society, and we then abandon the requirement for visibility which biblical religion places upon us. Secularism will have triumphed, freedom itself will be weakened, and we will have betrayed the living God. I believe that, together, we might engage contemporary American culture on two themes that speak even to secularists: (1) the relation between freedom and desire, and (2) the relation between individual and community. As pre-modern faiths in a post-modern culture, we bring something that is sometimes acutely felt to be lacking: a law deeper than the political for discerning right from wrong, and a communitarian ethos that speaks to contemporary loneliness, isolation, and alienation.

An Agenda for the Future

We need to envision an alternative to the society now being secularized by default. Rather than accepting a secular society where every religion is privatized, believers in interreligious dialogue could help shape a multi-religious society as the framework for a freer society. I use the term multi-religious rather than pluralistic. A multi-religious society would allow each religion to be itself, in all authenticity while, at the same time, through interreligious dialogue, contributing its own richness to the formation of a new culture, shaping a different society.

How would such a dialogue begin? It should begin at the beginning. Let us look again at Genesis and the Garden of Eden:

Even as they move away from a garden in which they walked with God and journey toward a celestial city, men and women work to shape a world in which they can become what God calls them to be. Only with difficulty can they be themselves if the basic harmony between nature and person is disrupted or if society is not organized to protect human dignity. Notice of a cultural crisis is given when there is no bridge to unite human achievements in the sciences with human accomplishments in the arts and when public institutions no longer mediate the divergent goals and individual efforts of all members of society. A healthy culture presupposes and fosters sensitivity to the full range of human capacities and possesses institutions able to integrate them. If culture is also to be related to faith, believers need . . . [an] anthropology that restores to human persons their integrity in such a way that they remain certain of their own identity and yet always open to goals which transcend their own particular experience.[39]

The Genesis story is the foundation for understanding ourselves not only as people of personal faith, but also as participants in public discourse. It represents one example of what our two traditions have in common—what we believe together—and is therefore one of the foundations for the faith we share. God's creation of the world is one of the central beliefs in both Judaism and Christianity. It tells us who we are and what the world is. The Book of Genesis is also a place in *interreligious* dialogue where we can discover the roots of the conflict with secularism, a conflict which exposes the various senses of what it means to be human. Biblical revelation itself enables us to hear Cardinal Cassidy's exhortation:

We must throw off all fear of the truth. Why should we be afraid of the truth? It is the truth that makes us free! What harm can come to us from a dialogue that goes beyond the discussion about problems and enters into the heart of what constitutes our identities as faith communities and also as human beings, in order to allow us to proceed along the path of common action?[40]

Or, as Dr. Hartman said:

Listening to other traditions doesn't have to destroy your own voice. Listening to the "other" can enrich your own voice.[41] . . . People often say that the greatest biblical commandment is: Love your neighbor as yourself. I claim that the greatest biblical commandment is: Love the stranger. Loving your neighbor is loving someone who is like you. It is not that difficult to love those who are like you or who can become like you. But can you love an "other" who remains an "other" to you? Can you respect the dignity of a tradition that is not digestible in your own categories or framework of experience?[42]

This, I believe, is the challenge and possibility that confronts us as we come to the tenth year of the Jerusalem Lecture series. If we are to

---

39. George, *Inculturation and Ecclesial Communion*, op. cit., 31.

40. Cassidy, op. cit., 11.

41. Hartman, op. cit., 25.

42. Ibid., 26.

make a contribution to the development of a new culture here, the biblical religions must find their respective voices and claim a new visibility. We must be heard and seen in the public square precisely as men and women of faith, eager to dialogue with all others, even secularists, as we have dialogued with one another.

In conclusion, let me again thank the American Jewish Committee, the Chicago Board of Rabbis, the Jewish Federation of Metropolitan Chicago and the Spertus Institute of Jewish Studies for your partnership with the Archdiocese of Chicago and for this opportunity to be the tenth Jerusalem Lecturer. May the God of Abraham, Isaac and Jacob bless us all.

Afterword

Michael C. Kotzin

I am grateful to the Rev. Thomas Baima for asking me to prepare this Afterword. When I began to think of what would be an appropriate approach to take in it, I found the material at hand evoking several poignant memories.

My first recollection has to do with the travels that got this project started. As Father Baima indicated in his Preface to this volume and as he notes in his Introduction, the Joseph Cardinal Bernardin Jerusalem Lecture, which is now an annual event in Chicago, originates from a lecture on "Anti-Semitism: The Historical Legacy and the Challenge for Christians" given by the late Cardinal himself in Jerusalem during the 1995 Catholic-Jewish trip which he led. That visit took place shortly after the Vatican established formal ties with the State of Israel, a historic event in Catholic-Jewish relations, and it grew out of the interfaith dialogue that had developed in Chicago over a number of years, greatly inspired by Bernardin's vision and sense of his vocation.

Traveling together in a land of central religious significance for each of our communities—and in a country of particular meaning for the individual and group identity of the Jewish members of the delegation—we were able to fulfill the traditional goals of interreligious dialogue by enhancing our respect for the "other" while intensifying our sense of self. For me, that dual effect was experienced with particular power the day we walked down the *Via Dolorosa*.

The impact of the location on the Cardinal was palpable. His very demeanor conveyed deep spirituality, expressing the profound meaning his religion had for him and strengthening the respect that I already had for him as a man of faith. At the same time, that Old City setting and its surroundings had very different resonance for me, heightening my sense of difference from him as I became all the more aware of my identity as a Jew with a particular history, set of traditions, tie to peoplehood, and connections with the place where we were.

Cardinal Bernardin was a great believer in setting an example. He wished to lead what we were told was the first ever trip to Israel in which a Cardinal headed a Catholic-Jewish delegation not only for the enriching experiences it would provide to each of us but also for the way that, in acting out this interfaith engagement, we would be modeling inter-religious experience for others. Those others included the Jews, Christians, and Muslims with whom we interacted on the trip on the one hand, and the people of Chicago on the other. The wall-to-wall Chicago media attention we received, also described by Father Baima in his Preface, was a vehicle for projecting that modeling image back home.

"We teach in a number of ways," Bernardin once wrote, including "by the programs and institutions we create." That observation leads me to another memory, this one stained with sadness. During our visit to Israel, I and Maynard Wishner, a prominent lay leader of the Federation, invited the Cardinal to deliver the keynote address at the Federation's annual meeting, which was scheduled for six months later. He agreed, not knowing that in between those two dates he would be diagnosed with cancer and would have to undergo difficult treatment for the disease.

When the scheduled date came he kept his commitment to speak, making that one of his first public appearances during the period when his cancer was in remission. My memory here is of greeting him at the entrance to the hotel meeting room, where hundreds of lunchtime guests awaited him, and of hearing him, with a familiar twinkle in the eye but with a now-drawn visage say: "Michael, I have something to announce in my speech that you are going to like." The "something" was his dec-laration that the Archdiocese was committing itself to working with its Jewish organizational partners from the trip to organize an annual lec-ture to sustain and advance the trip's impact on Catholic-Jewish rela-tions. That event, building on what the Cardinal himself had done in Jerusalem, is what came to be called the Joseph Cardinal Bernardin Jerusalem Lecture.

In its earliest years, the lecture series was tied to the Israel trip in another way as well, for the initial Jewish speakers—Professor Emil Fackenheim, who gave the first of the lectures in Chicago, and Rabbi David Hartman, who gave the third—had provided especially powerful experiences when the group met with each of them in Israel. Their Chicago presentations, along with the second lecture in the series, "Catholic-Jewish Relations: A New Agenda?" delivered by Edward

Cardinal Cassidy, then the President of the Pontifical Commission for Religious Relations with the Jews, set a high standard for the lectures, one which subsequent speakers have fully lived up to.

Sadly, Cardinal Bernardin lived long enough only to hear the first lecture. He was succeeded as Archbishop of Chicago by Francis Cardinal George, who has presided over each of the subsequent lectures in the series with his own sense of commitment to its purposes. While Cardinal Bernardin institutionalized the lecture series, Cardinal George, as Father Baima points out in his Introduction, advanced Israel-linked Jewish-Catholic cooperation of another sort by leading the Archdiocese to partner with the Jewish Federation in establishing a computer literacy project in the Israeli Christian Arab village of Fassouta. And while Cardinal Bernardin's lecture in Jerusalem was the progenitor of the Jerusalem Lecture series, Cardinal George provided the closing frame for the first decade of the series by being the guest speaker ten years later, on the topic "Catholics, Jews, and American Culture."

Interestingly enough, whereas both Cardinals spoke to the future, Cardinal Bernardin's lecture for the most part looked backward and talked about attitudes and behavior that were profoundly detrimental to the achievement of positive Jewish-Catholic relations, while Cardinal George looked greatly at the present moment and put the two religious groups together on one side of a divide that has secularism on the other side. As Cardinal George put it, they are two "pre-modern faiths in a post-modern culture." He closed his lecture by saying:

> This, I believe, is the challenge and possibility that confronts us as we come to the tenth year of the Jerusalem Lecture series. If we are to make a contribution to the development of a new culture here, the biblical religions must find their respective voices and claim a new visibility. We must be heard and seen in the public square precisely as men and women of faith, eager to dialogue with all others, even secularists, as we have dialogued with one another.

Though much happened in the world in the ten years between the two Cardinals' lectures, and though there have been additional developments in the dominant areas in which Jews and Catholics engage in the five years since Cardinal George gave his talk, some things remain the same, or nearly so. One of the most touching meetings held during the Israel trip with Cardinal Bernardin was a session with Prime Minister

Yitzhak Rabin. It was a time when Israel was participating in the Oslo Peace Process, when there was hope that reconciliation and peace between Israel and the Palestinians were on the horizon. But peace today seems no closer than it did then—perhaps even further away. And at the same time, although during the trip we had celebrated the establishment of Israel-Vatican ties at a lunch in Jerusalem with the Papal Nuncio, Andrea Cardinal Cordero Lanza di Montezemolo, the final details of the Israel-Vatican agreement have yet to be resolved. Furthermore, Cardinal Bernardin's call for the Vatican to open its Holocaust-era archives remains unrealized, and issues revolving around the Holocaust continue to surface from time to time in a way that affects Catholic-Jewish relations.

Meanwhile, the first decade of the series has by now been followed by another half decade of lectures, and the series goes on. It is always a high point on the interfaith calendar in Chicago, drawing significant audiences of people from both communities who invariably convey their appreciation for the opportunity to come together in that way.

Finally, then, while the delivery of each of these lectures has played an important part in advancing understanding and awareness of one another for Chicago's Catholics and Jews, thereby enhancing their relationship, this collection of the first ten years' worth of lectures will both expand the audience and keep those lectures alive, advancing the goals of dialogue in a different format. It is a result that we who have been partners in this enterprise locally hope will bring benefits both in Chicago and beyond.

About the Authors

Thomas A. Baima

The Rev. Dr. Thomas A. Baima is a priest of the Archdiocese of Chicago, a professor of systematic theology, and Vice Rector for Academic Affairs of the University of Saint Mary of the Lake/Mundelein Seminary.

Joseph L. Bernardin

His Eminence, the Late Joseph Cardinal Bernardin was Archbishop of Chicago from 1982 until his death in 1996.

Edward Idris Cassidy

His Eminence, Edward Cardinal Cassidy is the president emeritus of the Pontifical Council for Promoting Christian Unity.

Robert Chazan

Professor Robert Chazan is the S. H. and Helen R. Scheuer Professor of Hebrew and Judaic Studies at New York University.

Emil L. Fackenheim

The Late Professor Emil L. Fackenheim was Fellow of the Institute of Contemporary Jewry of the Hebrew University of Jerusalem and of the Jerusalem Institute of Public Affairs.

Richard A. Freud

Rabbi Dr. Richard A. Freud is Maurice Greenberg Professor of Jewish History and director of the Maurice Greenberg Center for Judaic Studies at the University of Hartford.

Francis E. George, OMI

His Eminence, Francis Cardinal George, OMI is Archbishop of Chicago.

David Hartman

Rabbi Dr. David Hartman is the founder and Director of the Shalom Hartman Institute in Jerusalem.

Arthur Hertzberg

The Late Rabbi Dr. Arthur Hertzberg was the Bronfman Visiting Professor of Humanities at New York University and Professor Emeritus of Religion at Dartmouth College.

Michael C. Kotzin

Dr. Michael C. Kotzin is Senior Counselor to the President of the Jewish United Fund/Jewish Federation of Metropolitan Chicago.

Bernard McGinn

Professor Bernard McGinn is the Naomi Shenstone Donnelley Professor of Historical Theology and the History of Christianity at the University of Chicago Divinity School.

Anthony J. Saldarini

The Late Professor Anthony J. Saldarini was professor of Bible at Boston College.

Robert Wilken

Professor Robert Wilken is the William R. Kenan, Jr. Professor of the History of Christianity at the University of Virginia.